THE HEALING MIRACLES

OF

COCONUT OIL

Revised Third Edition

BRUCE FIFE, N.D.
Foreword by Jon J. Kabara, Ph.D.

HealthWise

Colorado Springs, Colorado

The information in this book is provided for educational purposes. It does not replace the need for medical advice and counsel, especially in cases of serious illness.

Acknowledgments:
The photo on page 12 was graciously supplied by the Polynesian Cultural Center in Laie, Hawaii.

HealthWise Publications is an imprint of
Piccadilly Books, Ltd.
P.O. Box 25203
Colorado Springs, CO 80936, USA

International sales and inquiries contact:
 Empire Publishing Service
 20 Park Drive
 Romford Essex RM1 4LH, UK
or
 Empire Publishing Service
 P.O. Box 1344
 Studio City, CA 91614, USA

Library of Congress Cataloging-in-Publication Data
Fife, Bruce. 1952-
    The healing miracles of coconut oil/Bruce Fife.
       p. cm.
    Includes bibliographical references and index.
    ISBN 0-941599-51-5
    1. Coconut oil--Health aspects. 2. Fatty acids in human nutrition. I. Title.

QP752.F35 F545 2000
615'.3245--dc21   99-057917

Simultaneously published in Australia, UK, and USA
Printed in Canada

CONTENTS

FOREWORD

Jon J. Kabara, Ph.D.
Professor Emeritus, Department of Chemistry and Pharmacology
Michigan State University

Up until now only a small group of lipid (fat) researchers were familiar with the incredible health benefits of a unique group of saturated fats found in coconut oil. Most of those in the health care industry have been generally ignorant of these benefits, shunning coconut oil because of common misconceptions regarding dietary fat. But this is beginning to change as the amazing nutritional and therapeutic benefits of the tropical oils become better known.

In this book the reader will learn that not all saturated fats are unhealthy. In fact, there is a subgroup of saturated fats which actually have a positive effect on your health. This book provides a brief summary of the remarkable health benefits lipid researchers have slowly been uncovering regarding a unique group of saturated fats found in mother's milk and coconut oil known as "medium-chain fatty acids." The story is fascinating and can have a pronounced effect on your health.

Those of you that take the time to pick up this book may be surprised to learn that certain saturated fats (medium-chain fatty acids) promote good health. Contrary to what is generally believed by both the lay public and medical profession the saturated fats found in coconut oil are actually good for you. This should not be surprising because if coconut oil were unhealthy it would have been evidenced in populations who have used it for generations. There is no evidence of this. In fact, just the opposite is the case. Those populations who use coconut oil demonstrate a remarkable level of good health.

4

Historically coconut oil is one of the earliest oils to be used as a food and as a pharmaceutical. Ayurvedic literature long promoted the health and cosmetic benefits of coconut oil. Even today the Asian Pacific community, which may represent as much as half the world's population, uses coconut oil in one form or another. Many of these people enjoy remarkably good health and longevity. Studies on people who live in tropical climates and who have a diet high in coconut oil are healthier, have less heart disease, cancer, digestive complaints, and prostate problems. In North America and Europe popular cookbooks from the late 19th century often included coconut oil in many recipes, yet heart disease and cancer were almost unheard of at the time. Common sense would indicate that the saturated fats in coconut oil are not the poisons they are often made out to be.

Why then, all the negative publicity regarding coconut oil? Since it is thought that "saturated fats" are involved in heart disease, coconut oil was considered a health risk. Much of the information linking coconut oil and increased heart disease is, however, circumstantial at best and flawed at worst. Studies showing that dietary coconut oil raises blood cholesterol and increases the possible risk of heart disease were poorly conceived because the essential fats were not put into the diet. Populations using high levels of coconut oil always include other oils from vegetables and fish for a more balanced diet.

Both "scientific" and political propaganda by the American Soybean Association and the Center for Science in the Public Interest (or is it their own?) have joined forces in a campaign to replace tropical oils with polyunsaturated soybean oil from American farmers. Because of this campaign, food processors, restaurant, and theater chains have switched from coconut to polyunsaturated oils. Even dietetic and medical spokespersons blinded by negative publicity have supported the switch to polyunsaturated oils as heart healthy. This campaign has condemned all saturated fats as generically "poison." Both the lay and scientific press fail to describe the fact that certain subgroups of saturated fats have *positive* health benefits.

The abundance of documented scientific facts reviewed for this book will tell as Paul Harvey would say, "the rest of the story." As the story unfolds the reader can better appreciate the fact that "saturated fats" are classified into two primary categories: (1) long-chain fats and (2) short- and medium-chain fats. Each subgroup having markedly different biological effects. It will be shown that the overconsumption of polyunsaturated fats in our diet is more detrimental to our health than saturated fats found in tropical oils.

Not only is coconut oil not a "dietary poison" but it contains a remarkable fat called monolaurin. This medium-chain fat, first discovered in our laboratory, represents one of the most exceptional and inspiring group of fats found in nature. This unique fat available naturally from mother's milk and coconut oil is now commercially available as Lauricidin®. Monolaurin (Lauricidin®) is currently being tested in clinical trials as a treatment for genital herpes, hepatitis C, and HIV. Early clinical results have been very promising and show exciting possibilities for an important new weapon in alternative medicine.

Dr. Bruce Fife should be commended for bringing together in this very readable book the positive health benefits of coconut oil and especially monolaurin. The inquiring reader will have a new and more balanced view of the role of fat and especially saturated fats in our diet.

Dr. Jon J. Kabara has had a long career in lipid research. Beginning in 1948 as a research assistant at the University of Illinois, Department of Biochemistry to full professorship at the University of Detroit and then at Michigan State University where he served as Associate Dean and helped establish a new private College of Osteopathic Medicine. He was one of the first researchers to discover the antimicrobial properties of medium-chain fatty acids. He has been awarded 16 patents and has authored or co-authored more than 200 scientific publications including eight books. All of Dr. Kabara's awards and achievements in nutritional biochemistry and pharmacology are far too numerous to list here. He is considered by many to be one of the world's foremost authorities on dietary fats and oils.

® Trademark of Med-Chem Laboratories, Galena, IL 61036

6

A MIRACLE FOOD

AN ANCIENT HEALTH FOOD REDISCOVERED

Some years ago I was in a meeting with a group of nutritionists and one of the members of the group made the statement, "Coconut oil is *good* for you." We all gasped in disbelief. "Coconut oil healthy?" Preposterous, we thought. Everywhere we go we're told how bad coconut oil is because it is a source of "artery-clogging" saturated fat. How could coconut oil be good?

She knew we would doubt her statement and explained, "Coconut oil has been unjustly criticized and is really one of the *good* fats." She cited several studies proving to us that it wasn't the evil villain it was made out to be and actually provided many valuable health benefits. I learned that for several decades it has been used in hospital formulas to feed critically ill patients and that it is a major component of baby formula because it provides many of the same nutrients as human breast milk. Questions were raised: if it was as deadly as we are led to believe, why would they use it to nourish sick patients and feed infants? Would you give an unhealthy food to your new-born baby? It didn't make sense. I learned that coconut oil could be used to treat a number of common illnesses and is considered by the Food and Drug Administration (FDA) to be a safe, natural food. (It's on the FDA's exclusive GRAS list which means it is "Generally Regarded As Safe.")

After the meeting I was intrigued. I learned a lot, but it brought up many questions that troubled me. For instance, if coconut oil was good, why is it so often portrayed as being unhealthy? If the health benefits are for real, why haven't we heard of them before? Why don't we hear about the use of coconut oil in hospitals, baby formula, and elsewhere? If it's good for the sick and the very young, why wouldn't it be good for us as well? Why would the government include it on its list of safe foods if it was dangerous or unhealthy? Why aren't the studies on coconut oil better publicized? Why have we been misled...or have we? Perhaps coconut oil is bad and hospital patients and parents of formula-fed babies are being deceived. These and many more questions filled my mind. I had to find the answers.

I began a search to find out anything and everything I could about coconut oil. The first thing I discovered was that there was *very* little written about coconut oil in magazines and books. Even my nutritional textbooks were relatively silent on the subject. No one seemed to know much about it. Almost everything I came across in the "popular" health literature was critical, stating that coconut oil is bad because it is high in saturated fat. Each author seemed to parrot the other, giving no further explanation. It was almost like a royal decree had been sent out to all authors stating that they *must* say the exact same thing about coconut oil in order to be politically correct (but not necessarily accurate). Saying anything different was against the rules, and that was that. I did find a few, a very few, authors who stood up to this rhetoric and stated bluntly that coconut oil wasn't bad, but they didn't give much detail either. It seemed that nobody really knew anything about it.

The only place I could find cold, hard facts was in often-ignored research journals. Here I found a gold mine of information and I found the answers to all my questions. This was the best place for me to search because these journals report the actual results of studies and are not simply people's opinions, as are most material in popular magazines and books. There were literally hundreds of studies published in dozens of the most respected scientific and medical journals. What I learned was absolutely amazing. I found out that coconut oil is one of the most remarkable health foods available. I felt like I rediscovered an ancient health food that the world had almost forgotten about. I also learned why coconut oil has been maligned and misunderstood (we will get to that later and the answer may shock and even anger you).

I started using coconut oil myself and began recommending it to my clients.* I've witnessed it get rid of chronic psoriasis, eliminate dandruff, remove pre-cancerous skin lesions, speed recovery from the flu, stop bladder infections, overcome chronic fatigue, and relieve hemorrhoids, among other things. In addition to this, the scientific literature reports its

---

*I am a certified nutritionist and naturopathic physician, thus the N.D. after my name.

possible use in treating dental caries (cavities), peptic ulcers, benign prostatic hyperplasia (enlarged prostate), epilepsy, genital herpes, hepatitis C, and HIV/AIDS. Yes, as incredible as it sounds, I learned that coconut oil can be used to fight AIDS—a dreadful disease that up until now has been considered incurable! Many AIDS patients have already benefited. Let me relate one example.

In September of 1996 AIDS patient Chris Dafoe of Cloverdale, Indiana figured his time was running out. He'd lost a great deal of weight, lacked energy, and felt worse and worse with each passing day. The thing that drove the nail into his coffin was the lab results. The report showed he had a viral load of over 600,000—an indication of rampant HIV infection and a sign that he didn't have too much time left to live. So he made arrangements for his funeral, paying all expenses up front. Before he died, however, and while he still had some strength left, he wanted to take one last vacation—a dream vacation to the jungles of South America. He flew to the tiny Republic of Surinam and wound his way into the jungle where he stayed briefly among a group of Indians. While there, he ate the same foods as the natives. Every day he was served a dish of cooked coconut prepared by the natives.

"The Indian Chief told me," says Dafoe, "that they use the coconut as the basis for all their medicines. They also use the milk from the inside of the coconut and also use other plants and herbs from the jungle to make medicines. They eat cooked coconut every morning to help prevent illness." While there, Dafoe's health took a turn for the better, his strength and energy increased and he regained 32 pounds. Home again six weeks later he went in for another lab test. This time the results showed his viral load had plummeted to *undetectable levels*. The HIV virus that once flooded his body was no longer measurable.

He continues eating cooked coconut for breakfast every day, mixing it with hot cereal. He is convinced that it keeps the virus under control and allows him to enjoy good health. With a zest for life he says, "I feel great. I have more energy than ever."[1]

Another remarkable benefit of coconut oil is its ability to prevent heart disease. Yes, I said *prevent* heart disease. While for years we've been led to believe coconut oil promotes this condition, recent research proves otherwise. In fact, in the near future it may gain wide acceptance as a powerful aid in the fight against heart and other cardiovascular diseases.

I've continued to research coconut and other oils. I've been so impressed with the potential health benefits available from coconut oil that I felt an obligation to share what I've learned with the rest of the world. That's why I've written this book. Let me state up front that I do *not* sell coconut oil or have any financial interest in the coconut industry. My purpose in writing this book is to dispel myths and misconceptions and reveal to you some of the many healing miracles of coconut oil. What you will learn in this book may sound incredible, at times maybe even too incredible, but I didn't make this stuff up. Every statement I make in this book is verified by published scientific studies, historical records, and personal experience. If you want to check them out, references and additional resources are listed in the back of this book.

Whenever I talk about coconut oil, the first thing people think is, "Isn't that bad for you?" This may have been your reaction when you first saw this book. Stop and think about it for a minute. All you need to do is use a little common sense and you will see how ridiculous it is to think of coconut oil as being harmful. Coconuts (and coconut oil) have been used as a major source of food for thousands of years by millions of people in Asia, the Pacific Islands, Africa, and Central America. Traditionally these people have had much better health than those in North America and Europe who don't eat coconut.[2] Before the introduction of modern foods, many of these people depended almost entirely on coconut to sustain life. They didn't suffer from heart disease, cancer, arthritis, diabetes, and other modern degenerative diseases, at least not until they abandoned their traditional coconut-based diet and began eating modern foods. It should be, or soon will become, obvious to you that coconut oil isn't the evil villain it has been portrayed.

THE TREE OF LIFE

If you traveled the world looking for a people who enjoy a degree of health far above that found in most nations, a people who are relatively free from the crippling effects of degenerative disease, you couldn't help but be impressed with the natives who inhabit the islands of the South Pacific.

These people in their tropical paradise enjoy a remarkable degree of good health relatively free from the aches and pains of degenerative disease that plague most of the rest of the world. These people are robust and healthy. Heart disease, cancer, diabetes, and arthritis are almost unheard of—at least among those who live on the *traditional native diets*. Researchers have long noted that when these island people start to abandon their traditional diets in favor of Western foods, their health deteriorates. The more Westernized the people become, the more their diseases mimic those commonly found in the West.

Ian Prior, M.D., a cardiologist and director of the epidemiology unit at the Wellington Hospital in New Zealand, says this pattern has been very clearly demonstrated with Pacific Islanders. "The more an Islander takes on the ways of the West, the more prone he is to succumb to our degenerative diseases." He states that the further the Pacific natives move away from the diet of their ancestors "the closer they come to gout, diabetes, atherosclerosis, obesity, and hypertension."[3]

For centuries these people have lived on native foods without experiencing the degenerative diseases so common in our society. It wasn't until they began taking on the lifestyle and eating habits of the West that these diseases began to surface. While most of the people inhabiting the islands of the Pacific have adopted the use of modern foods, those who retain their native culture and diets remain remarkably free from the ills that plague most of the rest of the world. While many factors may be involved, an obvious influence is the change in diet among these people.

What is the miracle food these people eat that protects them from degenerative disease? What is this mysterious food that has been used throughout the tropical island cultures in the Pacific, yet is relatively uncommon in Western diets?

A survey of the types of foods common among these people would include bananas, mangos, papayas, kiwi, taro, sego palm root, and coconut. While all of these are common in the tropics, only a few are widely dispersed and used as staple food sources by millions of island inhabitants. Mangos, for example, are found only in limited locations and are not an important food source in most island populations. Bananas, likewise, while abundant in some areas, are relatively rare in others and do not contribute much if anything to the diets of the people in other localities.

The most universally eaten foods among the Polynesian and Asian communities around the Pacific are the roots of the taro and sego palm and the fruit of the coconut tree. These roots are rich sources of fiber and carbohydrate and form the staple diet of many island populations, much like rice or wheat do in other parts of the world. Nutritionally, however, these foods are inferior to rice and wheat, containing fewer vitamins and minerals per volume. Such foods could hardly be the secret of the islander's good health.

The only other food eaten universally throughout the area is the coconut. Could coconut be the miracle food that has made these people some of the healthiest on earth? Research over the past several decades indicates that this may be so. Coconuts have been used as a staple part of the diets of most all Polynesian, Melanesian, and many Asian peoples in this area for centuries. They are used as food, as flavoring, and made into beverages. They are highly prized for their rich oil content which is used for all cooking purposes.

11

Polynesian Cultural Center

Polynesians have learned how to climb tall coconut palms with ease in order to harvest fresh coconuts.

It is the oil that is perhaps the most remarkable ingredient in coconuts. Coconut oil is unique. No other oil used for human consumption, except for other palm fruits such as palm kernel oil (a relative of the coconut) is like it. In our modern society, where we are constantly being advised to reduce fat intake, it sounds strange to learn that eating any one particular type of oil can be healthy and actually prevent disease. But eating *more* oil may be one of the healthiest dietary changes you can make—if it's coconut oil.

We are told that in order to reduce the risk of heart disease we should limit fat consumption to no more than 30 percent of our total calorie intake per day. However, Polynesian peoples consume large quantities of fat in the form of coconut oil. For some, it comprises up to 60 percent of their total calorie intake—twice the limit recommend as prudent. The 30 percent limit is probably a good standard with oils typically eaten in Western countries, but coconut oil is different. It is one of the "good" oils that promotes better health. As researchers have studied coconut oil, it has emerged as the premiere dietary oil of all time, providing health benefits that surpass even those of other highly regarded oils.

Whenever coconut oil is mentioned, most people immediately think of saturated fat and, therefore, assume it must be bad. It's true that coconut oil is primarily a saturated fat. What people don't realize, however, is that there are many different types of saturated fat and all of them affect the body differently. The type of saturated fat found in coconut oil, a plant source, is different from the type found in animal products. The difference is dramatic and is fully documented by years of scientific research.

The therapeutic benefits of the unique oil found in coconuts are well known among lipid (oil) researchers. This oil is used in hospitals to feed patients who have digestive or malabsorption problems. It is commonly given to infants and small children who cannot digest other fats. It has been a primary ingredient in most commercial infant formulas. Unlike other fats, coconut oil protects against heart disease, cancer, diabetes, and a host of other degenerative illnesses. It supports and strengthens the immune system, thus helping the body ward off attack from infection and disease. It is unique among oils in that it promotes weight loss which has earned it the reputation of being the world's only low-calorie fat.

Coconut oil has a long and highly respected reputation in many cultures throughout the world, not only as a valuable food but also as an effective medicine. It is used throughout the tropics in many of the traditional systems of medicine. For example, in India it is an important ingredient in some of the Ayurvedic medical formulations. Ayurvedic medicine has been practiced in India for thousands of years and is still used

13

as the primary form of medical treatment by millions of people. In the Central American country of Panama, people are known to drink coconut oil by the glass to help them overcome sickness. They have learned over the generations that consuming coconut oil speeds recovery from illness. In Jamaica coconut is considered a health tonic good for the heart. In Nigeria and other parts of tropical Africa, palm kernel oil (which is very similar to coconut oil) is a trusted remedy for all types of illnesses. It has been used here with success for so long that it is the most commonly administered traditional remedy. [4] Among the Polynesian people the coconut palm is valued above all other plants for its nutritional and health-giving properties. The healing miracles of the coconut have long been recognized in those cultures where it is grown. Only recently are these benefits starting to become known to the rest of the world.

If you've been avoiding coconut oil because of its saturated fat content, you are among hundreds of thousands of others who have been purposely misled by self-serving commercial enterprises. At this point you may be skeptical and perhaps even resistant to the idea that coconut oil can be healthy. At one time, I felt the same way. But several years of intensive research into the scientific literature, as well as first-hand clinical use, has revealed a new image of this marvelous dietary oil. Much of the information presented in this book is so new that most health care professionals aren't even aware of it yet.

Using coconut oil for all your cooking needs may be one of the healthiest decisions you could ever make. In this book you will discover many of the health-promoting benefits coconuts and coconut oil can bring to you. You will also learn why many researchers now consider coconut oil to be the healthiest oil on earth. You will discover why many Asian and Polynesian people call the coconut palm "The Tree of Life."

WHY PACIFIC ISLANDERS DON'T GET HEART DISEASE

While having dinner with friends some time ago I happened to mention that coconut oil was the healthiest oil one could use. A member of the group objected to my statement and responded emphatically, "Coconut oil is unhealthy; it causes heart disease." My rebuke was quick and simple, "That must be why all the Pacific Islanders died off hundreds of years ago." My antagonist didn't know how to respond to this statement. The simple fact is: Pacific Islanders who live on traditional diets rich in coconut don't get heart disease.

Coconuts have traditionally been a staple in the diets of Pacific Islanders for thousands of years. They eat them by the pound every day. Common sense would tell you that if they were as harmful as we are led to believe, all the Islanders should have died off years ago. But until their adoption of modern foods, heart disease and other degenerative conditions were unheard of. Heart disease has only appeared in island populations after traditional foods consisting of coconuts and coconut oil were replaced by modern processed foods and refined vegetable oils.

The early explorers who visited the South Sea Islands in the 16th and 17th centuries described the Islanders as being exceedingly strong, vigorously built, beautiful in body, and kindly disposed. The Islanders gained a reputation for their beauty, excellent physical development, and good health. Some of the islands were viewed as the equivalent to the Garden of Eden where the inhabitants were near perfect in stature and appearance. Such observations may have even fueled interest in the folklore of a fountain of youth. Tales of a mystical island containing such a fountain had been popular for centuries in Europe and led explorers, such as Juan Ponce

15

DeLeon to search in vain for the mythical waters. While a fountain whose waters brought eternal youth was not to be found, the Islanders did have a fountain of youth of sorts. That fountain was in the fruit of the coconut tree, the Tree of Life, as they call it. The coconut with its life-giving water (the oil and milk) bestowed a level of youthful health on these people that far surpassed that of their European visitors.

It wasn't until relatively recently that science began to unlock the secrets to the Islanders' good health and discover the many healing miracles of coconut oil. Through the pioneering research of people like Weston A. Price, Ian A. Prior, Jon J. Kabara, and others, we now know that it was the coconut-based diet that was largely responsible for the Islanders' good health and youthful appearance. It was and still is the reason Pacific Islanders don't get heart disease.

DR. PRICE'S STUDIES
Coconut-Based Diets

The benefits of the native diet of the Pacific Islanders has been noted for decades. A remarkable series of studies of the health of island populations was conducted in the 1930s. These studies were carried out by Dr. Weston A. Price a dentist and nutritional researcher from Cleveland, Ohio. Dr. Price traveled to the Pacific Islands to study the relationship between the Islanders' health and their diet. His results were published in 1938 in a book titled *Nutrition and Physical Degeneration.* This book, which is still in print, is considered a classic in nutritional science.

His travels took him to numerous islands scattered over thousands of miles of the Pacific Ocean. He studied native populations in Hawaii, Somoa, Fiji, Tahiti, Raratonga, Nukualofa, New Caledonia, the Marquesas, and other islands. In the 1930s many of the people still lived as they had for generations, eating traditional foods. Commercial trade with the Islanders brought Western foods and influences to the ports of many of these islands. As a result, many Islanders had adopted the Western way of life and their foods. This provided Dr. Price an ideal setting to study the differences between native and modern diets and how they each affect health.

Being a dentist, Dr. Price focused his research on dental health but also made note of health in general. He examined and analyzed food and diets of the people. He immediately noticed the contrast in health between those who lived entirely on indigenous foods, such as coconut and taro root, and those who had abandoned their traditional diet for Western foods.

Wherever he found Islanders living on traditional foods, he noted that both their dental and physical health were excellent; but when the Islanders abandoned traditional foods and began eating modern foods, their health declined. In the absence of modern medical care, physical degeneration was pronounced. Dental disease, as well as infectious and degenerative diseases such as arthritis and tuberculosis became common. For instance, the differences between the New Caledonian islanders who lived inland and those who lived near the ports where modern foods were available was readily apparent. Speaking of the inland inhabitants Dr. Price noted, "The physical development of the primitive people, including their teeth and dental arches is of very high order. A comparison of the individuals living near the ports with those living in the isolated inland locations shows marked increase in the incidence of dental caries (cavities). For those living almost exclusively on the native foods the incidence of dental caries was only 0.14 percent; while for those using trade foods the incidence of dental caries was 26 percent." He went on to observe that there was also a "progressive development of degenerative diseases around the port."[1]

This wasn't an isolated phenomenon seen on only one or two islands. The same pattern repeated itself over and over again. In fact, every population he studied displayed this pattern. He found no exceptions.

Over all, Dr. Price found that the number of teeth affected by cavities among those who ate traditional native foods was only about 0.3 percent (3 out of every 1000 teeth examined) while the number of cavities in western-ized Islanders was typically as much as 30 percent (3 out of 10). He noted, as do many dentists nowadays, that the health of the mouth reflects the overall health of the individual. People with poor dental health also suffer from many other health problems. People who have good dental health are generally very healthy overall. Recent studies have verified this observa-tion. People who suffer with cavities and gum disease are more prone to develop other health problems. Some of the conditions associated with dental disease include: heart disease, stroke, atherosclerosis, diabetes, ul-cers, and pneumonia. Isn't it interesting that those Islanders who ate coconuts had the best dental health and no gum disease, while those who switched from coconut and other traditional fare to modern foods suffered poor dental health?

In all these island populations coconut, in one form or another, supplied a staple part of their diet. For some it was their primary source of food. The fat (primarily from coconuts) in their diet far exceeded those in the West, yet their health was far superior. Through Dr. Price's studies we see that eating coconuts and coconut oil didn't harm the Islanders one bit. If anything, it gave them a higher level of health than most of us.

The work of Weston A. Price established the fact that Pacific Islanders who maintained their traditional coconut-based diets weren't troubled with dental problems or other conditions such as heart disease. More recent research regarding the connection between dental health and other diseases has supported Dr. Price's findings. The contributions Dr. Price made to nutritional science are kept alive through the Weston A. Price Foundation. Their website (www.westonaprice.org) is full of informative articles on a variety of nutritional topics, including the benefits of coconut oil.

Dental Health and Heart Disease
A wise farmer when considering buying a horse always examines its mouth. He knows that the condition of the animal's mouth reflects the health of its entire body. No farmer in his right mind is going to pay top dollar for an animal with missing teeth or sore gums. Dental problems signal that other health problems are likely present. This is true with humans as well. This fact was recognized long ago and was the basis for the old focal-infection theory used in dentistry. This theory states that an oral infection can influence the health of the whole body. Based on this theory old-time dentists were inclined to pull all diseased teeth in hopes of preventing disease from spreading to other parts of the body. In the mid-20th century better dental techniques were developed, teeth were repaired without being pulled, and the focal-infection theory was ignored. A cavity could be cleaned and filled, germs which cause gum disease could be killed, and infected teeth could be saved with root canals and other procedures.

Fixing the teeth, however, doesn't stop the association between dental disease and health. People can have good-looking teeth but still have recurring episodes with dental disease as well as other health problems. In recent years the focal-infection theory has made a comeback. Poor oral health has been linked with numerous health problems including diabetes and ulcers, but the most striking correlation is with cardiovascular illnesses such as heart disease, stroke, and atherosclerosis.

A definite link between oral health and heart disease has been demonstrated. Several studies have found that heart disease patients have more tooth decay and higher rates of gum disease. The reverse is also true. Those with poor dental health are more likely to suffer a heart attack. Subjects in these studies had their dental health evaluated and then were monitored for several years to see if those with poor dental health were more likely to get heart disease. They were.[2] For example, Robert J. Genco, D.D.S., Ph.D. of the University of Buffalo, studied 1,372 people over a 10-year period and found that heart disease was three times more prevalent for those with gum disease.[3] In the National Health and Nutritional Examination Study published in the *British Medical Journal* (Vol. 306, pp. 688-691) people with inflammation of the gums had a 25 percent increased risk of heart disease. Risk was high even for those who had gum disease in the past as well as currently. From these studies it appears that those who have or have had dental infections have a much higher risk of developing heart disease.

Some researchers believe that oral bacteria that cause dental disease enter the bloodstream through small tears in the gums. In the circulatory system these bacteria can cause inflammation, increase blood clotting, and promote the formation of arterial plaque, all of which leads to heart disease as well as stroke and atherosclerosis.

Others have proposed that the bacteria responsible for heart and gum disease are present in the body due to poor diet and lifestyle choices which weaken the body's natural defenses. To some extent these bacteria are present in the body all the time, but if the body is strong and healthy, the bacteria could not reach numbers that would cause problems. In this view gum disease does not necessarily lead to heart disease; they each happen at the same time, more or less, as a result of the body's inability to adequately control the bacteria.

William Campbell Douglass, M.D., editor of the *Second Opinion* newsletter, has put it this way: "Your teeth are the window to your body's physical condition. They reflect your general state of health. If your teeth are deteriorating, *you* are deteriorating. Hardening of the arteries and decaying teeth are part of the same degenerative process. The one you can see, cavities, comes early in life. The other, atherosclerosis—heart attack, is not seen and comes later. They are a *continuum*—part of the same degenerative process leading to disease and death."

It seems that if you have good dental health you are likely to have good cardiovascular health as well. This is interesting because the Pacific Islanders that Dr. Price studied never brushed their teeth, never flossed, never used antibacterial mouthwash, and never saw dentists, yet they had exquisite dental health, that is, so long as they continued to eat their traditional, coconut-based diet. The Islanders' good dental health was a reflection of the absence of heart disease and other degenerative conditions.

THE PUKAPUKA AND TOKELAU STUDIES

It has long been observed that people of the Pacific Islands and Asia whose diets are high in coconut oil are surprisingly free from cardiovascular disease, cancer, and other degenerative diseases. Some of the most thorough research conducted on people who have a high-fat diet derived primarily from coconuts are the Pukapuka and Tokelau Island studies. These studies involved many researchers and extended for over a decade. The islands of Pukapuka and Tokelau lie near the equator in the South Pacific. Pukapuka is an atoll in the Northern Cooks Islands and Tokelau, another atoll, lies about 400 miles southeast. Both are under the jurisdiction of New Zealand. The populations of both islands have been relatively isolated from Western influences. Their native diet and culture remain much as it has for centuries. Pukapuka and Tokelau are among the more isolated Polynesian islands and have had relatively little interaction with non-Polynesians.

The coral sands of these atolls are porous, lack humus, and will not support the food plants that flourish on other tropical islands. Coconut palms and a few starchy tropical fruits and root vegetables supply the vast majority of their diets. Fish from the ocean, pigs, and chickens make up what little meat they eat. Some flour, rice, sugar, and canned meat are obtained from small cargo ships that occasionally visit the islands.

The standard diets on both islands are high in fat derived from coconuts but low in cholesterol. The diets are high in fiber but low in sugar. The major food source is coconuts. Every meal contains coconut in some form: the green nut provides the main beverage; the mature nut, grated or as coconut cream, is cooked with taro root, breadfruit or rice; and small pieces of coconut meat make an important snack food. Plants and fruitfish are cooked with coconut oil. In Tokelau, coconut sap or toddy is used as a sweetener and as leavening for bread.

The Tokelau and Pukapuka studies were begun in the early 1960s and included the entire populations of both islands. This was a long-term multidisciplinary study set up to examine the physical, social, and health consequences of the people who migrate from the island atolls to New Zealand, where they are exposed to Western foods and influences. The total population of the two islands consisted of about 2,500 people.

The researchers reported that the overall health of both groups was extremely good compared to Western standards. There were no signs of kidney disease nor hypothyroidism that might influence fat levels and no hypercholesterolemia (high blood cholesterol). All inhabitants were lean and healthy despite a very high saturated-fat diet. In fact, the populations as a whole had ideal weight-to-height ratios as compared to the Body Mass Index figures used by nutritionists. Digestive problems were rare, constipation uncommon. The people averaged two or more bowel movements a day. Atherosclerosis, heart disease, colitis, colon cancer, hemorrhoids, ulcers,

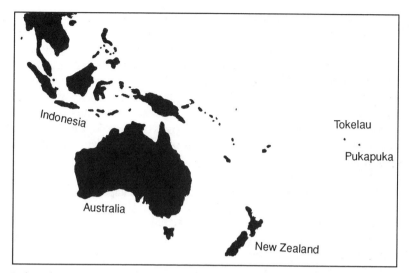

Pukapuka and Tokelau are located in the South Pacific, northeast of New Zealand. Both islands have remained relatively isolated from Western influences.

diverticulosis, and appendicitis are conditions with which they were generally unfamiliar.

Saturated Fat Consumption

The American Heart Association recommends that we get no more than 30 percent of our total calories from fat and that saturated fat should be limited to no more than 10 percent. The Tokelauans apparently aren't aware of these guidelines, because nearly 60 percent of their energy is derived from fat and most all of that is saturated fat derived largely from coconuts. The fat in the Pukapukan diet is also primarily from saturated fatty acids from coconut with total energy from fat being 35 percent.[4] Most Americans and others who eat typical Western diets get 32-38 percent of their calories from fat, most of which is in the form of *unsaturated* vegetable oils. Yet they still suffer from numerous degenerative conditions and weight problems. The islanders in this study consumed as much or more total fat and a far greater amount of saturated fat, yet they are relatively free from degenerative disease and are generally lean and healthy.

Considering the amount of saturated fat in their diet, Dr. Ian A. Prior and colleagues calculated their cholesterol levels. The calculations they used were based on rates observed in Western countries. The islanders had much lower cholesterol levels than predicted.

21

Actual blood cholesterol levels were 70 to 80 mg lower than predicted. Cholesterol levels of the Tokelauans were the higher of the two because they derived 57 percent of total calories from fat. About 50 percent of their total calorie intake comes from saturated fat. Their total food consumption, including imported flour, rice, sugar, and meat was also higher. Dietary cholesterol and polyunsaturated fatty acids of both groups were low. Pukapukans ages 25-54 consumed about 63 grams of saturated fat per day and only 7 grams of unsaturated fat. Tokelauans consumed about 130 grams of saturated fat per day and only 6 grams of unsaturated fat. The saturated fat they ate was primarily from coconuts and is different from most all other dietary saturated fats. The differences in the saturated fat of coconut and those of other foods will be discussed in following chapters.

Dietary Changes Affect Health Status

The migration of Tokelau Islanders from their island atolls to the very different environment of New Zealand is associated with changes in fat intake that indicate increased risk of atherosclerosis. This is associated with an actual *decrease* in saturated fat intake from about 50 percent to 41 percent of energy, an increase in dietary cholesterol intake to 340 mg and an increase in polyunsaturated fat and sugar. Fat changes include increased total cholesterol, higher LDL (bad cholesterol) and triglycerides, and lower HDL (good cholesterol) levels.[5]

Blood cholesterol becomes higher when they migrate to New Zealand despite the fact that the *total* fat content of their diet drops, declining from 57% in Tokelau, with 80% of that from coconut oil, to around 43% in New Zealand.[6] They eat more white bread, rice, meat, and other Western foods and less of their high-fiber, coconut-rich foods.

Ian Prior, who headed some of the studies of these two island populations, stated: "Vascular disease is uncommon in both populations and there is no evidence of the high saturated-fat intake having a harmful effect in these populations."[7]

The conclusion we can make from these island studies is that a high saturated-fat diet consisting of coconut oil is *not* detrimental to health and does *not* contribute to arteriosclerosis. Indeed, those people who eat coconut oil in place of other vegetable oils are amazingly free from the degenerative diseases which are so common in the West. They also have nearly ideal body weight and appear to be examples of perfect health. But when these people replace coconut oil in their diets with other oils and processed foods (which are typically loaded with polyunsaturated and hydrogenated oils) their health declines.

COCONUT OIL IS HEART HEALTHY

All of the criticism that has been aimed at coconut oil is based primarily on the fact that it is a saturated fat and saturated fat is known to increase blood cholesterol. No legitimate research, however, has ever demonstrated any proof that coconut-oil consumption raises blood cholesterol levels.

The reason coconut oil does not adversely affect cholesterol is because it is composed primarily of a group of unique fat molecules known as a medium-chain fatty acids (MCFA). These fatty acids are different from those commonly found in other food sources and are burned almost immediately for energy production, and so they are not converted into body fat or cholesterol and do not affect blood cholesterol levels. Numerous studies have clearly demonstrated that coconut oil has a *neutral* effect on cholesterol levels.[8, 9, 10, 11, 12, 13, 14, 15]

Even the ratio of HDL (good) cholesterol to LDL (bad) cholesterol is not changed.[16, 17] While coconut oil's direct effect on blood cholesterol has shown to be neutral, it may indirectly *lower* LDL (bad) cholesterol and *increase* HDL (good) cholesterol. This is because of its stimulatory effect on the metabolism (see Chapter 10 for a more complete discussion on metabolic effects). One of the factors that increases blood cholesterol is low metabolism. Because coconut oil stimulates metabolism it actually protects against high cholesterol.

In one study performed in the Philippines, for example, ten medical students tested diets consisting of different levels of animal fat and coconut oil. Animal fat is known to raise blood cholesterol. Total calories from dietary fat consisted of 20 percent, 30 percent, and 40 percent, using different combinations of coconut oil and animal fat. At all three levels with a ratio of 1:1, 1:2, and 1:3, animal fat to coconut oil, no significant change in cholesterol levels was observed. Only when the ratio was reversed so that animal fat consumption was greater than coconut oil and when total fat calories reached 40 percent was a significant increase in blood cholesterol reported. This study demonstrated that not only did coconut oil have no effect on cholesterol levels, it even reduced the cholesterol-elevating effects of animal fat.[18] Anyone who says coconut oil contributes to high blood cholesterol is either ignorant of the facts regarding medium-chain fatty acids (MCFA) or has some financial interest at stake.

A review of epidemiological* and experimental data regarding coconut-eating populations shows that dietary coconut oil does not lead to high

---

* Epidemiology is the study of disease in select populations.

blood cholesterol or coronary heart disease.[19] When native peoples change their diets and give up eating coconut oil in favor of refined polyunsaturated vegetable oils, their risk of heart disease has been shown to increase.[20, 21]

Dr. Ian Prior and colleagues found that island populations that ate very high amounts of saturated fat from coconut oil showed no signs of heart disease. But when they migrated to New Zealand and began eating less coconut oil and less saturated fat but more polyunsaturated fats, the incidence of heart disease and other illness greatly increased.[22] Those who blindly state that all saturated fats are unhealthy or that coconut oil consumption leads to heart disease are ignorant of the facts. There is no evidence to support the notion that the saturated fat in coconut oil is harmful.[23] Indeed, there is strong evidence now that coconut oil can help *prevent* heart disease.[24]

An even more important factor in relation to cardiovascular health is the blood's tendency to form clots. Special proteins in the blood called platelets cause clotting when they become sticky. Numerous studies have demonstrated that all fats—beef fat, lard, butter, vegetable oil, and even canola and olive oils—promote platelet stickiness. The more you eat, the stickier the blood gets, and the greater the risk of developing blood clots. The omega-3 fatty acids, like those found in fish oil, are an exception. They have the opposite effect on blood platelets. This is the main reason why they have been recommended for those at risk of heart disease.

Another group of fats that don't promote platelet stickiness are the MCFA in coconut oil. These fats are burned up immediately after consumption and, therefore, do not affect platelet stickiness either one way or the other. Of all the dietary fats, MCFA are the most benign.

People who traditionally consume large quantities of coconut oil as a part of their ordinary diet have a very low incidence of heart disease and have normal blood cholesterol levels. This has been well supported by epidemiological observations recorded in many studies. Those populations who consume large quantities of coconut oil have remarkably good cardiovascular health. Absent are the heart attacks and strokes characteristic in Western countries. After analyzing all available studies and reviewing epidemiological evidence, author and coconut researcher, P.K. Thampan concludes that there is absolutely no correlation between coconut oil consumption and heart disease.[25] If anything, coconut oil consumption is heart healthy.

In Sri Lanka, coconut has been the chief source of fat in the diet for thousands of years. The average consumption in the island country has been reported to be 90 coconuts per capita annually. When the consumption of coconut oil is also taken into consideration, the total consumption in terms of coconuts is 120 annually. Their heart disease rate is far lower than that of noncoconut-eating populations.

In the state of Kerala, in India, where large quantities of coconuts and coconut oil have traditionally been consumed, an average 2.3 out of 1,000 people suffered from coronary heart disease in 1979. A campaign against the use of coconut oil on the grounds that it is an "unhealthy" saturated fat decreased coconut oil consumption during the 1980s. Processed vegetable oils replaced it in household use. As a result, by 1993 the heart disease rate tripled! In Delhi, where the consumption of coconut products is negligible, 10 out of 1,000 people had heart disease in the same time period.[26] In Western countries where refined vegetable oil is the main source of fat, heart disease accounts for nearly half of all deaths. It seems that if you want to protect yourself from heart disease, you should replace your processed vegetable oils with coconut oil.

Not only does coconut oil not contribute to heart disease or any other health problem, it actually provides protection from them. If you want to prevent heart disease, you may want to add coconut oil to your diet. The marvelous anti-heart disease effects of coconut oil are discussed more thoroughly in Chapter 7.

Numerous scientific studies, observations of coconut eating populations, and even just plain old common sense would tell you that coconut oil, if anything, is heart healthy. So why all the negative publicity in the press about coconut oil? The answer to that question is found in the following chapter. There I explain why coconut oil is so severely criticized, and the reason has nothing to do with science.

25

THE TROPICAL OILS WAR

A CAMPAIGN OF TERROR

At this point you may be asking: "If coconut oil is as good as you say it is, why isn't it used more often?" The simple reason is money, politics, and misunderstanding. Everybody knows coconut oil is a saturated fat, and who wants to add saturated fat to their diet? We're constantly told to reduce our fat intake, especially saturated fat. The words "saturated fat" have almost become synonymous with "heart disease." Very few people know the difference between the medium-chain fatty acids (MCFA) in coconut oil and the long-chain fatty acids in meat and other foods. To most people, saturated fat is saturated fat—an evil substance lurking in foods waiting for the opportunity to attack and strike you down with a heart attack. Even medical professionals don't know there is a difference. Most don't even know there is more than one type of saturated fat (the different types are discussed in Chapter 4). If someone warns you not to eat coconut oil because it's a saturated fat, yet he has no idea that there are many different types of saturated fat, are you going to listen to him? Such people only repeat what they hear and have no understanding of fats and how they affect the body. Unfortunately, many health care workers and health and fitness writers fall into this category. Only recently has the truth about coconut oil been reemerging.

As far back as the 1950s, research began to show the health benefits of coconut oil. For many years it was considered a good oil with many nutritional uses. So how did coconut oil become a despised artery-clogging villain? Give credit to the American Soybean Association (ASA).

It began in the mid 1980s. At the time the media was stirred into a frenzy warning the public about a newly discovered health threat—coconut oil. Coconut oil, they proclaimed, was a saturated fat and would cause heart attacks. Everywhere you turned, any product that contained coconut or palm oil was criticized as being "unhealthful." In response to the seemingly overwhelming public response, movie theaters began cooking their popcorn in soybean oil. Food makers began switching from the tropical oils they had used for years to soybean oil. Restaurants stopped using tropical oils in favor of soybean and other vegetable oils. By the early 1990s, the tropical oils market had dwindled to a fraction of what it once was. The promoters of this media blitz declared a victory in their fight against tropical oils.

This war of oils, unfortunately, made every man, woman, and child in America (and elsewhere) its victim. The only winner was the soybean industry. Why are we the victims? Because the oil that replaced coconut and palm oils was *hydrogenated* vegetable oil (principally from soybeans)—one of the most health-damaging dietary oils in existence. It is ironic that these hydrogenated replacements contain as much saturated fat as the tropical oils.[1] But these replacements are not made from easily digested medium-chain fatty acids (MCFA), they are composed of toxic trans fatty acids. The result has been to replace healthy tropical oils with some very nasty, chemically altered vegetable oils. We are all victims because when we eat foods containing these oils our health suffers.

The entire campaign was a carefully orchestrated plan by the American Soybean Association (ASA) to eliminate competition from imported tropical oils. During the 1960s and 1970s, research indicated that some forms of saturated fat increased blood cholesterol. Since elevated cholesterol was recognized as a risk factor in the development of heart disease, saturated fat was, consequently, regarded as an undesirable food component and we were advised to reduce our intake of it. The prevailing opinion was that the less saturated fat you ate the better.

Capitalizing on the public's fear of saturated fat and its perceived association with heart disease, the ASA set out to create a health crisis. The crisis they planned would be so terrifying it would literally scare people away from using tropical oils. In 1986 the ASA sent a "Fat Fighter Kit" to soybean farmers encouraging them to write government officials, food companies, etc., protesting the encroachment of "highly saturated tropical fats like palm and coconut oils." The wives and families of some 400,000 soybean growers were encouraged to fan out across the country in a lobbying effort touting the health benefits of soybean oil. Well meaning, but misguided health groups such as the Center for Science in the Public Interest (CSPI) joined in the battle, issuing news releases referring to palm, coconut, and palm kernel oils as "artery-clogging fat."

CSPI, a non-profit consumer activist group, had been criticizing saturated fats since its founding in the 1970s. Like most nutritional advocates at the time, they mistakenly believed that all saturated fats were the same and attacked them with a vengeance. Encouraged by the publicity generated by the ASA, they began to intensify their attack. The tropical oils, being highly saturated, were severely criticized in their promotional literature, news releases, and lobbying efforts. It seemed the CSPI considered saturated fat to be the worst evil ever to face mankind. The ASA had found a powerful and vocal ally in its campaign to take over the tropical oil market.

For a group that claimed to be an advocate for responsible nutritional education, the CSPI was surprisingly ignorant regarding saturated fats, especially concerning MCFA. Instead of informing the public about the truth regarding saturated fats, they only succeeded in strengthening misconceptions and falsehoods. The CSPI's lack of knowledge concerning lipid biochemistry was revealed in a booklet they published called *Saturated Fat Attack*. While the laymen and many health care professionals may have been fooled by the information in this booklet, nutritional biochemist Mary G. Enig, Ph.D. says, "There were lots of substantive mistakes in the booklet, including errors in the description of the biochemistry of fats and oils and completely erroneous statements about the fat and oil composition of many of the products."[2] Most people, however, would not have known this, and the booklet and other inaccurate information distributed by the group succeeded in convincing many to completely shun tropical oils. CSPI's lack of accurate scientific knowledge made them an unsuspecting puppet for the ASA.

In October 1988, Nebraska millionaire Phil Sokolof, a recovered heart attack patient and founder of the National Heart Savers Association, jumped on the media bandwagon. He began running full-page newspaper advertisements accusing food companies of "poisoning America" by using tropical oils with high levels of saturated fat. Radically anti-saturated fat, he staged a blistering national ad campaign attacking tropical oils as a health danger. One ad showed a coconut "bomb" with a lighted wick and cautioned consumers that their health was threatened by coconut and palm oils. Before long everybody "knew" that coconut oil was a "bad" saturated fat.

Food manufacturers joined in too. Trying to profit off the anti-tropical oils sentiment they tried to add labels to their products which read "contains no tropical oil." The U.S. Federal Trade Commission ruled such labels illegal because the statement implied a health claim which portrayed the product as being better for not having tropical oil, but there was no evidence to back it up.

FICTION TRIUMPHS OVER FACT

Meanwhile, tropical oil exporters from Malaysia prepared a public relations campaign against what it called "vicious scare tactics" being used against its product. The tropical oil war was in full swing. At stake was the $3 billion-a-year vegetable oil market in the United States, where the dominant domestic soy oil producers had launched a vicious propaganda war against foreign competitors.

The tropical oil industry, having few allies and comparatively little financial muscle to retaliate, couldn't match the combined efforts of the ASA, CSPI, and others. Few would listen to the lone voices protesting the dissemination of the false information attacking tropical oils.

When the attack on coconut oil began, those medical and research professionals who were familiar with it wondered why. They knew coconut oil did not contribute to heart disease and that it provided many health advantages. Some even stepped forward to set the record straight. But by this time public sentiment had firmly sided with the ASA, and people refused to listen.

Researchers familiar with tropical oils were called on to testify on the health implications of these products. "Coconut oil has a neutral effect on blood cholesterol, even in situations where coconut oil is the sole source of fat," reported Dr. George Blackburn, a Harvard Medical School researcher who testified at a congressional hearing about tropical oils held on June 21, 1988. "These (tropical) oils have been consumed as a substantial part of the diet of many groups for thousands of years with absolutely no evidence of any harmful effects to the populations consuming them," said Mary G. Enig, Ph.D., an expert on fats and oils and a former research associate at the University of Maryland.[3]

Dr. C. Everett Koop, former Surgeon General of the United States, called the tropical-oil scare "foolishness." Commercial interests either trying to divert blame to others or ignorantly following the saturated-fat hysteria were "...terrorizing the public about nothing." Many misguided public interest groups have also condemned coconut oil because they believed all saturated fats were bad.

Dr. David Klurfeld, Chairman and Professor of the Department of Nutrition and Food Science at Wayne State University called the anti-tropical oils campaign "Public relations mumbo jumbo." He pointed out that tropical oils amounted to only about 2 percent of the American diet and that even if they were as bad as the ASA claimed, they wouldn't have much of an affect on health, "The amount of tropical oils in the U.S. diet is so low that there is no reason to worry about it. The countries with the highest palm oil intakes in the world are Costa Rica and Malaysia. Their heart disease rates and serum cholesterol levels are much lower than in western nations. This [tropical oils scare] never was a real health issue." Despite testimonials of respected medical professionals and lipid (oil) researchers, the media paid little attention. The saturated fat crisis was news and that got headlines. Major newspapers and television and radio networks picked up the anti-saturated-fat ads and developed alarming news stories. One such story was titled "The Oil From Hell." Those who knew the truth about coconut oil were ignored and even criticized by those brainwashed by the media blitz. Because of the frenzy stirred up by the ASA and their friends, the fictional message they trumpeted won out over scientific fact.

CURSE OF THE TRANS FATTY ACIDS

Catering to public sentiment, McDonald's, Burger King, and Wendy's restaurants announced they would replace the saturated fat they had used with more "healthful" vegetable oils. The switch to the new vegetable oils actually *increased* the fat content of the fried foods—hardly a healthful move. Tests by the Food and Drug Administration (FDA) and others found that french fries cooked in beef tallow absorbed *less* fat than those cooked in vegetable oil, which led to estimates that the switch to vegetable oil would more than double the fat content of fries and *increase* fat consumption.[4] Plus, the fat was *hydrogenated*, which is worse than beef tallow because it contains toxic trans fatty acids. Trans fatty acids have a greater negative effect on blood cholesterol than beef tallow and, therefore, are considered a greater risk for heart disease.

The ASA succeeded in producing a health crisis where none had existed. The general ignorance about nutrition by most people swayed them into siding with the soybean industry, which proves money and politics can override truth. In reality, there was no public outcry; the change was mainly brought about by an aggressive negative campaign. As a result, most major food companies, sensitive to consumer fear, reformulated hundreds of products, replacing tropical oils with hydrogenated oils. Since 1990, the fast food industry has been cooking french fries in hydrogenated vegetable oil instead of beef tallow and tropical oils. They made the change because of the prevailing opinion that vegetable oils were healthier than other oils.

Breads, cookies, crackers, soups, stews, sauces, candy, frozen and prepared foods of all sorts were typically made using tropical oils. Up until the late 1980s tropical oils were common ingredients in many of our foods. They were used extensively by the food industry because they gave foods many desirable properties. These plant-derived saturated fats, being highly stable, do not go rancid as polyunsaturated oils do. When tropical oils were used, foods remained fresh longer and were better for you. That's not the case any more. It's hard to find foods made with tropical oils nowadays.

As a result of the tropical oils war, coconut and palm oils have nearly disappeared from our food supply. The consequence is that we now consume far less of the health-promoting fatty acids found in coconut oil and much more of the health destroying trans fatty acids found in hydrogenated soybean oil. Nearly 80 percent of all the vegetable oil used in the United States today comes from soybeans. Three-fourths of that oil is hydrogenated (containing up to 50 percent trans fatty acids).[5] This amounts to an awful lot of nasty trans fatty acids that are in our foods now that weren't there before. For example, a single restaurant meal, which in 1982 contained only 2.4 grams of trans fatty acids, contains a whopping 19.2 grams today. The food is the same; only the oil is different. Because hydrogenated oils are used everywhere, we are cursed with trans fatty acids just about anytime we eat (unless we prepare our food from scratch).

Yes, we lost the war. We lost the many health benefits that can result from regular consumption of coconut products. But we gained too. We gained an increased chance of suffering from heart disease, cancer, diabetes, infectious disease, obesity, and immune dysfunction. These are conditions that have all been tied to the consumption of hydrogenated and partially-hydrogenated vegetable oils. Through the cunning marketing strategies of the ASA and the misguided efforts of public interest groups we have replaced a good health-promoting fat with a very destructive and harmful one.*

Even now the cinders of this war still burn. Many ill-informed writers and speakers continue to condemn coconut oil as containing "artery-clogging" saturated fat.** But who are you going to believe? Are you going to believe the soybean industry, which has a huge financial interest at stake or are you going to believe the Pacific Islanders who eat a great deal of coconut oil and have far better health than the rest of us? Are you going to believe the residents of Sri Lanka who eat lots of coconut oil but have one of the lowest rates of heart disease in the world? Personally, I believe those

---

* If you have any doubts about the aggressive tactics used by the soybean industry and harmful health effects of their products, I recommend you get on the Internet and look up www.soyonlineservice.co.nz. This information may shock you.
** The term "artery-clogging saturated fat" is a misnomer. The fat that collects in arterial plaque is primarily *un*saturated fats (74 percent) and cholesterol. Saturated fat does not collect in the arteries like poly- and monounsaturated fat because it is not easily oxidized and only oxidized fat ends up as arterial plaque. Vegetables oils are easily oxidized by over-processing and heating.

people who eat coconut oil and don't have heart disease. In Western countries we eat very little coconut oil but consume a significant amount of hydrogenated vegetable oils. The result? Heart disease is on a rampage. It is our number one killer.

Studies have clearly shown that natural coconut oil as a part of a normal diet has a neutral effect on blood cholesterol. Non-hydrogenated, non-adulterated coconut oil has absolutely no adverse health effects. Epidemiological studies show conclusively that populations that consume large amounts of coconut oil experience almost no heart disease as compared to other populations in which coconut oil is only a small part of the diet. If coconut oil did have any adverse health effects associated with it, we would see it reflected in the morbidity and mortality of countries which are high consumers of coconut oil. Yet, they are among the healthiest people in the world. Simple logic clearly refutes the ASA smear campaign. As you will discover in the following chapters, coconut oil offers so many health benefits it is correctly labeled "the healthiest oil on earth."

WHY COCONUT OIL IS DIFFERENT

In this chapter I will describe the differences between saturated and unsaturated fats and explain the reason why coconut oil is different from all the rest. Since the uniqueness of each oil depends on its chemical makeup, I am forced to described the differences in chemical terms. Unfortunately, when chemistry is discussed it is easy for those people who lack a scientific background to become confused. Please bear with me; I will make my explanation simple enough for the layman to understand. If you get confused, that's okay, skim through the material and go on to the next chapter. The purpose of this chapter is to provide you with a scientific foundation. You don't need to know chemistry in order to benefit from using coconut oil.

TRIGLYCERIDES

Doctors often use the term "lipid" in referring to fat. Lipid is a general term that includes several fat-like compounds in the body. By far the most abundant and the most important of the lipids are the triglycerides. When we speak of fats and oils we are usually referring to triglycerides. Two other lipids—phospholipids and sterols (which includes cholesterol)—technically are not fats because they are not triglycerides. But they have similar characteristics and are often referred to as fats.

What is the difference between a fat and an oil? The terms fat and oil are often used interchangeably. Generally speaking, the only real difference is that fats are considered solid at room temperature while oils remain liquid. Lard, for example, would be referred to as a fat, while corn oil is called an oil. Both, however, are fats.

When you cut into a steak, the white fatty tissue you see is composed of triglycerides. Cholesterol is also present, but it is intermingled within the meat fibers and undetectable with the naked eye. The fat that is a nuisance to us, the type that hangs on our arms, looks like jelly on our thighs, and can make your stomach look like a spare tire, is composed of triglycerides. It is the triglycerides that make up our body fat and the fat we see and eat in our foods. About 95 percent of the lipids in our diet, from both plant and animal sources, are triglycerides.

Saturated fat is a triglyceride; so is polyunsaturated fat. Triglycerides are composed of individual fat molecules known as *fatty acids*. It takes three fatty acid molecules to make a single triglyceride molecule.

FATTY ACIDS

There are dozens of different types of fatty acids. Scientists have grouped these into three general categories: saturated, monounsaturated, and polyunsaturated. Each category contains several members. So, there are many different types of saturated, monounsaturated, and polyunsaturated fats.

Each of the fatty acids, regardless of whether it is saturated or not, affects the body differently and exerts different influences on health. Therefore, one saturated fat may have adverse health effects, while another may promote better health. The same is true with monounsaturated and polyunsaturated fats. For example, olive oil has been hailed as one of the "good" fats because those people who eat it in place of other oils have less heart disease. Olive oil is composed primarily of a monounsaturated fatty acid called *oleic acid*. However, not all monounsaturated fats are healthy. Another monounsaturated fatty acid known as *erucic acid* is extremely toxic to the heart, more so than perhaps any other fatty acid known.[1] The difference between the two, chemically, is very slight. Likewise, some polyunsaturated fatty acids can also cause problems. On the other hand, the saturated fatty acids that are found in coconut oil have no harmful effects and actually promote better health. So we cannot say one oil is "bad" because it is saturated while another is "good" because it is monounsaturated or polyunsaturated. It all depends on the type of fatty acid and not simply on its degree of saturation.

No dietary oil is purely saturated or unsaturated. All fats and oils consist of a mixture of the three classes of fatty acids. To say an oil is saturated or monounsaturated is gross oversimplification. Olive oil is often called "monounsaturated" because it is *predominantly* monounsaturated, but like all vegetable oils, it also contains some polyunsaturated and saturated fat as well.

Animal fats are generally the highest in saturated fat. Vegetable oils contain saturated fat as well as monounsaturated and polyunsaturated fat. Most vegetable oils are high in polyunsaturated fats, the exception being palm and coconut oils which are very high in saturated fat. Coconut oil contains as much as 92 percent saturated fat—more than any other oil including beef fat and lard.

COMPOSITION OF DIETARY FATS

Fat	Saturated	Mono	Poly
Canola Oil	6	62	32
Safflower Oil	10	13	77
Sunflower Oil	11	20	69
Corn Oil	13	25	62
Soybean Oil	15	24	61
Olive Oil	14	77	9
Chicken Fat	31	47	22
Lard	41	47	12
Beef Fat	52	44	4
Palm Oil	51	39	10
Butter	66	30	4
Coconut Oil	92	6	2

SATURATION AND SIZE

We hear the terms saturated, monounsaturated, and polyunsaturated all the time, but what do they mean? What is a saturated fat saturated with? All fatty acids consist primarily of a chain of carbon atoms with varying numbers of hydrogen atoms attached to them. A molecule that has two hydrogen atoms attached to each carbon is said to be "saturated" with hydrogen because it is holding all the hydrogen atoms it possibly can. This type of fatty acid is called a saturated fat. A fatty acid that is missing a pair of hydrogen atoms on one of its carbons is called a monounsaturated fat. If more than two hydrogen atoms are missing, it's called a polyunsaturated fat. Wherever a pair of hydrogen atoms is missing, the adjoining carbon atoms must form a double bond (see examples on the following page). This is important because this double bond produces a weak link in the carbon chain which, as we will see in the next chapter, can have a dramatic influence on health.

The concept of saturation can be described by using an analogy with a school bus full of kids. The bus could represent the carbon chain and the students the hydrogen atoms. Each seat on the bus can hold two students just as each carbon can hold two hydrogen atoms. A bus filled to capacity so there are no empty seats would be analogous to a saturated fat. No more

Saturated Fatty Acid

```
    H   H   H   H   H   H   H   H   H   H   H   H   H   H   H   H   H   O
    |   |   |   |   |   |   |   |   |   |   |   |   |   |   |   |   |   ‖
H - C - C - C - C - C - C - C - C - C - C - C - C - C - C - C - C - C - C - O-H
    |   |   |   |   |   |   |   |   |   |   |   |   |   |   |   |   |
    H   H   H   H   H   H   H   H   H   H   H   H   H   H   H   H
```

Saturated fats are loaded, or saturated, with all the hydrogen (H) atoms they can carry. The example shown above is stearic acid an 18-carbon saturated fat commonly found in beef fat.

Monounsaturated Fatty Acid

```
    H   H   H   H   H   H   H   H               H   H   H   H   H   H   H   O
    |   |   |   |   |   |   |   |               |   |   |   |   |   |   |   ‖
H - C - C - C - C - C - C - C - C - C = C - C - C - C - C - C - C - C - C - O-H
    |   |   |   |   |   |   |   |   |   |   |   |   |   |   |   |   |
    H   H   H   H   H   H   H   H   H   H   H   H   H   H   H   H   H
```

If one pair of hydrogens were to be removed from the saturated fat, the carbon atoms would form double bonds with one another in order to satisfy their bonding requirements. The result would be an unsaturated fat. In this case it would form a monounsaturated fatty acid. The example shown is oleic acid, an 18-chain monounsaturated fatty acid which is found predominantly in olive oil.

Polyunsaturated Fatty Acid

```
    H   H   H   H   H           H           H   H   H   H   H   H   H   O
    |   |   |   |   |           |           |   |   |   |   |   |   |   ‖
H - C - C - C - C - C - C = C - C - C = C - C - C - C - C - C - C - C - C - O-H
    |   |   |   |   |   |   |   |   |   |   |   |   |   |   |   |   |
    H   H   H   H   H   H   H   H   H   H   H   H   H   H   H   H
```

If two or more pairs of hydrogen atoms are missing and more than one double carbon bond is present, it is referred to as a polyunsaturated oil. The example illustrated is linoleic acid an 18-chain polyunsaturated acid. This is the most common fat in vegetable oils.

students can fit on the bus. If two students get off the bus and leave one seat vacant, that would be analogous to a monounsaturated fat. If four or more students get off the bus leaving two or more empty seats, that would be like a polyunsaturated fat. A school bus that is only half filled would be like a fatty acid that is *very* polyunsaturated.

The length of the fatty acid chain, or size of the school bus, is also important. Some fatty acids contain only two carbon atoms while others have as many as 24 or more. The two-carbon fatty acid would be like a bus that has only two seats, so that it can carry a maximum of four students— two in each seat. A fatty acid with 24 carbons would be like a long bus with 24 seats, allowing room for 48 students.

Acetic acid, found in vinegar, has a chain only two carbon atoms long. A longer acid chain may have four, six, eight, or more carbon atoms. Naturally occurring fatty acids usually occur in even numbers. Butyric acid, one type of fatty acid commonly found in butter, consists of a four-carbon chain. The predominant fatty acids found in meats and fish are 14 or more carbon atoms long. Stearic acid, common in beef fat, has an 18-carbon chain. The 14- to 24-carbon fatty acids are known as long-chain fatty acids (LCFA).* Medium-chain fatty acids (MCFA) range from 8 to 12 carbons and short-chain (SCFA) range from 2 to 6 carbons. The length of the carbon chain is a key factor in the way dietary fat is digested and metabolized and how it affects the body.

The degree of saturation and length of the carbon chain of the fatty acids determine their chemical properties and their effects on our health. The more saturated the fat and the longer the chain, the harder the fat and the higher the melting point. Saturated fat, like that found in lard, is solid at room temperature. Polyunsaturated fat, like corn oil, is liquid at room temperature. Monounsaturated fat is liquid at room temperature, but in the refrigerator it begins to solidify slightly and becomes cloudy or semi-solid. Short-chain fatty acids (SCFA) are soft and fluid while long-chain fatty acids (LCFA) become thick or waxy. Butter, which contains a mixture of short- and long-chain saturated fatty acids, is very soft when not refrigerated and melts easily when the room temperature rises on warm days. Most vegetable oils have very low melting points and, therefore, are liquid.

---

* Three fatty acids joined together by a glycerol molecule make a triglyceride. The glycerol molecule acts like a backbone so-to-speak for the triglyceride. All glycerol molecules look exactly alike, but the fatty acids may vary in size and degree of saturation. When three fatty acids of similar length are joined together by a glycerol molecule, the resulting molecule is referred to as long-chain triglyceride (LCT), medium-chain triglyceride (MCT), or short-chain triglyceride (SCT).

FATTY ACIDS

Fatty Acid	No. of Carbons	No. of Double Bonds	Common Source
SATURATED FATTY ACIDS			
Acetic	2	0	Vinegar
Butyric	4	0	Butterfat
Caproic	6	0	Butterfat
Caprylic	8	0	Coconut oil
Capric	10	0	Palm oil
Lauric	12	0	Coconut oil
Myristic	14	0	Nutmeg oil, butterfat
Palmitic	16	0	Animal and vegetable oil
Stearic	18	0	Animal and vegetable oil
Arachidic	20	0	Peanut oil
MONOUNSATURATED FATTY ACIDS			
Palmitoleic	16	1	Butterfat
Oleic	18	1	Olive oil
Erucic	22	1	Rapeseed oil (Canola)*
POLYUNSATURATED FATTY ACIDS			
Linoleic	18	2	Vegetable oil
Alpha-linolenic	18	3	Linseed oil
Arachidonic	20	4	Lecithin
Eicosapentaenoic	20	5	Fish oils
Docosahexaenoic	22	6	Fish oils

* Rapeseed oil contains as much as 55% erucic acid—a very toxic fatty acid. Through the process of genetic engineering the erucic acid content has been reduced to less than 1%. To distinguish this genetically altered oil from the original it is given the name canola oil. This is the canola oil found in our foods.

Fatty acids commonly found in foods.

The fats found in animal tissue, as well as our own bodies, are mainly the triglycerides of stearic, palmitic, and oleic acids. Oleic acid is a monounsaturated fat. Stearic and palmitic acids are saturated fats.

The saturated fat found in food consists of a mixture of the different types. Milk, for example, contains palmitic, myristic, stearic, lauric, butyric, caproic, caprylic, and capric acids. Each of these fatty acids exerts different effects on the body which are governed by the length of the carbon chain and the degree of saturation.

Saturated fatty acids with up to 26 carbon atoms (C:26) and as few as 2 (C:2) carbons in the chain have been identified as constituents of fats. Of these, palmitic acid (C:16) is the most common, occurring in almost all fats. Myristic (C:14) and stearic (C:18) acids are other common saturated fatty acids.

The melting points of the saturated fatty acids increase with carbon chain length. Esters of fatty acids with more than 18 carbon atoms are characteristic constituents of waxes. Fatty acids less than 10 or greater than 22 carbons long are not generally abundant in nature.

Saturated fats have received a lot of criticism for their role in raising blood cholesterol. While some saturated fats do raise blood cholesterol, others do not. To say that all saturated fats raise cholesterol is simply not true. Myristic (C:14) and palmitic (C:16) acids exert the greatest cholesterol raising effect. Stearic (C:18) and most of the shorter chain saturated fatty acids (less than 12 carbons) do *not* raise blood cholesterol.

Short-chain fatty acids (SCFA) are relatively rare in nature. The most common sources are found in vinegar and butter. Medium-chain fatty acids (MCFA) are also relatively rare but found in moderate concentrations in some tropical plants. Long-chain fatty acids (LCFA) are by far the most common fatty acids found in nature. Long-chain fatty acids provide the most efficient or compact energy package and thus make the best storage fats in both plants and animals. Fat cells in our bodies and those of animals are almost entirely long-chained. The fatty acids in most plants, whether saturated or unsaturated, are almost entirely of the long-chained variety.

The fats in our foods are composed almost entirely of long-chain fatty acids. Most oils contain no SCFA or MCFA. Those that do have only minimal amounts and are, therefore, insignificant. Very few foods contain any appreciable amount of the short- or medium-chain fatty acids, and all of them are saturated. Milk contains tiny amounts of the shorter chain fatty acids. These fats are concentrated in the making of butter and comprise about 12 percent of the total fat content. Tropical nuts and oils are by far the greatest dietary source of medium-chain fatty acids.

TROPICAL OILS ARE UNIQUE

Coconut oil and its relatives, palm and palm kernel oils, are unique in that they contain the highest natural source of medium- and short-chain fatty acids. This is what makes them different from all other dietary oils and what gives them their incredible health-promoting properties.

Palm oil contains only a small amount of medium-chain fatty acids (MCFA). Coconut and palm kernel oils are by far our richest dietary sources of these important fatty acids. Palm kernel oil contains 58 percent MCFA and coconut oil 64 percent. Because they are both composed predominantly of MCFA, their effects on health are characterized by the chemical and biological properties associated with these fats. Much of the information in this book discusses the many health aspects of MCFA derived from tropical oils.

In summary, the fats and oils in our diet are predominantly triglycerides. Each triglyceride molecule is comprised of three fatty acids. Those fatty acids that are fully loaded with hydrogen atoms and have no double carbon bonds are called saturated fats; those that have one or more double bonds are unsaturated fats. The carbon chains that make up the fatty acids can be as short as two carbons or as long as 24. Most all of the fatty acids stored as body fat are long-chain fatty acids (in the form of long-chain triglycerides). Fats in our foods, if not used immediately as an energy source, are stored as fat tissue on our bodies. Coconut oil is composed predominantly of medium- and short-chain fatty acids and, therefore, has a totally different effect on the body than the typical long-chain fatty acids (both saturated and unsaturated) found abundantly in meat and vegetable oils. As you will see in the following chapters, medium-chain fatty acids in our foods are broken down and used predominately for energy production and thus seldom end up as body fat or as deposits in arteries or anywhere else. They produce energy, not fat.

OILS AND YOUR HEALTH

SATURATED FAT AND CHOLESTEROL

Saturated fat has been labeled a dietary villain that we should avoid at all costs. We buy lean cuts of meat, non-fat milk, and low-fat foods of all types in order to limit our intake of this dreaded substance. But why is saturated fat so bad? There is really only one reason; saturated fat is easily converted by the liver into cholesterol. Eating too much saturated fat can raise blood cholesterol levels which, in turn, is believed to increase the risk of heart disease.

Contrary to popular belief, neither saturated fat nor cholesterol *cause* heart disease. This is a fact that all fat researchers and medical professionals know, but many of the rest of us do not. High blood cholesterol is only one of many so-called *risk factors* associated with heart disease. What this means is that those people who have heart disease sometimes also have elevated blood cholesterol levels. Not all people with high blood cholesterol develop heart disease and not everyone with heart disease has high blood cholesterol. If high blood cholesterol were the cause of heart disease, *everybody* who dies from this disease would have elevated cholesterol levels, but they don't. In fact, most people who have heart disease do *not* have high blood cholesterol.[1]

Other risk factors associated with heart disease include high blood pressure, age, gender (being male), tobacco use, diabetes, obesity, stress, lack of exercise, insulin levels, and homocysteine levels. High blood cholesterol is no more the cause of heart disease than age or being a male is. It's guilty only by association.

Blood levels of homocysteine is one of the most accurate of the risk factors. Homocysteine is an amino acid derived from protein found in meat, milk, and other foods. Recent research has shown that homocysteine levels in the blood are much more strongly associated with heart disease than cholesterol.[2] In fact, homocysteine may help raise blood cholesterol. The association of high blood cholesterol with heart disease may be due more from homocysteine (derived primarily from protein found in meat and dairy products) than from cholesterol (or saturated fat).

The important thing to remember from all this is that neither saturated fat nor cholesterol *cause* heart disease. Furthermore, saturated fat is not the only substance that your liver converts into cholesterol. Other fats, as well as carbohydrate, also end up as cholesterol in our bodies. Carbohydrate is the main nutritional component of all fruits, vegetables, and grains. To infer that only saturated fat raises blood cholesterol is grossly inaccurate and misleading. Some foods raise blood cholesterol more than others. Some have little or no effect depending on many metabolic factors. Medium-chain saturated fatty acids, like those found in coconut oil, are burned up immediately to create energy and, therefore, have a neutral effect on blood cholesterol!

PLATELETS AND BLOOD CLOTS

The mechanism that causes blood to stick together to form clots is influenced by dietary oils. The clotting agents in blood are called platelets. Platelets are tiny protein particles that look like plates. When you cut yourself, they stick together, forming a clot which prevents you from bleeding to death. In healthy people, the blood becomes sticky only when it comes in contact with a wound or injury. If you could reach inside the body and touch healthy blood while it was surging around your body, it would feel slippery. But in recent heart attack victims, the blood in their bodies has been found to be about 4.5 times stickier than in normal people. If you could look at your blood under a microscope you would be able to see platelets sticking to each other and to artery walls. When platelets stick to walls, they form clots which can block the flow of blood. When a blood clot forms in the heart it can cause a heart attack, in the carotid artery that feeds the brain, a stroke.

A common criticism of saturated fat is that it increases platelet adhesiveness (blood stickiness), thus promoting the development of blood clots. Some of the long-chain saturated fats do increase platelet stickiness, but so do most polyunsaturated fats found in vegetable oils. All dietary oils both saturated and unsaturated, with the exception of two, *increase* platelet stickiness. Even olive oil increases blood clot risk.[3] The two exceptions are the omega-3 fatty acids (e.g., flaxseed oil, fish oil) and the medium-chain fatty acids (e.g., tropical oils). So, when you eat corn, safflower, soybean, cottonseed, canola, and peanut oils you are increasing your risk of suffering a heart attack or stroke. Eating omega-3 and medium-chain fatty acids reduces that risk.

FREE RADICALS

Research over the past three decades has identified a key player in the cause and development of degenerative disease and aging. That player is the free radical.

Simply stated, a free radical is a renegade molecule (or atom) that has lost an electron in its outer shell, leaving an unpaired electron. This creates a highly unstable and powerful molecular entity. These radicals will quickly attack and steal an electron from a neighboring molecule. The second molecule, now with one less electron, becomes a highly reactive free radical itself and pulls an electron off yet another nearby molecule. This process continues in a destructive chain reaction that may affect hundreds and even thousands of molecules.

Once a molecule becomes a radical, its physical and chemical properties are permanently changed. When this molecule is part of a living cell, it affects the function of the entire cell. Free radicals can attack our cells, literally ripping their protective membranes apart. Sensitive cellular components like the nucleus and DNA, which carries the genetic blueprint of the cell, can be damaged, leading to cellular mutations and death.

The more free radicals that attack our cells, the greater the damage and the greater the potential for serious destruction. If the cells that are damaged are in our heart or arteries, what happens? If they are in the brain, what happens? If they are in our joints, pancreas, intestines, liver, or kidneys, what happens? Think about it. If the cells are damaged, dysfunctional, or dead, can these organs fulfill their intended purpose at optimal levels, or do they degenerate?

Free-radical damage has been linked to the loss of tissue integrity and to physical degeneration. As cells are bombarded by free radicals the tissues become progressively impaired. Some researchers believe that free-radical destruction is the actual cause of aging.[4] The older the body gets, the more damage it sustains from a lifetime accumulation of attack from free radicals.

Today some sixty or so degenerative diseases are recognized as having free radicals involved in their cause or manifestation.[5] Additional diseases are regularly being added to this list. Research that linked the major killer diseases such as heart disease and cancer to free radicals has expanded to include atherosclerosis, stroke, varicose veins, hemorrhoids, hypertension, wrinkled skin, dermatitis, arthritis, digestive problems, reproductive problems, cataracts, loss of energy, diabetes, allergies, failing memory, and other degenerative conditions.

The more free radicals to which we are exposed, the more damage occurs to our cells and tissues, which increases our chances of developing the conditions listed above. We are exposed to free radicals from the pollutants in the air we breath and from the chemical additives and toxins in the foods we eat and drink. Some free-radical reactions occur as part of the natural process of cellular metabolism. We can't avoid all the free radicals in our environment, but we can limit them. Cigarette smoke, for example, causes free-radical reactions in the lungs. Certain foods and food additives also cause destructive free-radical reactions that affect the entire body. Limiting your exposure to these free-radical causing substances will reduce your risk of developing a number of degenerative conditions. In this regard, the types of oil you use have a very pronounced effect on your health.

POLYUNSATURATED OILS

When nutritionists tell us to reduce fat intake, we automatically think only of saturated fat. But the recommendation is to reduce *all* fats, including polyunsaturated fats. In an attempt to reduce saturated fat people often substitute vegetable oils for those of animal origin. Many vegetable fats, however, are no better than the animal fats we try so hard to avoid. In some cases they can be even worse!

The thing that makes vegetable oils potentially harmful is the *unsaturation*. The double-carbon bonds in the molecule of the polyunsaturated oil are highly vulnerable to oxidation and free-radical formation.

Polyunsaturated oils become toxic when they are oxidized. This is what causes rancidity. Rancidity occurs when oils are exposed to oxygen, heat, or light (sunlight or artificial light). Oxidation causes the formation of harmful free radicals. The longer a bottle of oil sits, the more opportunity for oxidative damage. Oil stored in clear plastic bottles is exposed to damaging radiation from light. Any polyunsaturated oil which is heated, becomes oxidized. The higher the temperature, the greater the degree of oxidation. Cooking foods at high temperatures accelerates oxidation. Numerous studies, some published as early as the 1930s, have reported the toxic effects of consuming heated oils.[6]

Oils oxidize easily when they are heated or exposed to oxygen. When oils are extracted from seeds, they are immediately exposed to oxygen, heat, and light, so the oxidation process has already started before the oil even leaves the factory. By the time we buy the oil in the store it has already gone rancid to some degree. The more processing an oil undergoes the more chance it has of oxidizing. The safest vegetable oils to use are those processed at low temperatures and packaged in dark containers. Cold pressed oils are minimally processed so they retain most of their natural antioxidants. These antioxidants are important because they retard spoilage by slowing down oxidation and free-radical formation.

Polyunsaturated Fatty Acid

Double-carbon bonds are vulnerable to free-radical attack

Oils are masters of deception. You can't tell a rogue from a saint. They all pretty much look alike. The most toxic vegetable oil can appear as sweet and pure as those that are freshly extracted under ideal conditions.

Jurg Loliger, Ph.D. of the Nestle Research Center in Switzerland, states in the authoritative book *Free Radicals and Food Additives* that primary oxidation products of vegetable oils have no objectionable flavor or taste, but the secondary degradation products are generally very potent flavor modifiers and can modify the structure of the product.[7] So pure vegetable oil may be very rancid but give no indication of this because it doesn't affect its taste or smell. You can eat rancid vegetable oil and not realize it; if mixed with other substances, the free-radical reactions may cause these other substances to produce an unpleasant smell and taste. The disagreeable odor of soured milk is a result of rancid fats affecting proteins and other milk components. When the proteins in the milk are damaged by free radicals they produce a most putrefying smell.

While vegetable oils are stored in warehouses, transported in hot trucks, and sitting on the store shelves, they are going rancid. They are not refrigerated. They are usually bottled in clear containers where light can penetrate and create more free radicals. These oils may sit around exposed to warm temperatures and light for months before they are sold. But because pure vegetable oil does not produce any noticeable signs of rancidity, we assume them to be safe. *All* conventionally processed and refined vegetable oils are rancid to some extent by the time they reach the store.

To make matters worse, the vegetable oils we buy sit in our kitchen cupboards for months. And when we use them they are almost always cooked with our food. The cooking accelerates the oxidizing process making the oil even more rancid and unhealthy. Cooking also creates toxic *trans fatty acids* as well. Trans fatty acids raise blood cholesterol levels even more than saturated fat does and have been linked to several degenerative conditions, including cancer.

All vegetable oils should be sealed in air tight, opaque containers, and stored in the refrigerator. While this won't completely stop free-radical generation, it will slow it down. If you have oils that have not been stored this way, throw them out now. Your health is more important than the few cents they cost. If your store doesn't carry these types of oils, check the resources in the back of this book.

The majority of vegetable oils today, even many health food store brands, are highly processed and refined. In the refining process, the oil is separated from its source with petroleum solvents and then boiled to evaporate the solvents. The oil is refined, bleached, and deodorized, which involves heating to temperatures of about 400° F (200° C). Chemical preservatives are frequently added to retard oxidation.

The less processing an oil undergoes, the less harmful it is. The most natural oils are extracted from seeds by mechanical pressure and low temperatures, and without the use of chemicals. Oils derived by this process are referred to as "expeller pressed" or "cold pressed." These are the only vegetable oils you should eat. But be careful, even these oils are subject to oxidation and must be packaged and stored properly.

SATURATED FATS

One distinct advantage that all saturated fats have over unsaturated fats (mono- and polyunsaturated fats) is that they don't have any missing hydrogen atoms or double bonded carbons. This means that they are *not* vulnerable to oxidation and free-radical formation like unsaturated fats are.

Food manufacturers have known this for decades. They've added saturated fats (often coconut and palm kernel oils) to foods because they help prevent spoilage caused by free radicals.

Over the years the tropical oils have been replaced in most foods by hydrogenated and partially hydrogenated oils. Hydrogenation is a process where an unsaturated vegetable oil is chemically altered to form a more saturated fat. Increasing the saturation makes the oil less susceptible to spoilage and is cheaper than animal or tropical oils. Hydrogenation involves heating oils to high temperatures while bombarding them with hydrogen atoms, thus creating toxic trans fatty acids. These artificial fats are structurally different from natural fats. Our bodies can handle natural fats, but trans fatty acids have no place in our bodies and are linked to many health problems. Shortening and margarine are two hydrogenated oils which should be completely eliminated from your diet.

In the 1950s and 1960s when saturated fat was first being associated with elevated cholesterol, researchers began looking for other potentially adverse effects caused by saturated fat. They reasoned that if excessive consumption of saturated fat increased the risk of developing heart disease, it might be associated with other health problems as well. Researchers began studying the relationship between saturated fat and cancer. What they found surprised them. When compared with other oils, it appeared that saturated fat had a protective effect against cancer rather than a causative one. Processed polyunsaturated oils were identified as *promoting* cancer and the higher the degree of unsaturation, the greater the risk.[8]

Other conditions such as asthma, allergies, memory loss, and senility also showed a greater degree of occurrence among people who use refined polyunsaturated oils rather than saturated fats. Another problem with these polyunsaturated oils is their influence on the immune system. Our immune system is what keeps us healthy. Polyunsaturated oils suppress the immune system, making us more vulnerable to disease and premature aging. Unsaturated fats not only suppress the immune system but can even kill white blood cells.[9] The health of your immune system to a large part determines your ability to ward off disease and remain healthy. Researchers believe that for the most part, free radicals are to blame for these conditions. When you eat conventionally processed polyunsaturated oils, the type typically sold at grocery stores, you are just shortening your life by providing a doorway for disease.

Because saturated fat has no double-carbon bonds—the weak links that are easily broken to form free radicals—they are much more stable under a variety of conditions. They can be exposed to heat, light, and oxygen without undergoing any appreciable degree of oxidation or free-radical formation. For this reason, they are preferred in use with food, especially if the food is going to be cooked or stored for any length of time. Saturated fat remains stable even when heated to normal cooking temperatures. This is why it is far superior to polyunsaturated oil for cooking purposes. This fact has been known and used in the food industry for many decades.

Coconut oil, being a highly saturated fat, is the least vulnerable of all the dietary oils to oxidation and free-radical formation and, therefore, is the the safest to use in cooking. Also, since it is composed primarily of medium-chain fatty acids, it is not like the long-chain saturated fatty acids that raise blood cholesterol levels. And unlike most all saturated and unsaturated oils, it does not promote platelet stickiness that leads to blood clot formation. Compared to other oils, coconut oil is rather benign, causing no harm. Replacing the refined vegetable oils you are now using with coconut oil can help eliminate the many health problems caused by consuming oxidized oils. While coconut oil's apparent harmlessness is a definite advantage, it is not the primary reason it is so good. In the following chapters you will learn why coconut oil is considered by many to be the healthiest oil on earth and why it has been called a low-fat fat.

TRANS FATTY ACIDS

Trans fatty acids are artificial fatty acids created by technology and are foreign to the human body. Because these fats are unlike the natural fatty acids needed for good health, our bodies are incapable of utilizing them in a productive manner. It's like pouring apple cider into the gas tank of your car—it gums up the works. Cars are designed to run on gasoline, not apple cider. The sugars in the apple juice will cause the engine to freeze up. In like manner, trans fatty acids cause our cells to freeze up, so to speak, leaving them dysfunctional. The more trans fatty acids eaten, the greater the cellular destruction until entire tissues and organs become seriously affected. Disease is the result.

Where do we get trans fatty acids? Unfortunately, as a result of modern food processing they are everywhere. Trans fatty acids are formed when monounsaturated and polyunsaturated oils are heated to high temperatures. Charles T. McGee, M.D., in his book *Heart Frauds,* relates the following experience:

> "My first introduction to fatty acids came during a medical meeting in 1976. Dr. Alsoph Corwin, Professor Emeritus of Chemistry at Johns Hopkins University, presented what he called a cooking demonstration. This was highly unusual for a medical meeting. There he stood wearing his apron, looking like a chef on a television cooking program.
>
> "Dr. Corwin held up a glass beaker full of vegetable oil which had been collected by the age-old technique of crushing vegetable seeds in a press. With the room lights off he exposed

the oil to an ultraviolet light in front of a white screen. The screen stayed white.

"He then held the beaker of oil over the flame of a bunsen burner, brought it to a boil, and again exposed it to the UV light. A light pink color was projected on the screen. It was obvious something in the oil had changed. Dr. Corwin explained that molecules of fatty acids in the oils had been polymerized by the heat. Polymerization involves changes in chemical bonds."

Dr. McGee goes on to explain that the change that occurred in this demonstration was the creation of trans fatty acids. Heat converts normal unsaturated fatty acids into toxic trans fatty acids. This process occurs whenever vegetable oil is heated.

In the extraction, refining, and deodorizing process vegetable oils are heated to temperatures up to 400° F (200° C) for extended periods of time. Between 15-19 percent of the fatty acids in conventionally processed liquid vegetable oils are trans fatty acids. Cold processed oils don't contain trans fatty acids unless they are heated to high temperatures during food preparation. It's ironic that people will buy cold pressed oil at the health food store and then turn it into a health hazard by cooking with it.

Vegetable oils are often *hydrogenated* to turn them into solid fats. In the process of hydrogenation, higher temperatures and longer exposure times create a far greater number of trans fatty acids. Shortening and margarine are hydrogenated oils. On average they contain about 35 percent trans fatty acids, but some brands may run as high as 48 percent.

"These are probably the most toxic fats ever known," says Walter Willett, M.D., professor of epidemiology and nutrition at Harvard School of Public Health. Dr. Willett disagrees with those who say that the hydrogenated fats found in margarine or shortening are less likely to raise cholesterol than the saturated fats found in butter: "It looks like trans fatty acids are two to three times as bad as saturated fats in terms of what they do to blood lipids."[10]

Dr. Willett isn't alone; many researchers believe trans fatty acids have a greater influence on the development of cardiovascular disease than any other dietary fat.[11] Studies now clearly show that trans fatty acids can contribute to atherosclerosis and heart disease. For example, in animal studies, swine fed a diet containing trans fatty acids developed more extensive atherosclerotic damage than those fed other types of fats.[12]

The *New England Journal of Medicine* reported the results of a 14-year study of more than 80,000 nurses (*New England Journal of Medicine,* November 20, 1997). The research documented 939 heart attacks among the participants. Among the women who consumed the largest amounts of trans fats, the chance of suffering a heart attack was 53 percent higher than among those at the low end of trans fat consumption.

Another interesting fact uncovered by this study was that total fat intake had little effect on the rate of heart attack. Women in the group with the largest consumption of total fat (46 percent of calories) had no greater risk of heart attack than those in the group with the lowest consumption of total fat (29 percent of calories).

The researchers, from the Harvard School of Public Health and Brigham and Women's Hospital in Boston, who conducted the study said this suggested that limiting consumption of trans fats would be more effective in avoiding heart attacks than reducing overall fat intake. About 15 percent of the fat in the typical Western diet is trans fat.

Trans fatty acids affect more than just our cardiovascular health. According to Mary Enig, Ph.D., when monkeys were fed trans fat-containing margarine in their diets, their red blood cells did not bind insulin as well as when they were not fed trans.[13] This suggests a relationship with diabetes. Trans fatty acids have been linked with a variety of adverse health effects including cancer, heart disease, MS, diverticulitis, complications of diabetes, and other degenerative conditions.[14]

Hydrogenated oil is a product of technology and may be the most destructive food additive currently in common use. If you eat margarine, shortening, hydrogenated or partially hydrogenated oils (common food additives), then you are consuming trans fatty acids.

Many of the foods you buy in the store and in restaurants are prepared with or cooked in hydrogenated oil. Fried foods sold in grocery stores and restaurants are usually cooked in hydrogenated oil. Many frozen, processed foods are cooked or prepared in hydrogenated oils. Hydrogenated oils are used in making french fries, biscuits, cookies, crackers, chips, frozen pies, pizzas, peanut butter, cake frosting, candy, and ice cream substitutes such as mellorine.

The processed vegetable oils you buy in the store aren't much better. The heat used in the extraction and refining process also creates trans fatty acids. So that bottle of corn or safflower oil you have on the kitchen shelf contains trans fatty acids even though it has not been hydrogenated. Unless the vegetable oil has been "cold pressed" or "expeller pressed," it contains trans fatty acids. Most of the common brands of vegetable oil and salad dressings contain trans fatty acids.

Whenever monounsaturated and polyunsaturated oils are used in cooking, especially at high temperatures, trans fatty acids are formed. So even if you use cold pressed oil from the health food store, if you use it in your cooking, you are creating unhealthy trans fatty acids. The purpose of buying the "healthy" oil is defeated if you cook it.

You might ask: does the amount of trans fatty acids that are produced when you heat oils at home pose any real danger? Studies show diets containing heat-treated liquid corn oil were found to produce more atherosclerosis than those containing unheated corn oil.[15] So, *yes any polyunsaturated vegetable oil becomes toxic when heated.* And even a small amount, especially if eaten frequently over time, will affect your health.

Saturated fats from any source are much more tolerant to temperatures used in cooking and do *not* form trans fatty acids; therefore, they make much better cooking oils. Saturated fats are the only fats that are safe to heat and cook with. Many people, however, are hesitant to use saturated fat because of concern about heart disease. But what if there was a saturated fat that was heart healthy? You could use that in your cooking without fear. Coconut oil is such a fat. It is not only resistant to heat but is an excellent oil for improving overall health.

MCT OILS

Before ending this chapter I need to discuss medium-chain triglyceride (MCT) oils. MCT oils have recently become increasingly popular in sports nutrition and in intravenous formulas used in hospitals. You are likely to encounter this term in foods and supplements sold at health stores if you haven't already. Another term you'll see used for MCT oil is "fractionated coconut oil."

As you learned in the last chapter, fatty acids are usually packaged in groups of three. These packages are called triglycerides. Medium-chain triglyceride (MCT) oils are simply oils composed of 100 percent medium-chain fatty acids (MCFA). These fatty acids are derived from coconut or palm kernel oils. Since the medium-chain fatty acids are associated with many health benefits, manufacturers have developed an oil composed entirely of them. Coconut oil, in comparison, contains only 64 percent MCFA.

Some of the unique health benefits of the medium-chain fatty acids found in coconut oil have been known and used since the 1950s. Because of this, coconut and MCT oils have been and still are used in hospitals to treat malabsorption syndrome, cystic fibrosis, epilepsy, and to improve protein and fat metabolism and mineral absorption.[16, 17, 18] Because of their superior nutritional benefits MCFA are used in hospital formulas to nourish seriously burned or critically ill patients.[19] Coconut oil, and more recently MCT oil, has been an important ingredient in commercial baby formulas and is essential in hospital formulas for treating and nourishing premature infants. Athletes use MCFA to reduce and control weight and increase exercise performance. For these reasons, you will see MCT or coconut oils listed in the ingredient labels on many sports drinks as well as baby formulas. You may also see MCT or fractionated coconut oil sold by itself for use as a dietary or cooking oil.

It's interesting to note that if you ask the soybean industry about coconut oil they will tell you its a deadly poison and will cause all types of health problems. They will try to persuade you that you should eat their man-made, disease-causing hydrogenated oils instead. They ignore the fact that hydrogenated oil is now known to promote heart disease, cancer, and other illnesses. Yet coconut and MCT oils are used to treat and heal hospital patients, improve the endurance and performance of athletes, and nourish babies. What would you rather eat, an oil that is safe and healthy enough to nourish newborn babies or one that has been shown to cause health problems? You have a choice.

The health benefits of MCFA in coconut oil are many. Each of the individual MCFA exert somewhat different yet complementary effects on the body, and all are important. The percentages of MCFA in coconut oil are lauric acid (48%), caprylic acid (8%), and capric acid (7%) in addition to other beneficial fatty acids. Unlike coconut oil, MCT oil consists almost entirely of just two fatty acids. MCT oil is approximately 75 percent caprylic acid and 25 percent capric acid. In my opinion, this is a major drawback because it contains little or no lauric acid which is probably the most important MCFA. As you will see in Chapter 6, lauric acid is an extremely important nutrient which provides some very valuable health benefits. Coconut oil, rich in lauric acid, contains a complete set of MCFA as well as other nutrients. It provides a balance of several fatty acids rather than just two and, unlike MCT, is completely natural. The fatty acids in MCT oil are extracted and purified from coconut oil making it a manufac-tured rather than a natural oil.* For these reasons, I believe coconut oil to be a better dietary source for medium-chain fatty acids.

---

* The soap and cosmetic industry use lauric acid in the manufacture of cleansing agents. This leaves capric and caprylic acids behind as by-products that can be cheaply used for other purposes. While not used in the cosmetic industry, these medium-chain fatty acids have important nutritional and pharmaceutical applica-tions. They are used in a variety of supplements, dietary formulas, and compose the bases of MCT oil.

NATURE'S MARVELOUS GERM FIGHTER

THE AGE OF SUPERGERMS
A New Breed of Germ

"There's nothing else we can do," the doctor said as the 57-year-old kidney patient lay dying. For nine months Dr. Gibert desperately tried one antibiotic after another, but nothing worked. The man's blood remained flooded with bacteria, slowly poisoning his body.

"We tried six or seven different medications. Some we didn't think would work. But we had nothing else to try," said Gibert, an infectious-disease specialist at the Veterans Affairs Medical Center. Even experimental drugs proved useless. Sometimes the man's blood tested clean, but within days the infection came roaring back. One strain of bacteria would die but a few antibiotic-resistant bacteria would take the place of their more vulnerable cousins. Then they multiplied by the billions. The patient sensed his doctor's frustration.

"I guess you're going to tell me I'm dying," he sighed discouragingly.

"Nothing is working," she confided, "there are no more options."

Antibiotics, the miracle drugs of the 20th century, had been useless against this new strain of bacteria, and within days the man died of a massive bacterial infection of the blood and heart.

Today people are suffering and dying from illnesses that science predicted 40 years ago would be wiped off the face of the earth. Infectious illnesses like tuberculosis, pneumonia, and sexually transmitted disease, which were considered conquered through the use of antibiotics, have made a frightening comeback. Infectious diseases are now the third leading killer of Americans, behind cancer and heart disease, and are becoming a global threat. The world's population has never been more vulnerable to emerging and reemerging infections, wrote Dr. Joshua Lederberg, a Nobel prize winner for research in the genetic structure of microbes, in an editorial in the *Journal of the American Medical Association.*

Experts say our overuse of antibiotics is largely to blame: antibiotics encourage proliferation of drug-resistant bacteria. The Centers for Disease Control and Prevention (CDC) examined death records nationwide and found 65 deaths among every 100,000 people were caused by infectious disease, up from 41 of every 100,000 deaths 12 years earlier.

In 1946, just five years after penicillin came into wide use, doctors discovered a staphylococcus bacteria that was not vulnerable to the drug. Pharmacologists developed new antibiotics, but new drug-resistant bacteria appeared. As new drugs were developed, new strains of bacteria arose. By developing new drugs to combat the new strains of bacteria pharmacologists thought they would be able to stay ahead. Slowly, scourges such as tuberculosis, bacterial pneumonia, septicemia (blood poisoning), syphilis, gonorrhea, and other bacterial infections were vanquished, or so it seemed. People still died from these ills, but not so many. In recent years disease-causing bacteria have been staging a powerful comeback. We are in a new age of germ warfare—the age of the "supergerm."

Today every disease-causing bacterium have versions that resist at least one of medicine's 100-plus antibiotics. Some of these supergerms resist almost all known antibiotics. Drug-resistant tuberculosis now accounts for one in seven new cases. Several resistant strains of pneumococcus, the microbe responsible for infected surgical wounds and some children's ear infections and meningitis, appeared in the 1970s and are still going strong. Thousands of patients are now dying of bacterial infections that were once cured by antibiotics. It isn't that their infections were immune to every single drug, but rather that by the time doctors found an antibiotic that worked, the rampaging bacteria had poisoned the patient's blood or crippled some vital organ.

While medications are still an important defense against bacterial infections, the emergence of supergerms has increased our vulnerability to many diseases we thought would soon be rare or extinct.

Food Poisoning—A Growing Problem

Another growing concern in recent years is the sanitation practices in the food processing industry. Food poisoning caused by bacteria is becoming a serious concern. Meat is the most common source of harmful bacteria. It easily becomes contaminated in slaughterhouses and warehouses where sanitary conditions are often deplorable. Because of the prevalence of contamination in meat, we are continually advised to cook all meat thoroughly before eating. Even a tiny speck of blood on a cutting board or knife can transfer the bacteria to raw foods, leading to illness or even death. The Centers for Disease Control and Prevention (CDC) estimate that in the United States up to three-quarters of all cases of food poisoning are directly linked to ground beef. A batch of ground beef might contain portions of meat from as many as 100 cows, any one of which may have been contaminated. It only takes a microscopic amount of meat from one infected animal to contaminate an entire batch of meat and then this large batch of meat is divided and sent to dozens of stores and restaurants. The most notable outbreak occurred in 1993. Seven hundred people who ate Jack in the Box hamburgers became ill, some sustaining permanent kidney damage, and at least four children died. E. Coli, the culprit in the Jack in the Box outbreak, kills an estimated 100 people a year in the U.S. and sickens 25,000 others.

Even foods we normally regard as safe can be a problem. For example, we think milk that has been pasteurized to be free from harmful germs, but contamination can occur after pasteurization. In 1994 a truck that was contaminated with salmonella from a previous cargo of raw eggs delivered tainted pasteurized milk to an ice cream factory in Minnesota. The ice cream made from that milk was then shipped to stores in several states, causing an estimated 224,000 cases of food poisoning, the largest single food poisoning outbreak in U.S. history. Since then there have been over 50 major outbreaks in this country.

A recent report in the *American Medical News* stated, "Food-borne pathogens—the bacteria, chemicals, viruses, parasites and unknown agents that can cause illness when ingested—pose a growing threat to the public health."[1] Between 6.5 million and 81 million Americans experience food-borne illnesses each year and about 9,000 die as a result. While most cases don't end in death, food poisoning is far more common than we are aware. Some experts estimate that as much as half of the flu cases that occur each year are really reactions to food poisoning. The bout with the flu you experienced last fall may very well have really been food poisoning. Contamination has become a growing problem not just with meat but all types of foods. Our fruits and vegetables aren't even safe. Unpasteurized apple cider, lettuce, and strawberries have also caused widespread outbreaks of food poisoning. While cooking destroys disease-causing bacteria, many fruits and vegetables are eaten raw. The only other thing you can do is wash your produce and hope you've cleaned it adequately enough. Then if you do become sick, antibiotics and your body's own recuperative powers are your only defense. But what if you're infected with one of the supergerms—say a strain of staphylococcus that is resistant to most antibiotics—what do you do? You better hope your immune system is strong enough to overcome it.

All Viruses Are Supergerms

Antibiotics still work for most bacterial infections; viruses, however, are another matter. They are all, in a sense, supergerms because there are no drugs that can effectively kill them. Antibiotics are only useful against bacteria, not viruses. To date, no drugs have been developed that can effectively eradicate viruses and cure the illnesses that they cause. Antiviral drugs may reduce the severity of the infections but do not eliminate them completely. That is why there is no cure for the common cold—a viral infection. When you get a viral infection such as a cold, flu, herpes, or mononucleosis, there is little the doctor can do for you. The doctor's only option is to help you feel a little more comfortable by reducing the severity of the symptoms while your body fights the infection.

The most effective weapon against viruses are vaccines, but these are used to prevent disease not treat it. Vaccines use dead or weakened viruses that are injected into the body. The body recognizes a vaccine as a viral infection and mounts a feverish attack by producing its own "antiviral" compounds called antibodies. These vaccines, however, have the potential to cause infections and other illnesses, so they aren't completely safe. Viruses are continually mutating and new strains emerging so vaccines to most aren't available. Our only real protection against viral infections is our body's own natural defenses.

Because there is no cure for viral infections, they can become deadly, especially in individuals with depressed immunity. Many children and elderly die each year from flu that ordinarily would not be fatal. One of the most hideous outbreaks in modern times is AIDS, caused by the human immunodeficiency virus (HIV). This virus attacks the cells of the immune system, leaving the person vulnerable to infection by any number of opportunistic organisms. Infection by these organisms eventually causes the victim's death. As yet, none of the antiviral drugs can stop it.

We are in the age of supergerms. Medications can't be relied on to protect us against all infectious organisms. We need something more to boost our immune systems and help us fight these troublesome invaders.

A SUPER ANTIMICROBIAL

We live in an environment teaming with microorganisms. They are in the air we breath, the food we eat, the water we drink, and even live on our

56

skin. Many of these germs cause disease. Some have become drug-resistant supergerms. Fortunately, nature has provide us a number of medicinal plants to help protect us from attack by these harmful pests. The coconut is one of these.

When you catch a cold or get the flu, how long does it stay around? For most people it lasts several days to a week or more. There is no medicine, no cure for the common cold or the flu. When you get sick you have to let your body fight its own battle. That's why it takes so long to get rid of it.

Not too long ago an associate of mine said she felt like she was coming down with the flu. She had the beginnings of a sore throat, sinus congestion, and inklings of fatigue. I told her, "Take 2-3 tablespoons of coconut oil mixed in a glass of lukewarm orange juice with every meal."

She looked at me inquisitively as if to say, "You've got to be joking. How is coconut oil going to help?"

From earlier discussions she knew coconut oil had many nutritional benefits but doubted it would help with her infection. I didn't tell her it would cure her or that it would even make her feel any better. "Trust me," I said, "take it and see what happens."

During the first day the symptoms got worse as they usually do with seasonal infections. Normally, the flu gets progressively worse for the first few days until the body has had time to rally its defenses sufficiently to fight the invading infection. The next day, instead of getting worse, the symptoms started to get better. By the end of third day the symptoms were all but gone. Three days that's all it took. She was surprised. "I never had an infection that lasted only three days," she said.

How could coconut oil stop the flu? One of the most amazing aspects of coconut oil is its ability to fight infections. When coconut oil is eaten the body transforms its unique fatty acids into powerful antimicrobial power-houses capable of defeating some of the most notorious disease-causing microorganisms. Even the supergerms are vulnerable to these lifesaving coconut derivatives. Coconut oil is, in essence, a natural antibacterial, antiviral, antifungal, and antiprotozoal food.[2-10]

Coconut oil's antimicrobial effects come from its unique composition of MCFA. All of these fatty acids (when converted into free fatty acids or monoglycerides) exhibit antimicrobial properties, some to a greater extent than others. This is an exciting area of research because it involves a readily available food source that can be used to both treat and prevent infectious illness. Wouldn't it be more pleasant to eat your favorite foods cooked in coconut oil to fight an infection rather than choke down a handful of antibiotics and suffer with their side effects? Eating a pizza made with coconut oil or a pudding made of coconut milk sounds a lot more appetizing than swallowing a bunch of nasty-tasting pills. Such a scenario may be possible. Researchers are currently working on formulations derived from the MCFA in coconut oil to produce concentrated antimicrobial dietary supplements and pharmaceuticals.[11]

Coconut oil is composed of 48 percent lauric acid (a 12-chain saturated fatty acid), 7 percent capric acid (a 10-chain saturated fatty acid), 8 percent caprylic acid (an eight-chain saturated fatty acid), and .5 percent caproic acid (a 6-chain saturated fatty acid). These medium-chain fatty acids give coconut oil its amazing antimicrobial properties and are generally absent from all other vegetable and animal oils with the exception of butter.

Human breast milk and the milk of other mammals all contain small amounts of MCFA. This is why butter, which is concentrated milk fat, also contains MCFA. Milk with its medium-chain fatty acids protects the newborn baby from harmful germs at its most vulnerable time in life while its immune system is still developing. For years medium-chain fatty acids have been added to infant formula as protection and because they supply easily digestible nutrients. A mother who consumes coconut oil will have more MCFA in her milk to help protect and nourish her baby.

The potential coconut oil has in treating and preventing a wide assortment of infections is truly astounding, ranging from the flu* to life-threatening conditions such as AIDS. Treating individuals infected with HIV, the virus that causes AIDS, by feeding them MCFA has recently shown great promise and research is now underway in this area. Eating coconut oil may be a simple solution to many illnesses we face today. Laboratory tests have shown that the MCFA found in coconut oil are effective in destroying viruses that cause influenza, measles, herpes, mononucleosis, hepatitis C, and AIDS; bacteria which can cause stomach ulcers, throat infections, pneumonia, sinusitis, earache, rheumatic fever, dental cavities, food poisoning, urinary tract infections, meningitis, gonorrhea, and toxic shock syndrome; fungi and yeast which lead to ringworm, candida, and thrush; and parasites which can cause intestinal infections such as

---

* Unlike most flu viruses, the virus that causes the common cold (rhinovirus) does not have a lipid coat and, therefore, is not vulnerable to the action of MCFA. Cold and flu symptoms are often very similar and it is difficult to tell which infection is present. In either case, however, coconut oil may be beneficial. Infections of any type depress the immune system often allowing other germs to multiply, compounding the problem. If the infection is caused by a cold the MCFA will help kill these other troublesome microorganisms thus relieving stress on the immune system allowing it to more effectively fight the cold virus.

giardiasis. The marvelous thing about using coconut oil to treat or prevent these conditions is that while it is deadly to disease-causing microorganisms, it is harmless to humans. The fatty acids that make coconut oil so effective against germs are the same ones nature has put into mother's milk to protect her children. If it's safe enough for a newborn baby, it is safe enough for us. Nature made MCFA to nourish and protect us against infectious illnesses.

Medical researchers develop marvelous synthetic drugs to fight infections, but all of them are accompanied by undesirable side effects. Some are highly toxic. Coconut oil is nature's own antimicrobial weapon, and being a food that has withstood the test of time, it is totally safe. While drugs may be necessary to treat certain illnesses, if you regularly eat coconut oil your chances of being infected with these illnesses may be greatly reduced.

As research continues, coconut oil may prove to be one of the best internal antimicrobial substances available without a doctor's prescription. Simply adding coconut oil to your daily diet may provide you with substantial protection from a wide range of infectious illnesses. If you feel you are coming down with the flu, eating dried coconut or foods prepared with coconut oil may help you fight off the infection. If you have children it may be the means to protect them against many childhood illness such as earaches and measles. Along with good dental hygiene it might help to protect young teeth from developing cavities and periodontal disease. Eating something as ordinary as a pizza made with coconut oil may be one of the healthiest things you can do for yourself and your children.

NATURAL GERM FIGHTER

Fatty acids are essential to our health. We must have them in order to supply the building blocks for tissues and hormones. Every cell in our bodies must have a ready supply of fatty acids in order to function properly. Nature put fatty acids in our foods for a purpose. Your body recognizes them and knows what to do with them. MCFA are natural substances the body knows how to use for its benefit. They are harmless to us while they are deadly to certain microorganisms.

MCFA are antibacterial, antifungal, antiviral, and antiparasitic. While caprylic acid (C:8), capric acid (C:10), and myristic acid (C:14) all demonstrate antimicrobial properties, lauric acid (C:12) has greater antiviral activity. This is important because there are few substances that can effectively fight viruses. Lauric acid (and other MCFA), unlike all drugs, have no undesirable or harmful side effects.

As far back as 1966 Dr. Jon J. Kabara, a professor of pharmacology and researcher at Michigan State University, reported on the antimicrobial activity of lauric acid. Because of concerns about viral contamination in foods, early research focused on the antiviral effects of lauric acid. It was soon discovered that lauric acid also exhibited antibacterial and antifungal effects as well. In fact, all the MCFA seem to share this characteristic. Most bacteria and viruses are encased in a coat of lipids (fats). The fatty acids that make up this outer membrane or skin hold together the organism's DNA and other cellular materials. But unlike our skin, which is relatively tough, the membrane of these microorganisms is nearly fluid. The fatty acids in the membrane are loosely attached, giving the membrane a remarkable degree of mobility and flexibility. This unique property allows these organisms to move, bend, and squeeze through the tiniest openings.

Lipid-coated viruses and bacteria are easily killed by MCFA, which primarily destroy these organisms by disrupting their lipid membranes. Medium-chain fatty acids, being similar to those in the microorganism's membrane, are easily attracted to and absorbed into it. Unlike the other fatty acids in the membrane, MCFA are much smaller and, therefore, weaken the already nearly fluid membrane to such a degree that it disintegrates.[12, 13] The membrane literally splits open, spilling its insides and killing the organism. Our white blood cells quickly clean up and dispose of the cellular debris. MCFA kill invading organisms without causing any known harm to human tissues.

Our bodies have many ways of protecting us from microorganisms that can cause us harm. The strong acid excreted in our stomachs, for example, kills most organisms that we may eat with our foods. In our bloodstream, microorganisms are attacked and killed by our white blood cells. Our first line of defense against any harmful organism, however, is our skin. In order to inflict harm, microorganisms must first penetrate the skin's protective barrier. While the skin is permeable to some degree, it is also equipped with chemical weapons to help it ward off attack. One of these weapons is the oil secreted by our sebaceous (oil) glands. Sebaceous glands are found near the root of every hair. This oil is secreted along the hair shaft to lubricate the hair and skin. Some have described this oil as "nature's skin cream" because it prevents drying and cracking of the skin. It also has another very important function. It contains medium-chain fatty acids to fight invading microorganisms. A thin layer of oil on the skin helps protect us from the multitude of harmful germs our skin comes into contact with each day.

The antimicrobial power of MCFA are utilized naturally by our own bodies. They are found in mother's milk to protect and nourish her babies;

60

LIPID COATED MICROORGANISMS KILLED BY LAURIC ACID

Below are some of the pathogenic organisms reported to be inactivated by lauric acid.

Lipid Coated Viruses

Human immunodeficiency virus (HIV)
Measles virus
Herpes simplex virus
Herpes viridae
Sarcoma virus
Syncytial virus
Human lymphotropic virus (Type 1)
Vesicular stomatitis virus (VSV)
Visna virus
Cytomegalovirus
Epstein-Barr virus
Influenza virus
Leukemia virus
Pneumonovirus
Hepatitis C virus

Lipid Coated Bacteria

Listeria monocytogenes
Helicobacter pylori
Hemophilus influenzae
Staphylococcus aureus
Streptococcus agalactiae
Groups A, B, F, & G streptococci
Gram-positive organisms
Gram-negative organisms (if pretreated with chelator)

Numerous laboratory studies have shown that lauric acid effectively kills many disease-causing microorganisms.

they are also utilized on our skin to shield us from infectious intruders. They are non-toxic to us and create no toxic by-products. They are completely safe and natural. Lipid researcher Jon J. Kabara, Ph.D., speaking of the safety of using fatty acids for medicinal purposes says, "Fatty acids and derivatives tend to be the least toxic chemicals known to man. Not only are these agents nontoxic to man but are actual foods and in the case of unsaturated fatty acids are essential to growth, development, and health."[14]

LAURIC ACID

Technically speaking, coconut oil as it is found in fresh coconuts has little, if any, antimicrobial properties. Coconuts can be attacked by fungi and bacteria like any other fruit or nut. I know this sounds contrary to what I've stated above, but the beauty of this is that when we *eat* the oil, our bodies convert it into a form that is deadly to troublesome microbes, yet remains harmless to us.

All dietary oils, including coconut, are composed of triglycerides. Triglycerides are nothing more than three fatty acids hooked together by a glycerol molecule. When oil is eaten the triglycerides break apart into diglycerides (two fatty acids joined by a glycerol), monoglycerides (a single fatty acid attached to a glycerol), and free fatty acids. It is the monoglycerides and free fatty acids that have the antimicrobial properties. The most active are lauric acid and capric acid and their monoglycerides—monolaurin and monocaprin.

In regards to their antimicrobial properties, the monoglycerides and free fatty acids are active and the diglycerides and triglycerides are inactive. The antimicrobial properties of coconut oil (which consists of triglycerides), therefore, become active only when ingested or otherwise converted into free fatty acids or monoglycerides.

The medium-chain fatty acid that appears to have the greatest overall antimicrobial effect is lauric acid (and monolaurin). This is the largest of the MCFA consisting of a string of 12 carbon atoms.

Coconut and palm kernel oils are by far the richest natural sources of this super nutrient, comprising nearly 50 percent of their fat content. Milk fat and butter are a distant second consisting of about 3 percent. These are the only food sources we have that contain significant amounts of lauric acid. Unlike the tropical oils, all vegetable oils are completely deficient in this and other MCFA.

Lauric acid was first identified in the fruit and seed of the bay laurel tree which grows in the Mediterranean region. The healing properties of this oil were recognized in ancient times. In Italy, France, Greece, Turkey, and

Morocco the oil was used as a folk medicine to improve digestion, as a salve for bladder and skin diseases, and to provide protection against insect stings. It wasn't until the 1950s and 1960s that scientists began to unlock its healing secrets. Although laurel seeds contain 40 percent lauric acid, coconut and palm kernel oils provide a more abundant source. The medical research on lauric acid and other MCFA is derived predominantly from the tropical oils.

Because of the many health benefits derived from lauric acid, researchers have recently been experimenting with ways to increase the amount of it available in our foods. They have been working with a variety of plants in an effort to increase their lauric acid content. Recently scientists have genetically engineered a new variety of canola called laurate canola that contains 36 percent lauric acid. In time this new canola may wind up being used in a variety of foods.

The research demonstrating the many health benefits of the medium-chain fatty acids and their monoglycerides has been so compelling that companies are now marketing dietary supplements containing these products. Sold under many different brand names, Lauricidin® is a monolaurin supplement currently available from many health food stores and health care professionals. Dozens of health care clinics in the United States are actively using these supplements to treat patients and achieving extraordinary success. For example, HIV-infected individuals using these supplements under clinical supervision have reported significant improvement in health.[15] Most monolaurin supplements come in 300 mg capsules.

Dietary supplements and genetically engineered vegetable oils are two ways in which the food and health industry is trying to increase our exposure to lauric acid. By far the best and richest natural sources of lauric acid are coconuts and coconut oil. For instance, 1 tablespoon of dried shredded coconut contains about 2 grams of lauric acid. A tablespoon of pure coconut oil contains 7 grams. Besides lauric acid, coconut products also contain other MCFA such as capric acid (7 percent) and caprylic acid (8 percent) both of which also provide many beneficial effects on health, which may be lacking in non-coconut sources.

BACTERIA

Until the discovery of antibiotics, medical science had little at their disposal to fight bacterial infections; all they could really do was make the patient as comfortable as possible while the body battled the disease. Drugs have now become the standard weapon against disease-causing bacteria, but there are some natural products—foods and herbs—which also exhibit

BACTERIA KILLED BY MEDIUM-CHAIN FATTY ACIDS

Bacterium	Diseases Caused
Streptococcus	throat infections, pneumonia, sinusitis, ear ache, rheumatic fever, dental cavities
Staphylococcus	staph infection, food poisoning, urinary tract infections, toxic shock syndrome
Neisseria	meningitis, gonorrhea, pelvic inflammatory disease
Chlamydia	genital infections, lymphogranuloma venereum, conjunctivitis, parrot fever pneumonia, periodontitis
Helicobacter pyloris	stomach ulcers
Gram positive organisms	anthrax, gastroenteritis, botulism, tetanus

antibiotic properties, that have been used for generations with some degree of success. One of these is coconut oil.

The fatty acids found in coconut are powerful antibiotics. They are known to kill bacteria which can cause throat and sinus infections, pneumonia, ear infections, stomach ulcers, venereal disease, and dental cavities, to name just a few. The table above lists some of the bacteria MCFA are effective against and the common diseases these organisms cause.

The standard treatment for all these bacterial infections is to use antibiotics, and this may be necessary in life-threatening situations. It is conceivable that instead of taking a drug for every single infection, we may simply eat foods that will kill these organisms. Onions, garlic, and echinacea are edible plants that are commonly used for this purpose already. Coconut appears to be another food that can serve this purpose, perhaps far better than any of the other natural antibiotics.

Take a look at stomach ulcers, for example. A recent analysis estimated that 90 percent of all stomach ulcers are caused by H. pyloris bacterium and not excess acid as once believed. MCFA kill H. pyloris. In order to treat stomach ulcers there may come a time that your doctor will simply recommend eating more foods cooked in coconut oil. Using the oil regularly may even prevent the infection altogether. This may also be true with ear infections, pneumonia, food poisoning, and a host of other infectious illnesses. This is an exciting possibility that needs to be investigated more thoroughly. You don't need to wait five or ten years, however, for the research to be completed before you can benefit from using coconut oil; because it's safe to use, you can add it into your diet now without fear.

One of the drawbacks with using antibiotics is that they generally kill a variety of bacteria both good and bad. Our intestines are the home to many "friendly" bacteria that cause no harm and are, in fact, necessary for good health. These friendly bacteria help digest nutrients, synthesize important vitamins (such as vitamin K) which are essential for good health, and compete for space with pathogenic or disease-causing bacteria and yeasts. A healthy human will have abundant intestinal bacteria, which prevent disease-causing troublemakers such as candida. Candida is a single-celled fungus or yeast cell that typically inhabits the intestinal tract. As long as good bacteria outnumber the candida and keep it under control this yeast poses little threat.

When people take antibiotics, these good bacteria are often killed along with the disease-causing ones. This leaves yeast, such as candida which is not affected by antibiotics, to grow unrestrained, proliferating and overrunning the intestinal tract. The consequence is a yeast overgrowth or infection. Such infections can last for years causing a wide variety of symptoms ranging from headaches to digestive problems. Often people have systemic candida infections without even knowing it. This is why antifungal medications or probiotics should be taken whenever antibiotics are used. A probiotic supports the growth of friendly bacteria but not the disease-causing kind.

One of the good things about lauric acid is that it kills lipid-coated bacteria but does not appear to harm the friendly intestinal bacteria.[16] The MCFA also have antifungal properties so not only will they kill disease-causing bacteria and leave good bacteria alone, they will also kill candida and other fungi in the intestinal tract, further supporting a healthy intestinal environment.

YEAST AND FUNGI

Norma Galante, a Boston college student, went to her local medical clinic complaining of vaginal itching and a slight discharge. The physician took a culture of the discharge and examined it under the microscope. He diagnosed a mild bacterial infection and prescribed an antibiotic.

When Norma took the medication, however, it only made the symptoms worse. She went back to the doctor and he gave her another antibiotic. It didn't work either. She tried again, and again but he couldn't find a medication that would help. "I kept going back to the clinic, and the doctors kept prescribing different antibiotics," Norma says. Out of frustration, the physicians finally prescribed a topical anti-candida cream to see if that would be of any help. While candida is not affected by antibiotics it can be treated topically with anti-fungal creams and suppositories. Her symptoms subsided. She felt relieved. At last she thought her problem was solved.

Yeast infections are persistent and often recur. This was the case with Norma. It wasn't long before she had another infection. The medications she used seemed to relieve the symptoms, but within a few months they would flare up again. Before long she began to develop other fungal infections like athlete's foot and skin rashes (ringworm). Fungal infections of one sort or another became an ongoing nuisance. She felt chronically fatigued. Everything she did seemed to tire her. She became depressed. "The doctors didn't have any answers," she recalls. "To them I had a minor problem, but I was living with the itching and the fatigue every day; it wasn't a minor problem for me."

After receiving little help from her doctors she began searching for an answer herself. She scoured health food stores for books and information on yeast infections. After studying these materials she realized she was suffering from a systemic or entire body candida infection. She cut sugar out of her diet and began taking a dietary supplement derived from coconut oil called caprylic acid. It worked! Both the vaginal yeast and skin infections healed. Without the constant strain of fighting the infection her energy returned. She was able to function normally again without feeling constantly fatigued. "I was so relieved to find something that brought my energy back," she says.[17]

One of the most widespread health problems in Western society is caused by the fungus Candida albacans. Many women are familiar with this troublesome pest because it is a common cause of vaginal yeast infections. It is also the same organism that causes oral thrush and diaper rash in babies. Candida is a single-celled fungus or yeast cell that inhabits the intestinal tract and mucus membranes of every living person on the earth. Within days after birth, newborns are infected and have a budding colony living in their digestive tract. Normally, competition from friendly bacteria and the cleansing action of our immune system keep candida numbers low and prevent them from causing any adverse health problems. But when the immune system is compromised or friendly bacteria in our gut are killed by taking antibiotics, a candida infection can quickly flare up. A single course of antibiotics can lead to a raging candida infection. Approximately 75 percent of women experience vaginal yeast infections at one time or another. Vaginal yeast infections are typically treated as if they were only localized in one area of the body. Many people, however, have systemic infections in which candida grows out of control overrunning the digestive tract and affecting the entire body, including the reproductive system. Systemic yeast infections called candidiasis (or yeast syndrome) affect the entire body and can afflict men as well as women. Symptoms are numerous and varied (see table below) and even doctors have difficulty identifying the problem.

Because it is not easy to identify, hundreds of thousands of women and men are plagued with candidiasis without even realizing it. Vaginal yeast infections or oral yeast infections (thrush) can be identified by the white discharge they produce. Recurring vaginal yeast infections are one of the signs of a systemic infection. But you can have candidiasis without an active vaginal yeast infection. Anyone who has taken antibiotics, birth control pills, steroids, or immunosuppresive drugs is at high risk of having a systemic yeast infection, even if no noticeable symptoms are evident.

PROBLEMS COMMONLY ASSOCIATED WITH SYSTEMIC CANDIDA INFECTIONS

General: fatigue, headache, digestive problems, joint pains, depression, memory loss, irritability, allergies

Women: persistent vaginitis, menstrual irregularities, recurrent bladder problems

Men: persistent or recurrent jock itch or athlete's foot, prostatitis, impotence

Children: ear infections, hyperactivity, behavior and learning problems

Source: Crook, W. 1985, *The Yeast Connection*

Typical symptoms also include fatigue, depression, allergy symptoms, and recurring fungal skin infections (athlete's foot, jock itch, ringworm, etc.). Skin fungus can afflict any part of the body from the head to the toe. Dry flaky skin that persists despite the use of hand lotion and skin creams could very well be a fungal infection. Often what people call psoriasis is really a fungal infection. Dandruff is caused, in part, by skin fungus. Preadolescent children are the primary victims of scalp ringworm (tinea capitis), a skin fungus similar to athlete's foot. Not until puberty do glands secrete oil containing medium-chain fatty acids that help protect the scalp from skin fungus (see Chapter 11 for more information on skin health).

One of the most potent non-drug or natural yeast-fighting substances is caprylic acid, a medium-chain fatty acid derived from coconut oil. Caprylic acid in capsule form is commonly sold as a dietary supplement in health food stores. It is very effective against candida and other forms of fungi. It is even effective mixed with a little coconut oil or vitamin E oil as a topical application for fungal skin infections. I've seen fungal infections that have lasted for months clear up in a matter of days using caprylic acid and a little coconut oil. It works just as effectively inside the body, killing fungi without the least bit of harm. Polynesian women who eat their traditional coconut-based diet rarely if ever get yeast infections. Eating coconut oil on a regular basis, as the Polynesians do, would help to keep candida and other harmful microorganisms at bay.

The efficiency of caprylic acid is reportedly so favorable that many supplement manufacturers put it in their products used to fight systemic and vaginal yeast infections. John P. Trowbridge, M.D., President of the American College of Advancement of Medicine and author of the book *The Yeast Syndrome*, highly recommends caprylic acid as an aid to fight systemic candida infections.

William Crook, M.D., the author of *The Yeast Connection* and recognized authority on yeast infections, also recommends it. He reports that many physicians have used it successfully and that it works especially well for those patients who have adverse reactions to antifungal drugs.[18] It is reported that caprylic acid is just as effective as nystatin, the most popular antifungal prescription drug, but without the side effects.

The only effective cure for candidiasis has been dietary changes and medications. Caprylic acid is a natural yeast fighter that has been used very successfully in place of the drugs. Caprylic acid is often sold in combination with anti-fungal herbs in dietary supplements designed to help those with yeast infections. Caprinex (Nature's Way), Capricin (Professional Specialties), Mycostat (P & D Nutrition), and Caprystatin (Ecological Formulas) are the names of some of the anti-candida supplements available.

68

It is interesting that people who eat a lot of coconuts live in areas where yeast and fungi are extremely plentiful, yet they are rarely troubled by infections. Only in more temperate climates where processed vegetable oils are the main source of dietary fat are yeast infections, skin fungus, acne, and other skin infections big problems.

PARASITES

There are two general groups of parasites. One consists of worms such as tape worms and roundworms. The second category is the protozoa, one-celled organisms. Parasites infect the intestines of both humans and animals and can cause a great deal of intestinal distress. We often associate parasites with Third World countries and poor sanitation, but parasites are a problem everywhere, even in North America. In countries where sanitation is a priority people mistakenly assume that no problem exists and they don't need to worry. Parasites are everywhere, waiting for the opportunity to latch onto an unsuspecting host. Backpackers have long been aware of the danger of drinking water from streams and lakes. Open water even in the backcounty is often contaminated with parasites waiting for a host.

Bert Thomas, a 45-year-old geologist, was a wilderness enthusiast. He loved hiking, rock climbing and mountain biking and was an excellent athlete. In the spring of 1994 he took his three children and went backpacking in the Wyoming wilderness. Always mindful about the dangers of drinking surface water, even in a seemingly pristine wilderness, he made sure to boil or filter every drop of water they drank.

On his return home he began to experience bouts with diarrhea and became increasingly fatigued. He lost all energy and stopped participating in the outdoor sports that had become a regular part of his life. He began to lose weight, suffer from dizzy spells, and became short of breath. Doctors were unable to find a cause for his problems. Because the illness began soon after his return home from Wyoming, a stool sample was tested for parasites. The tests came back negative. Over the next six months in an attempt to find the cause of his illness he was treated for ulcers, had blood tests, abdominal scans, and X rays. Symptoms became worse. He began having blackouts and heart palpitations and was hospitalized. Monitoring his heart revealed a serious abnormality called arrhythmia. It was assumed this was the cause of his dizzy spells and blackouts. He was given medication to control the arrhythmia but after a while stopped taking it because of the side effects. Despite the negative tests from the stool specimen, his doctor gave him medication to treat giardia because there was little else they could do.

He felt dramatic relief of the diarrhea and regained much of his former energy. As Bert found out, a common problem with tests for parasites is that they are often wrong. A negative reading doesn't necessarily mean there are no parasites present.

His heart palpitations and dizziness continued and seemed to become aggravated when he attempted to exercise. He went to another doctor, an expert in intestinal disease, who recognized the symptoms immediately as giardiasis. Another stool test was performed to make sure that the giardia had been eradicated. It was.

While the parasites may have been removed, the damage done by them wasn't. Intestinal permeability tests showed Bert was having trouble absorbing nutrients and was suffering from a mineral deficiency. He was given a multiple vitamin and mineral supplement. Within a month Bert reported a 90 percent reduction in heart palpitations and dizziness and was able to resume his favorite sports. It took nine months on high doses of supplements for his body to recover completely from the damage caused by the giardia infection.

It was assumed that Bert became infected with giardia while he was in the wilderness, but that may not be so. Tap water can also be a source of contamination. The water treatment process doesn't remove all contaminants and parasites. Single-celled organisms such as cryptosporidium and giardia are particularly troublesome because they can often slip through water purification treatment unharmed. Since these organisms are protected by a tough outer coat, the chlorine added to municipal water supplies to kill germs has little effect on them. Because of their small size, very fine filters are needed to trap them, and complete elimination of these parasites from tap water isn't possible. Drinking-water regulations are designed to reduce, but not necessarily eliminate, parasite contamination; so even water systems that meet government standards may not be free of parasites. Water supplies must be constantly monitored to detect levels above acceptable limits, even then there exists the potential for giardia infection. The most susceptible are those who have a weak immune system incapable of mounting an effective defense against the organism. This is seen mostly in the very young and the elderly and those affected with other immune-suppressing illnesses such as AIDS.

Giardia and cryptosporidium normally live in the digestive tracts of many mammals. Public water supplies can become infected with these organisms when they are contaminated by sewage or animal waste. Although you may not hear about it, outbreaks occur all the time, usually in smaller cities and occasionally in large metropolitan areas. In 1998 the three million residents of Sydney, Australia were advised by the Health Department to boil all their tap water because high concentrations of giardia and cryptosporidium were detected in the city's water supply. In this instance most people were spared from infection because they were warned in time. Unsafe water is an embarrassment to the water department of any city and sometimes officials are unwilling to admit that a problem exists until it's too late. This is apparently what happened in Milwaukee, Wisconsin in 1993. A breakdown in water sanitation permitted cryptosporidium to contaminate the city's drinking water for a week. As a result, a hundred people died and 400,000 suffered stomach cramps, diarrhea, and fever that are characteristic of the parasite. Recent outbreaks have occurred in several cities in California, Colorado, Montana, New York, Pennsylvania, and Massachusetts to name just a few.

Cryptosporidium is believed to be in 65 to 97 percent of the nation's surface waters (rivers, lakes, and streams), according to the Centers for Disease Control and Prevention (CDC). About half of our tap water comes from treated surface water. Giardia is a much bigger problem. It is commonly found in the pretreated water system used by some 40 million Americans and has caused epidemics in several small cities.

Giardiasis ranks among the top 20 infectious diseases that cause the greatest morbidity in Africa, Asia, and Latin America. It is the most common parasite diagnosed in North America. The CDC estimates that two million Americans contract giardiasis every year.[19]

Giardia can live in a variety of water sources: streams, ponds, puddles, tap water, and swimming pools. Infection is spread by contact with an infected source. You don't have to drink contaminated water to become infected. Giardiasis can spread by sexual contact, poor personal hygiene, hand-to-mouth contact, and from food handlers who don't wash their hands thoroughly. If your hands are exposed to contaminated water, animals, people, or feces (e.g., litter boxes, diapers), it could spread to you. Shoes can come in contact with animal droppings and bring it inside the home. Veterinary studies have shown that up to 13 percent of dogs are infected. Any pet can become a source of infection for humans although they may not show signs of infection.

Infection can come from the most unsuspected sources. One family get-together proved this point. A few days after a party 25 people who attended reported gastrointestinal distress. They were all found to be infected with giardia. On investigation, suspicion fell on the fruit salad. It was discovered that the salad became infected by the food preparer who hadn't properly washed her hands. She had a diapered child and a pet rabbit at home both of which tested positive to giardia.

A study at Johns Hopkins Medical School a few years ago showed antibodies against giardia in 20 percent of randomly chosen blood samples from patients in the hospital. This means that at least 20 percent of these patients had been infected with giardia at some time in their lives and had mounted an immune response against the parasite.

Giardia is rampant in day-care centers. A study in 1983 showed 46 percent of those who were infected were associated with day-care centers or had contact with diaper-age children. It is estimated that 20 to 30 percent of workers in day-care centers harbor giardia.[20] In a study done in Denver, Colorado with 236 children attending day-care centers, it was found that 38 (16%) were infected.[21]

Symptoms of infection are similar to those of the flu and often misdiagnosed. We don't usually think of parasites when be feel "under the weather." I wonder how many times when the "flu" goes around that the real cause is parasites in the water supply? Symptoms vary. In acute cases symptoms are usually most severe and can include any of the following listed in order of prevalence:

diarrhea	headaches
malaise (a sense of ill being)	anorexia
weakness	abdominal bloating
abdominal cramps	flatulence
weight loss	constipation
greasy, foul-smelling stools	vomiting
nausea	fever

Infection can persist for weeks or months if left untreated. Some people undergo a more chronic phase that can last for many months. Chronic cases are characterized by loose stools and increased abdominal gassiness with cramping, depression, fatigue, and weight loss. Some people may have some symptoms and not others while some may not have any symptoms at all.

Giardiasis can be mistaken for a number of other conditions including the flu, irritable bowel syndrome, allergies, and chronic fatigue syndrome. Many people are diagnosed and treated for these other conditions without finding relief.

Even if giardia is diagnosed and treated, it can damage the intestinal lining causing chronic health problems that persist for years after the parasite is gone. Food allergies, including lactose (milk) intolerance can develop. Damaged intestinal tissues become leaky. This is often referred to as leaky gut syndrome. Toxins, bacteria, and incompletely digested foods are able to pass through the intestinal wall into the bloodstream, initiating an immune response. Sinus congestion, aches and pains, headaches, swelling, and inflammation—all typical symptoms of allergies—are the result.

Loss of intestinal integrity can lead to gastrointestinal discomfort known as irritable bowel syndrome (IBS). Dr. Leo Galland, an expert in gastrointestinal disease, demonstrated that out of a group of 200 patients with chronic diarrhea, constipation, abdominal pain, and bloating, half of them were infected with giardia. Most of these patients had been told they had irritable bowel syndrome. He notes that parasitic infection is a common event among patients with chronic gastrointestinal symptoms and many people are given a diagnosis of irritable bowel syndrome without a thorough evaluation.

Another consequence of poor intestinal integrity is fatigue resulting from malabsorption of important nutrients. If the condition persists it can lead to chronic fatigue syndrome. A giardia infection can be so draining on the immune system that it causes fatigue. Again the cause is often misdiagnosed. A giardia epidemic in Placerville, California, for example, was mysteriously followed by an epidemic of chronic fatigue syndrome. In 1991 Dr. Galland and colleagues published a study of 96 patients with chronic fatigue and demonstrated active giardia infection in 46 percent. In another study of 218 patients whose chief complaint was chronic fatigue, Dr. Galland found that 61 patients were infected with giardia.[22] His conclusion is that giardia may be an important cause of chronic fatigue syndrome.

Coconut oil may provide an effective defense against many troublesome parasites including giardia. Like bacteria and fungi, giardia can't stand up against MCFA. Research has confirmed the effectiveness of MCFA in destroying giardia and possibly other protozoa.[23, 24, 25] By using coconut oil and other coconut products every day, you may be able to destroy giardia before it can establish a toehold. In doing so you also eliminate the possibility of developing food allergies, chronic fatigue, and other related symptoms. If you're currently troubled with these conditions, coconut oil used liberally with meals may provide a source of relief. Because MCFA are quickly absorbed by the tissues and converted into energy it seems logical that those suffering from chronic fatigue would gain a great deal of benefit. Foods prepared with coconut oil, or even fresh coconut make a great energy booster.

Another possible use for coconut is for the removal of intestinal worms. In India it has been used to get rid of tapeworms. In one study it was reported that treatment with dried coconut, followed by magnesium sulfate (a laxative), caused 90 percent parasite expulsion after twelve hours.[26] The authors of some pet books apparently have had success with coconut and recommend feeding animals ground coconut as a means to expel intestinal parasites. In India coconut oil is rubbed into the scalp as a treatment to remove head lice.

Tapeworms, lice, giardia, candida, bacteria, viruses, and germs of all sorts can be eliminated or at least held in check with coconut oil. For infections and intestinal complaints it seems like coconut oil is one of the best natural medicines you can use.

A SHIELD AGAINST DISEASE

Tropical diseases such a malaria and yellow fever have plagued mankind for centuries. Throughout history, whenever people from moderate climates settled or traveled in areas covered by tropical jungles, they've been plagued with disease. Even today people who travel in these areas must be cautious.

When the territory of French Guiana was established in the 1676, settlers from France were encouraged to immigrate to and colonize the new land. The territory, covered with a thick tropical rain forest, was located on the northern coast of South America. Many attempts were made to establish permanent settlements but all failed disastrously. Disease decimated the settlers. In 1762 an ambitious attempt at organized colonization failed dismally when a group of 12,000 French settlers, far more Europeans than had ever been seen there before, arrived in the area. After just three years, fewer than 1,000 remained alive. Most of the survivors eventually returned to France. Over the years all attempts to establish settlements failed disastrously and the colonies were all but abandoned. In order to keep a foothold in the new world, Guiana was turned into a penal colony in 1852. The notorious Devil's Island was part of this prison system. Like the settlers before them, the prisoners who were forced to live in this disease-infested country often died of malaria. Nine out of every ten prisoners sent to Devil's Island died before completing their sentences. Those few who survived were released with the hope that they would populate the area and establish a permanent settlement.

The building of the Panama Canal in Central America provides another example. Excavation for the canal was started in 1883 by a French company using French laborers. Within a short period of time serious troubles arose. Malaria and yellow fever decimated the workers. Progress slowed to a crawl. New workers where shipped in to replace those who died from disease. The death rate was so high that able-bodied workers were in short supply. Faced with insurmountable odds caused by the decimation of the workforce, the company went broke. Another French company took on

74

the challenge in 1894. Work progressed slowly until 1899. By this time thousands more French workers had died and the project was again abandoned. The United States took over the task in 1904. Draining the marshes to kill the mosquitoes that carried the disease helped greatly, but didn't completely eliminate the problem. After 10 more years of battling disease and worker shortages, the canal was finally completed. No other modern peacetime undertaking in history has cost so many lives.

Similar stories have occurred time and time again throughout history. Whenever people go into tropical jungles for any length of time disease follows. The curious thing about this is why the people who are living in these areas don't succumb to disease. The natives in French Guiana lived among the settlers without being decimated. The Indians of Panama have lived in the jungles for generations without problem. What is it that protects them? Researchers have been unable to find any genetic reason for their resistance. Locals who move out of the area and return several years later are often susceptible to disease just like any other outsider.

I believe the local people are protected because of the types of food they eat, in particular coconuts. It is in these tropical climates that coconuts grow abundantly and supply a valuable food source for the local inhabitants. It is as if the coconut were put there purposely not only to serve as a primary source of food but to protect people from disease. In his studies of African natives, Dr. Weston A. Price noted that those who consumed traditional local foods did not suffer from insect-borne diseases such as malaria. Tropical climates are breeding grounds for all types of disease-causing organisms, yet indigenous peoples have lived in these places generation after generation without problem. Only those people from other climates, who eat virtually no coconut or other native plants, have a difficult time surviving.

Herbalists have noted for years that in regions where certain diseases are common, medicinal plants grow that can cure these diseases. This is why every culture in the world has a form of traditional medicine based on the use of local herbs. The people who live in the tropics where coconut grows are protected to some extent from malaria, yellow fever, and other common infectious organisms. The people in Panama have discovered the importance of coconut as a means of staying healthy. When they feel an illness coming on they increase their consumption of coconut, particularly the milk and the oil. Likewise, Africans in tropical areas will drink palm kernel oil whenever they get sick.

Before the onset of WWII, American contractors went to the Panama Canal zone to build airstrips, submarine bases, and barracks for the military. Workers from the city as well as natives from the jungles of Central

America and the Caribbean came in to provide the labor. Coconut was an important source of food for these natives. In 1940 many of the natives still lived a relatively isolated existence. Many spoke neither Spanish or English. Local labor was preferred, because over the years it was noticed that indigenous people were more resistant to disease and worked harder. One of the contractors, William Bockus, Jr., observed: "There were two striking differences between these Indians and the majority of the other workers. They were *never* sick and they were slim and trim. These guys would work steadily all day long in the swamps in mud and rain without complaint. Foremen had to tell them to take rest periods, believe it or not. They also never missed a day's work."[27] This is a far cry different from just a few years earlier when malaria and yellow fever devastated the French and American workers.

In my opinion the coconut is one of God's greatest health foods and, when consumed as part of your regular diet, can protect you against a host of infectious illnesses. Eating coconuts and coconut oil can provide you with some degree of protection from a wide variety of disease-causing organisms.

Coconut oil may not be able to cure all disease, but it can help prevent many illnesses, relieve stress on the immune system, and allow the body to resist disease better. A person who is aware of the health benefits of coconut oil but doesn't use it is like the person who jumps out of an airplane and never opens his parachute. You've got a parachute that can protect you from a number of nasty diseases, it would be foolish not to take advantage of it.

A NEW WEAPON
AGAINST HEART DISEASE

One of the biggest tragedies of our time concerning diet and health is the mistaken belief that coconut oil is a dietary villain that causes heart disease. Ironically, it may be one of best things you can eat to help protect you from heart disease. Instead of being a villain, as it is often made out to be, it is in reality a saint. By eating coconut oil you can *reduce* your chances of suffering a heart attack! One of the most exciting discoveries about coconut oil is its potential to prevent heart disease.

As you have seen in Chapter 2, coconut oil does not increase either blood cholesterol or triglyceride levels, nor does it promote platelet stickiness (excessive blood-clot formation). Because it stimulates metabolism it may, in fact, promote lower cholesterol. Studies in the 1970s and 1980s indicated that coconut oil is heart friendly even though saturated fat at the time was being accused of promoting heart disease. Coconut oil consumption was found to have many factors associated with a *reduced* risk of heart disease compared to other dietary oils namely, lower body fat deposition, higher survival rate, reduced tendency to form blood clots, fewer uncontrolled free radicals in cells, lower levels of blood and liver cholesterol, higher antioxidant reserves in cells, and lower incidence of heart disease in population studies.[1]

From this evidence alone coconut oil should be viewed as heart healthy or at least benign as far as heart disease is concerned. But there is another factor, even more important, that reveals coconut oil as not simply a benign bystander but as a very important player in the battle against heart disease. The evidence is so remarkable that coconut oil may soon become a powerful new weapon used against heart disease.

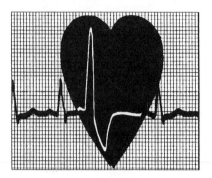

Coconut oil is a heart-healthy oil that may help protect you from heart disease and stroke.

ATHEROSCLEROSIS AND HEART DISEASE

To understand how coconut oil can help prevent heart disease you need to have a basic understanding of how the disease develops. Heart disease is caused by atherosclerosis (hardening of the arteries) which is manifest by the formation of plaque in the arteries. If you asked most people what causes atherosclerosis, they would probably tell you it was from too much cholesterol in the blood. This idea is called the cholesterol or lipid hypothesis of heart disease. While still loudly proclaimed in the popular press (and by the soybean industry), this theory has never really fit clinical observation or scientific studies and has since been replaced with the response-to-injury hypothesis.[2]

What causes plaque to build up in the arteries and atherosclerosis to develop? When we think of hardened arteries, we generally associate it with cholesterol. Cholesterol, however, doesn't simply come dancing freely down the artery and suddenly decide to stick somewhere. Cholesterol is used by the body to patch up and repair injuries to the arterial wall. In fact, cholesterol isn't even necessary for atherosclerosis or the formation of plaque. Contrary to popular belief, the principle component of arterial plaque is not cholesterol but protein (mainly scar tissue). Some atherosclerotic arteries contain little or no cholesterol.

According to the response-to-injury hypothesis, atherosclerosis initially develops as a result of injury to the inner lining of the arterial wall. The injury can be the result of a number of factors such as toxins, free radicals, viruses, or bacteria. If the cause of the injury is not removed, further damage may result and as long as irritation and inflammation persist, scar tissue continues to develop.

Special blood clotting proteins called platelets circulate freely in the blood. Whenever they encounter an injury they become sticky and adhere to each other and to the damaged tissue, acting somewhat like a bandage to facilitate healing. This is how blood clots are formed. Injury from any source triggers platelets to clump together or clot and arterial cells to release protein growth factors that stimulate growth of the muscle cells within the artery walls. A complex mixture of scar tissue, platelets, calcium, cholesterol, and triglycerides is incorporated into the site to heal the injury. This mass of fibrous tissue, not cholesterol, forms the principle material in plaque. The calcium deposits in the plaque cause the hardening which is characteristic of atherosclerosis.

Contrary to popular belief, plaque isn't simply plastered along the inside of the artery canal like mud in a garden hose. It grows *inside* the artery wall, becoming part of the artery wall itself. Arterial walls are surrounded by a layer of strong circular muscles which prevent the plaque from expanding outward. As the plaque grows, because it can't expand outward, it begins to push inward and close the artery opening, narrowing the artery and choking off blood flow.

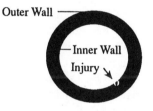

Injury occurs on the inside surface of the artery.

Plaque begins to develop inside artery wall.

Plaque buildup causes the wall of the artery to bulge inward restricting blood flow.

Platelets gather at the site of injury to form blood clots, plugging the holes in the damaged vessel. But if the injury persists or if the blood is prone to clotting, clots may continue to grow to the point that they completely block the artery. An artery already narrowed by plaque can easily be blocked by blood clots. When this process occurs in the coronary artery which feeds the heart, it is referred to as a heart attack. If it happens in the carotid artery that goes to the brain, the result is a stroke. Atherosclerosis leads to heart disease and other cardiovascular problems.

CHRONIC INFECTION AND ATHEROSCLEROSIS

Although many risk factors are associated with heart disease, none have actually been proven to cause the illness. Lack of exercise is a risk factor just as high blood cholesterol is, but neither one actually causes heart disease. If the lack of physical activity caused heart disease, then everyone who doesn't exercise would die of a heart attack, but they don't. Likewise, everyone with high cholesterol doesn't get heart disease and everyone who has heart disease doesn't have high cholesterol. Risk is only an observed association and not necessarily a cause. A substantial proportion of people with heart disease, however, do not have any of the standard risk factors.[3] The actual cause of heart disease is elusive and appears to be multifactorial.

One area of investigation that is gaining a great deal of interest is the relationship between *chronic infection* and atherosclerosis. It appears that there is a cause and effect relationship associated with persistent low-grade infections and heart disease. Recent research has shown that certain microorganisms can cause or are at least involved in the development of arterial plaque which leads to heart disease.

A large number of studies have reported associations between heart disease and chronic bacterial and viral infections.[4] As far back as the 1970s researchers identified the development of atherosclerosis in the arteries of chickens when they were experimentally infected with a herpes virus. In the 1980s similar associations were reported in humans infected with a number of bacteria (e.g., Helicobacter pylori and Chlamydia pneumoniae) and certain herpes viruses (particularly cytomegalovirus). In one study, for example, Petra Saikku and colleagues at the University of Helsinki in Finland found that 27 out of 40 heart attack patients and 15 out of 30 men with heart disease carried antibodies related to chlamydia, which is more commonly known to cause gum disease and lung infections. In subjects who were free of heart disease, only seven out of 41 had such antibodies. In another study at Baylor College of Medicine in Houston, Texas, researchers found that 70 percent of patients undergoing surgery for atherosclerosis carried antibodies to cytomegalovirus (CMV), a common respiratory infection, while only 43 percent of controls did.

More evidence supporting the link between infection and cardiovascular disease showed up in the early 1990s when researchers found fragments of bacteria in arterial plaque. One of the first to discover microorganisms in atherosclerotic plaque was Brent Muhlestein, a cardiologist at the LDS Hospital in Salt Lake City and the University of Utah. Muhlestein and colleagues found evidence of chlamydia in 79 percent of plaque specimens taken from the coronary arteries of 90 heart disease patients. In comparison, fewer than four percent of normal individuals had evidence of chlamydia in artery walls. Animal studies provided more direct evidence that bacteria might contribute to chronic inflammation and plaque formation. Muhlestein showed that infecting rabbits with chlamydia measurably thickens the arterial walls of the animals. When the animals were given an antibiotic to kill the chlamydia, the arteries became more normal in size.[5]

Some of the bacteria associated with atherosclerosis are also involved in the development of dental cavities and gum disease. Studies by James Beck of the University of North Carolina and others looked at dental data and found that those people with dental infections tended to have a higher rate of heart disease and strokes. These studies helped establish the link between dental health and heart disease. The connection between dental health and general health had been observed for decades. Weston A. Price, D.D.S., observed this during his studies of the Pacific Islanders in the 1930s. Those who had the best overall health also had the best dental health which, by the way, were those who regularly ate coconuts and coconut oil.

At least one out of every two adults in developed countries have antibodies to Helicobacter pylori, Chlamydia pneumoniae, or cytomegalovirus (CMV). The presence of antibodies does not necessarily indicate an active infection or the presence of atherosclerosis, but it is a sign that infection has occurred at some time. It's common for infections from these organisms to persist indefinitely. Once infected with herpes, for example, the virus remains for life. The effectiveness of the immune system determines the degree of trouble the virus may cause. The weaker the immune system the more likely an infection will hang on and cause problems. When these microorganisms enter the bloodstream they can attack the artery wall, causing chronic low-grade infections that lack any noticeable symptoms. As microorganisms colonize an artery wall, they cause damage to arterial cells. In an effort to heal the injury, blood platelets, cholesterol, and protein combine in the artery wall, setting the stage for plaque formation and atherosclerosis.[6] As long as the infection and inflammation persist, plaque continues to develop. Infection can both initiate and promote growth of atherosclerosis in arteries which, in turn, leads to heart disease.[7, 8]

At this point, researchers are not ready to say infection is responsible for every case of heart disease. Other factors (e.g. free radicals, high blood pressure, diabetes, etc.) can also cause injuries to the arterial wall and initiate plaque formation. Also, not all infections promote atherosclerosis. Only when the immune system is incapable of controlling the infection is there cause for alarm. Anything that may lower immune efficiency such as serious illness, poor diet, exposure to cigarette smoke, stress, and lack of exercise (i.e. many of the typical risk factors associated with heart disease) will also open up the body to chronic low-grade infections that can promote atherosclerosis.

We now know that, at least in some cases, heart disease may be treated with antibiotics. Antibiotics are limited because they work only against bacteria; infections caused by viruses remain unaffected. However, there is something that will destroy both the bacteria (Helicobacter pylori and Chlamydia pneumonia) and viruses (CMV) that are most commonly associated with atherosclerosis and that is MCFA or coconut oil. Yes, believe it or not. The MCFA in coconut oil are known to kill all three of the major types of atherogenic organisms. Not only can coconut oil help protect you from ulcers, lung infections, herpes, and such, but also heart disease and stroke. If you want to avoid dying from heart disease you should be eating coconut oil, not avoiding it!

FREE-RADICAL INJURY

Another major cause of arterial injury that can lead to atherosclerosis is from free radicals. These renegade molecules cause damage to cells and tissues wherever they are allowed to roam. A number of substances in our foods and environment can cause the formation of destructive free radicals.

Probably the most dangerous dietary substances to the heart and arteries are oxidized lipids (fats). When fats go rancid they oxidize, during this process free radicals are formed. It is interesting to note that only oxidized fats and oxidized cholesterol are found in arterial plaque. Non-oxidized fats and cholesterol do *not* accumulate in plaque. Only those fats that have been damaged by oxidation are harmful to the heart and arteries.

Oxidized fats are abundant in our modern diet. Processed vegetable oils are particularly bad. These refined oils have been stripped of the natural antioxidants that protect them from oxidation and free-radical generation. As a result, these oils can begin to oxidize and form free radicals while they

STANDARD RISK FACTORS FOR ATHEROSCLEROSIS

• Gender (being male)
• Glucose intolerance (diabetes)
• Heredity (history of CVD prior to age 55 in family members)
• High blood cholesterol/triglyceride levels
• High blood pressure
• Lack of exercise
• Obesity (30% or more overweight)
• Smoking
• Stress
• High insulin levels

Risk factors for disease are situations that are associated or correlated with the occurrence of a disorder but not proven to be the cause. The more risk factors one has the greater the risk or chance of suffering from a particular disease.

are still being processed and bottled. When you buy them at the store they already contain dangerous free radicals. If you or a restaurant use them in cooking the heat greatly accelerates oxidation and free-radical formation. When these damaged oils are consumed they release a horde of very chemically active free radicals into the bloodstream which attack the lining of the arteries causing inflammation and injury.

Another major source of free radicals is tobacco smoke and polluted air. When smoke is inhaled free radicals enter the lungs and are absorbed into the bloodstream where they can attack the arteries. This is why smoking is one of the strongest risk factors for heart disease.

The only way to stop a free radical is with an antioxidant. Antioxidants are molecules that neutralize free radicals making them harmless. Numerous studies have shown that diets high in fruits and vegetables rich in antioxidants (vitamins A, C, E, and beta-carotene) reduce the risk of heart disease and stroke. If antioxidants are readily available in the bloodstream they can protect the arteries from free-radical injury and reduce risk of heart disease.

We can get antioxidants in fresh fruits and vegetables, but most people don't eat enough of these to provide significant protection. Antioxidant supplements can help. Another way to fight free radicals is with coconut oil. Unlike other vegetable oils, coconut oil is chemically very stable and is not oxidized easily. In fact it is so resistant to free radical attack that it acts as

83

an antioxidant helping to prevent the oxidation of other oils. Coconut oil then can help protect the heart and arteries from free-radical induced injury and, therefore, helps *reduce* the risk of heart disease.

A NEW APPROACH TO
HEART DISEASE PREVENTION

Coconut oil protects the heart and arteries from injury caused by bacteria, viruses, and free radicals. By removing the cause of arterial injury, coconut oil prevents further damage allowing the arterial walls to heal, thus not only reducing risk of heart disease but actually promoting healing.

Coconut oil also seems to have a direct effect on the heart itself. I believe that it may help regulate heart function. I've seen people lower their heart rate and blood pressure when they start using coconut oil. For example, Maria, a heart disease patient, was told by her cardiologist that she had only five years to live. One of the common symptoms of heart disease is cardiac arrhythmia—an accelerated irregular heartbeat. She suffered so severely from arrhythmia that her doctor insisted she have a pacemaker implanted in her chest. She refused. She tried many natural methods but her symptoms persisted and worsened. I told her about coconut oil and she began taking it like a dietary supplement—4 tablespoons a day. The very first day she reported that her arrhythmia decreased by about 50 percent. She reported that it was the calmest her heart had been in years. Nothing she had ever tried before had worked this well. She continues to take coconut oil and her heart is functioning more normally now. It appears that her heart likes coconut oil.

While I was overjoyed to hear of Maria's success, it really wasn't a surprise. People who are familiar with coconut have learned that it helps the heart. As they say in Jamaica, "Coconut is a health tonic, good for the heart."

Heart disease, stroke, and atherosclerosis account for nearly half of all the deaths in most developed countries. Statistically, nearly one out of every two people you know will die from one of these cardiovascular conditions. In countries where people eat a lot of coconut products cardiovascular disease is much less frequent. In Sri Lanka, for example, where coconut oil is the primary dietary fat, the death rate from heart disease is one of the lowest in the world.[9] In areas of India, where coconut oil has been largely replaced by other vegetable oils, cardiovascular disease is on the rise. People have been encouraged to switch from their traditional cooking oils such as coconut oil in favor of processed vegetable oils that are promoted as "heart-friendly." Researchers involved with studies on diet and heart disease in India are now recommending the return to coconut oil to *reduce* the risk of heart disease. This recommendation is based on their findings of increased occurrence of heart disease as coconut oil is replaced by other vegetable oils.[10]

MONEY, POLITICS, AND HEART DISEASE

Unlike the standard treatments for heart disease, coconut oil is cheap, has no adverse side effects, and is readily available to everyone. This, however, may also be a drawback. Because it is a natural product that is already widely available, pharmaceutical and medical industries have no desire to fund studies or promote interest in this area. There is no profit for them. Since most of the information on MCFA and coconut oil are buried in scientific literature, few people are aware of the benefits. Knowledge about the true health aspects of coconut oil has to come from experienced clinicians, authors, and researchers who are familiar with the true facts about coconut oil. Yet they face an up-hill battle because they must fight prejudice and misguided popular opinion that is fueled by powerful profit-seeking enterprises.

As knowledge of the benefits of coconut oil increases, the soybean industry and their friends will step up their efforts to confuse the public with unfounded criticism and research funding designed to hide the truth and to make their products appear more desirable. Biased research in favor of the funding institution or industry happens all too often. Smear campaigns like those sponsored in the 1980s and early 1990s will undoubtedly continue.

The soybean industry's attack on tropical oils was built on the accusation that these oils cause heart disease. This is ironic because replacing tropical oils with hydrogenated vegetable oils has actually increased heart disease deaths.[11] And they know it. As far back as the 1950s hydrogenated oils were suspected of causing heart disease.[12] The soybean industry, fully aware that hydrogenated oils caused health problems, attempted to discourage and even suppress studies which presented unfavorable results. In the book, *What Your Doctor Won't Tell You*, author Jane Heimlich tells about one researcher who, after publishing the results of a study unfavorable to hydrogenated oils, found that she could no longer find funding.[13] The purpose of her research, she thought, was to discover truth and increase knowledge, not promote a product, but this didn't set well with the vegetable oil industry and they refused to fund any of her future studies.

The truth about hydrogenated oils and trans fatty acids eventually emerged. Like the tobacco industry which denied for years that cigarette smoke caused cancer, the soybean industry has denied that trans fatty acids promote heart disease. They cunningly diverted the public's attention to saturated fats and tropical oils, pointing a finger and calling them the troublemakers. In the 1980s and early 1990s, as the soybean industry's campaign against tropical oils raged, study after study implicated hydrogenated oils in contributing to heart disease as well as a number of other health problems. Aware of the growing evidence against hydrogenated oils, the soybean industry conveniently avoided discussing this in their anti-tropical oil campaign. They always implied that tropical oils should be replaced by "vegetable oils." They didn't say what type of vegetable oil, but they knew all along that it would be *hydrogenated* vegetable oil.

At this same time many of the health benefits of coconut oil and MCFA had been well established in certain circles. Hospitals were routinely using them in formulas to nourish infants and critically ill patients and to treat certain health problems. They were used in all commercial baby formulas. The soybean industry was well aware of this, but the general public didn't know. They knew their product was inferior to coconut oil and had to create a health scare to turn public opinion to their favor.

Food manufacturers, fearful of customer opinion, began removing tropical oils from their products. But to duplicate the same desirable effects the tropical oils gave to foods required another saturated fat. In most cases ordinary vegetable oils just wouldn't work. They go rancid far too quickly, and because they are more liquid than the tropical oils, they often give food a less desirable shape and texture. For example, if you tried substituting vegetable oil for shortening or butter in a cookie recipe, the cookies wouldn't hold their shape. As they cook they will spread out in a thin layer on the cookie sheet, kind of like a snow ball melting on a hot day, a result totally unacceptable for commercial bakeries.

Hydrogenated vegetable oils, however, are artificially saturated, giving them baking properties similar to natural saturated fats. So when tropical oils were removed from the ingredients of commercially prepared foods they were all replaced with hydrogenated or partially-hydrogenated oils. The result was more sales and profits for the soybean industry and many, many more deadly trans fatty acids in our diet.

It's all too clear now that trans fatty acids are a serious threat to health. Numerous studies have demonstrated their health-damaging effects. The negative effects on blood fat levels is twice that of saturated animal fats.[14] This indicates that hydrogenated oil is twice as bad as saturated fat in promoting heart disease. What makes this even worse is that during cooking, hydrogenated oil is absorbed into foods more readily than saturated fat so that you get *more* fat per serving. What are the results?

Researchers estimate that in the United States, consumption of trans fatty acids causes at least *30,000 premature deaths a year!*[15]

It appears that the soybean industry in its effort to capture a larger market and gain greater financial profits has caused untold pain and suffering by contributing to, rather than reducing, the incidence of heart disease, stroke, atherosclerosis, and other diseases. Are they about to admit they fooled everybody, that tropical oils aren't so bad after all, and that we would be better off without hydrogenated oils? Not likely. I predict they will fight even harder to keep from losing sales regardless of the health consequences to the public. So you are likely to continue to run across anti-tropical oil and pro-hydrogenated vegetable oil news for some time. Keep in mind that the companies that make hydrogenated oils send biased "educational" materials to health care professionals and health magazines and newsletter editors all the time, so your doctor may be confused on the issue.

As you have seen in this chapter, coconut oil is not only heart-friendly but provides some degree of protection against atherosclerosis and heart disease. Don't let self-serving enterprises scare you. It would be to your benefit to ignore marketing propaganda and use coconut oil in place of hydrogenated oils whenever possible.

EAT YOUR WAY TO BETTER HEALTH

Have you or someone you know ever been in a serious car accident? I mean serious enough that you had to be rushed to the hospital and spend time in the intensive care unit. Or maybe you've come down with a life-threatening illness. Or perhaps due to age you've been hospitalized to treat some degenerative condition. In any of these situations, whether you lived or died depended on the care you received in the hospital. Often this required you to be fed intravenously or through a tube. In the intensive care unit there would be others, some suffering from complications from genetic diseases such as cystic fibrosis or epilepsy and perhaps even premature infants struggling to survive their first few weeks of life. In each of these cases you and these other patients can give some of the credit for your recovery to coconut oil. Yes, in one form or another, coconut oil was part of your treatment.

Regardless of the condition, recovery requires good nutrition. Food scientists have long noted the nutritional benefits of MCFA. Coconut oil, or some derivative of it, is used in hospital formulas to feed the very young, the critically ill, and those who have digestive problems. It makes up a vital part of the solutions fed to patients intravenously or through a tube inserted down the throat.* In fact, if you were ever given formula as a baby, you

---

* In emergencies when commercial IV solutions are not available doctors in tropical climates will use coconut water instead. Often referred to as "coconut milk", fresh coconut water is naturally free from germs and has many mineral salts, sugars, and medium-chain fatty acids that are capable of nourishing a patient who is incapable of consuming or digesting ordinary food. Coconut water has helped save the lives of

took advantage of the health-promoting properties of coconut oil. MCFA from coconut oil have been added to baby formula for decades. Why do they use it? Because the MCFA in coconut oil are easily digested, absorbed, and put to use nourishing the body. Unlike other fats, they put little strain on the digestive system and provide a quick source of energy necessary to promote healing. This is important for patients who are using every ounce of strength they have to overcome serious illness or injury. It's no wonder why MCFA are added to infant formulas. Actually, whether you were breast or formula fed as an infant you consumed MCFA. Why? Because MCFA are not only found in coconut oil but are natural and vital components of human breast milk. MCFA are considered *essential* nutrients for infants as well as for people with serious digestive problems like cystic fibrosis. Like other essential nutrients, you must get them directly from the diet.

One of the first scientifically recognized benefits of MCFA is the unique manner in which they are digested and utilized by the body. These fats provide nutritional benefits that can improve overall health of both the sick and the well, the young and the old. Even athletes are now using them to boost performance and control weight. Unfortunately, few foods nowadays contain MCFA; the best source is coconut oil. By adding coconut oil to your diet you can literally eat your way to better health.

DIGESTION AND NUTRIENT ABSORPTION

For at least five decades researchers have recognized that the MCFA were digested differently than other fats. This difference has had important applications in the treatment of many digestive and metabolic health conditions and since that time MCFA have been routinely used in hospital and baby formulas.

The digestive health advantages of medium-chain fatty acids (MCFA) over long-chain fatty acids (LCFA) are due to the differences in the way our bodies metabolize these fats. Because the MCFA molecules are smaller, they require less energy and fewer enzymes to break them down for digestion. They are digested and absorbed quickly and with minimal effort.

MCFA are broken down almost immediately by enzymes in the saliva and gastric juices so that pancreatic fat-digesting enzymes are not even

---

hundreds of seriously sick and injured people. Its greatest use has been to combat dehydration and electrolyte depletion in wounded soldiers. During WWII the Japanese used coconut water as an emergency IV solution. Later during the Vietnam conflict North Vietnamese doctors did the same thing.

essential.[1] Therefore, there is less strain on the pancreas and digestive system. This has important implications for patients who suffer from digestive and metabolic problems. Premature and ill infants especially, whose digestive organs are underdeveloped, are able to absorb MCFA with relative ease, while other fats pass through their systems pretty much undigested. People who suffer from malabsorption problems such as cystic fibrosis, and have difficulty digesting or absorbing fats and fat soluble vitamins, benefit greatly from MCFA. They can also be of importance for people suffering from diabetes, obesity, gallbladder disease, pancreatitis, Crohn's disease, pancreatic insufficiency, and some forms of cancer.

As we get older our bodies don't function as well as they did in earlier years. The pancreas doesn't make as many digestive enzymes, our intestines don't absorb nutrients as well, the whole process of digestion and elimination moves at a lower rate of efficiency. As a result, older people often suffer from vitamin and mineral deficiencies. Because MCFA are easy to digest and improve vitamin and mineral absorption they should be included in the meals of older people. This is easy to do if the meals are prepared with coconut oil.

Unlike other fatty acids, MCFA are absorbed directly from the intestines into the portal vein and sent straight to the liver where they are, for the most part, burned as fuel much like a carbohydrate. In this respect they act more like carbohydrates than like fats.[2]

Other fats require pancreatic enzymes to break them into smaller units. They are then absorbed into the intestinal wall and packaged into bundles of fat (lipid) and protein called *lipoproteins*. These lipoproteins are carried by the lymphatic system, bypassing the liver, and then dumped into the bloodstream, where they are circulated throughout the body. As they circulate in the blood, their fatty components are distributed to all the tissues of the body. The lipoproteins get smaller and smaller, until there is little left of them. At this time they are picked up by the liver, broken apart, and used to produce energy or, if needed, repackaged into other lipoproteins and sent back into the bloodstream to be distributed throughout the body. Cholesterol, saturated fat, monounsaturated fat, and polyunsaturated fat are all packaged together into lipoproteins and carried throughout the body in this way. In contrast, MCFA are not packaged into lipoproteins but go to the liver where they are converted into energy. Ordinarily they are not stored to any significant degree as body fat. MCFA produce energy. Other dietary fats produce body fat.

Inside each of our cells is an organ called the mitochondria. The energy needed by the cell to carry on its functions is generated by the mitochondria. Mitochondria are encased in two membranous sacs which normally require special enzymes to transport nutrients through them. MCFA are unique in that they can easily permeate both membranes of the mitochondria without the need of enzymes and thus provide the cell with a quick and efficient source of energy. Longer chain fatty acids demand special enzymes to pull them through the double membrane, and the energy production process is much slower and taxing on enzyme reserves.

Because of the above advantages, coconut oil has been a lifesaver for many people, particularly the very young and the very old. It is used medicinally in special food preparations for those who suffer digestive disorders and have trouble digesting fats. For the same reason, it is also used in infant formula for the treatment of malnutrition. Since it is rapidly absorbed, it can deliver quick nourishment without putting excessive strain on the digestive and enzyme systems and help conserve the body's energy that would normally be expended in digesting other fats. Medium-chain fatty acids comprise a major ingredient in most infant formulas commonly used today.

METABOLISM AND ENERGY
Eating foods containing MCFA is like putting high octane fuel into your car. The car runs smoother and gets better gas mileage. Likewise, with MCFA your body performs better because it has more energy and greater endurance. Because MCFA are funneled directly to the liver and converted into energy, the body gets a boost of energy. And because MCFA are easily absorbed by the energy-producing organelles of the cells, *metabolism increases*. This burst of energy has a stimulating effect on the entire body.

The fact that MCFA digest immediately to produce energy and stimulate metabolism has led athletes to use them as a means to enhance exercise performance. Studies indicate this may be true. In one study, for example, investigators tested the physical endurance of mice who were given MCFA in their daily diet against those that weren't. The study extended over a six-week period. The mice were subjected to a swimming endurance test every other day. They were placed in a pool of water with a constant current. The total swimming time until exhaustion was measured. While at first there was little difference between the groups of mice, those fed MCFA quickly began to out-perform the others and continued to improve throughout the testing period.[3] Tests such as this demonstrated that MCFA had the ability to enhance endurance and exercise performance, at least in mice. Another study using human subjects supported the animal studies. In this study conditioned cyclists were used. The cyclists pedaled at 70 percent of maximum for two hours, then immediately embarked on a 40

K time trial ride (lasting about an additional hour) while drinking one of three beverages: a MCFA solution, a sports drink, or a sports drink/MCFA combination. The cyclists who drank the sports drink/MCFA mixture performed the best during the time trial.[4]*

Because of these and similar studies many of the powdered sports drinks and energy bars sold at health food stores contain MCFA to provide a quick source of energy.** Athletes and other active people looking for nutritional, non-drug methods to enhance exercise performance have begun using them.

Although many studies have shown MCFA to boost energy and endurance, there are other studies which have shown little or no effect, at least when MCFA mixtures are taken in a single oral dose. Studies generally show that a single oral dose has little measurable effect. In studies where animals were fed MCFA as a part of their daily diet, however, the results were more significant. From this evidence it appears that the best way to increase energy and endurance is to consume MCFA on a daily basis and not a single time just before or during competition.

It's easy to see why athletes would be interested in gaining greater endurance and energy, but what about non-athletes? MCFA can do the same for them. If eaten regularly, MCFA can provide a boost in energy and performance of daily activities. Would you like to increase your energy level throughout the day? If you get tired in the middle of the day or feel you lack energy, adding coconut oil to your daily diet may provide you with a much needed boost to help carry you through.

Besides increasing your energy level, there are other very important benefits that results from boosting your metabolic rate: it helps protect you

---

* The authors of the study theorized that the MCFA gave the cyclists an additional source of energy, thus sparing glycogen stores. Glycogen, the energy stored in muscle tissue, would have been used up during the three-hour ride. The more glycogen in the muscles the greater an athlete's endurance. So any substance that can conserve glycogen while providing energy would be useful to endurance athletes. In a follow-up study to test the glycogen sparing theory, participants cycled at 60% of their maximum for three hours while drinking one of three beverages as was done in the earlier study. Following the exercise, muscle glycogen levels were measured and found to be the same for all three groups. The conclusion was that MCFA did not spare glycogen stores, yet did improve performance. The improvement in performance was not due to glycogen sparing and must be attributed to some other mechanism.

** The medium-chain fatty acids (MCFA) most often used in sports drinks and energy bars are in the form of medium-chain triglyceride oil (MCT oil). They are usually indicated as "MCT" on food, supplement, and infant formula labels.

You can enjoy a higher level of energy by consuming coconut oil every day.

from illness and speeds healing. When metabolism is increased, cells function at a higher rate of efficiency. They heal injuries quicker, old and diseased cells are replaced faster, and young, new cells are generated at an increased rate to replace worn-out ones. Even the immune system functions better.

Several health problems such as obesity, heart disease, and osteoporosis are more prevalent in those people who have slow metabolism. Any health condition is made worse if the metabolic rate is slower than normal, because cells can't heal and repair themselves as quickly. Increasing metabolic rate, therefore, provides an increased degree of protection from both degenerative and infectious illnesses.

NATURE'S PERFECT FOOD
Nature's Nectar

Among all the foods in nature there is one that stands head and shoulders above all the rest. That food is mother's milk. Milk was designed by nature to supply all the nutrients a baby needs for the first year or so of life. It contains a perfect blend of vitamins, minerals, proteins, and fats for

Breast milk is nature's perfect food.

optimal growth and development. Without question breast milk is one of the wonders of nature.

Children who are breastfed not only take in important nutrients from the milk, but they also receive antibodies and other substances necessary to protect them against childhood illnesses such as ear infections, later in life.

Breastfed children are healthier than those who are not. They have better teeth and jaw formation, they are less prone to allergies, have better digestive function, and are better able to fight off infectious disease. Research suggests that breastfed children may even develop higher intelligence. Recognizing the superiority of nature, scientists have attempted to make baby formula match mother's milk as closely as possible.

An important component of breast milk is medium-chain fatty acids, principally lauric acid. Lauric acid is also the primary saturated fatty acid found in coconut oil. Apparently nature thought it essential to the baby's health to include it. Nature has a reason for everything it does. It doesn't do things, such as putting MCFA in milk, just for the fun of it.

Some of the important reasons medium-chain fatty acids are included in milk are improved nutrient absorption and digestive function. As noted earlier, pancreatic enzymes aren't even necessary to digest them. They also help to regulate blood sugar levels. Another very important function is that medium-chain fatty acids protect the baby from harmful microorganisms. The baby's immature immune system is supported by the antibacterial, antiviral, antifungal, and antiparasitic properties of these vital fatty acids. In fact, without these unique saturated fats, the baby would probably not survive long. It would become malnourished and highly susceptible to a myriad of infectious diseases.

Milk Quality and MCFA

Milk that is rich in medium-chain fatty acids is vital for the healthy growth and development of the child. For this reason, MCFA are added to most, if not all, baby formulas. Yet, these fatty acids are not exactly the same as those found naturally in mother's milk. At one time formula manufacturers used pure coconut or palm kernel oils and many brands still do. But MCT oil is used in some formulas. MCT oil is a product of industry containing 75 percent caprylic acid and 25 percent capric acid with little or no lauric acid—the most important antimicrobial MCFA. Lauric acid is also the most abundant MCFA found naturally in mother's milk. The ratio of lauric acid to other MCFA in coconut oil is similar to that in mother's milk. The reason MCT oil is used in place of the more expensive coconut oil is due to economics rather than concerns for health. Don't get me wrong, caprylic and capric acids are good, but not as good as lauric acid, and not as good as a combination of all three, as nature intended.

Just as the fatty acid content and quality of formula can be altered, so can human breast milk. Breast milk is, without question, the best choice of food for babies. Not all breast milk is the same however. The quality of the milk is influenced by the mother's health and diet. Breast milk is made from the nutrients the mother consumes. If she doesn't eat the right amount of nutrients, her body will pull them out of her own tissues. If the mother is deficient in these vital nutrients herself, then the milk she produces will also be deficient. Similarly, if she eats foods containing toxins (such as trans fatty acids) her milk may contain them as well. Eating wisely is very important for pregnant and nursing women and their babies.

The mammary glands produce small amounts of all the medium-chain fatty acids—vital components in human breast milk. They are there because they are easy for an infant's immature digestive system to absorb and utilize. They help give the baby the nutrients and energy it needs to grow and develop properly. Because they also have antimicrobial properties they give the infant some degree of protection against viruses such as HIV and herpes, bacteria such a chlamydia and H. pyloris, fungi such as candida, and protozoa such as giardia.

Both animal and human studies have shown MCFA to be an important component in mother's milk for the proper growth and development of their offspring. For example, when pregnant and lactating pigs were fed diets containing either long-chain fatty acids (vegetable oil) or medium-chain fatty acids (coconut oil) there was a pronounced difference in the survival and growth rates. The piglets whose mothers received the MCFA grew faster and healthier and had a survival rate of 68% compared to 32%. This was particularly true with piglets which were born underweight.[5]

The same thing appears to happen in humans. For example, coconut oil was added to the formula of 46 very low-birthweight babies to see if supplementation was capable of enhancing their weight gain. The group with the coconut oil gained weight quicker. The weight gain was due to physical growth and *not* fat storage.[6] The babies gained more weight and grew better with the coconut oil because their bodies were able to digest it easily. The vegetable oils, to a great extent, passed through their digestive tracts undigested and thus deprived them of nutrients they needed for proper development. MCFA not only allow infants to absorb needed fats, but they improve the absorption of fat-soluble vitamins, minerals, and protein.[7, 8]

Human milk fat has a unique fatty acid composition. The primary fat is saturated, comprising about 45-50 percent of the total fat content. The next most abundant fat is monounsaturated which makes up about 35 percent of the milk fat. Polyunsaturated fat comprises only 15-20 percent of the total. A significant portion of the saturated fat in human breast milk can be in the form of MCFA. Sadly, many mothers produce very little. This can have dramatic consequences on the health of their children.

If breast milk does not contain enough MCFA, an infant can suffer from nutritional deficiency and become vulnerable to infectious illness. Therefore, it is important that mother's milk contain as much MCFA as nature will allow. This can be done with diet. Given an ample supply of food containing medium-chain fatty acids, a nursing mother will produce a milk rich in these health-promoting nutrients.[9] While cow's milk and other dairy products contain small amounts, the foods richest in medium-chain fatty acids are the tropical oils, principally coconut oil.

The levels of these antimicrobial fatty acids can be as low as 3 to 4 percent, but when nursing mothers eat coconut products (shredded coconut, coconut milk, coconut oil, etc.) the levels of MCFA in their milk increase significantly. For instance, eating 40 grams (about 3 tablespoons worth) of coconut oil in one meal can temporarily increase the lauric acid in the milk of a nursing mother from 3.9% to 9.6% after 14 hours.[10] The content of caprylic and capric acids are also increased. "This gives an important benefit," says Mary G. Enig, Ph.D. an expert in lipid chemistry and Fellow of the American College of Nutrition. "The milk has increased amounts of the protective antimicrobials lauric acid and capric acid, which gives even greater protection to the infant." If the mother consumes coconut oil every day while nursing, the MCFA content will be even greater.

Preparation by the mother should start before the baby is born. Pregnant women store fat to be used later in making their milk. After the baby is born the fatty acids stored in the mother's body and supplied by her daily diet are used in the production of her milk. If she has eaten and continues to eat foods which supply ample amounts of MCFA, particularly lauric acid and capric acid (the two most important antimicrobial medium-chain fatty acids), her milk will provide maximum benefit to her baby. These mothers can have as much as 18 percent of the saturated fatty acids in their milk in the form of lauric and capric acids.

If the mother did not eat foods containing MCFA and does not eat them while nursing, her mammary glands will only be capable of producing about 3 percent lauric acid and 1 percent capric acid. Her child will lose a great deal of the nutritional benefits as well as the antimicrobial protection the infant could have otherwise had.

Protection from Illness

One of the major characteristics of human breast milk is its ability to protect infants from a myriad of infectious illnesses during a time when their immune systems are immature and incapable of adequately defending themselves. The antimicrobial substances in milk that protect the child from a world teaming with infectious germs and parasites are the MCFA found in the triglycerides or fat molecules in the milk. There are some illnesses that even an adult with a healthy immune system may have difficulty fighting off. If the baby is not protected with an adequate amount of MCFA in his or her milk, exposure to such an infection could result in serious illness.

When a nursing mother is infected with such an illness, her child is also vulnerable. Mothers infected by certain viruses can pass the infection on to their infants through breastfeeding. In these cases breastfeeding is not recommended. This is particularly true when the mother is infected with a dangerous virus such as HIV. Research suggests that mothers who include a source of lauric acid, such as coconut oil, in their diets have lower risk of infecting their nursing infants. Adding coconut to the diet would be beneficial because it would provide increased lauric and capric acid to the mother's milk, thus reducing the risk of transferring the virus.

While HIV-infected mothers are usually advised not to breastfeed their young for fear that the virus may be transferred, there is no feasible option in some parts of the world. Many women in resource-poor areas do not have the financial means to buy infant formula. Breastfeeding is really their only option. Adding coconut products and coconut oil to the mother's diet is the only practical defense these women have against passing the AIDS virus to their children.

It has been recommended that HIV-infected mothers who are breastfeeding consume 24-28 grams/day of lauric acid and 3-4 grams/day of capric acid to prevent the transfer of the virus. Since coconut oil is nearly 48 percent lauric acid and 7 percent capric acid, this requirement would be met if the mother ate about 50-55 grams of coconut oil each day. A tablespoon is equivalent to 14 grams. So $3^1/_2$ tablespoons of coconut oil a day would provide the recommended amount of both lauric and capric acids.

Other viral infections such as those that cause measles, herpes, mononucleosis, and such are also a threat to nursing infants. Pregnant women and nursing mothers can help protect their children by eating an abundant amount of coconut oil or products that contain coconut oil, such as shredded coconut or coconut milk.

Any mother or expectant mother who desires a healthy, well-developed baby should consider adding coconut oil to her diet. She will not only assure better health for her children but will benefit greatly herself.

MCFA are vital nutrients and protectors found naturally in human milk. They are deadly enough to kill the AIDS virus yet gentle enough to nourish a premature infant to health. As we grow to adulthood and beyond, our bodies begin to wear down. MCFA can help nourish and protect us, as it does infants, from infectious and degenerative disease. It appears that coconut oil provides many health benefits to those who are very young and those who are very old and all those in between.

COCONUT OIL AS A MEDICINE

Let me take you to the jungles of Northern Brazil, far from civilization. Imagine yourself as a modern-day explorer venturing into the Amazon rain forest fighting pesky mosquitoes and wading through knee-deep swamps. One morning you wake up sweating like an ice cube in the hot July sun. A fever rages out of control interspersed by brief periods of icy chills. Every muscle in your body feels like it's twisted into knots; the strain has sapped your strength and you lie exhausted, almost too weak to move. With no modern medicine or doctors to help, you seek assistance from the local natives. Your health, and perhaps even your life, depends on the skill of the tribal medicine man. His treatment consists of a porridge made from coconut. You're fed this meal every day. Under the watchful care of the medicine man you gradually regain your strength and soon you're well enough to go on your way.

This story is not beyond belief. The natives of South and Central America regard coconut as both a food and a medicine. It helps to keep them healthy in a climate infested with malaria, yellow fever, and other tropical diseases. If you go along the coasts of Somalia and Ethiopia the locals would give you palm kernel oil if you were sick—a traditional remedy used for most all ills. Whether you are on an island in the Caribbean, an atoll in the Pacific Ocean, or along the coast of Southeast Asia or India, it is likely that the native people would give you coconut in some form as part of your treatment. Wherever the coconut palm grows the people have learned of its value as a source of food and as a medicine. This is why it is hailed as the Tree of Life.

Coconut Folk Medicine

People from many diverse cultures, languages, religions, and races scattered around the globe have revered the coconut as a valuable source of both food and medicine. Wherever the coconut palm grows the people have learned to recognize its importance as an effective medicine and for thousands of years coconut and coconut oil have held a respected and valuable place in local folk medicine.

Herbalist James A. Duke has noted that coconut and coconut oil are used as folk remedies to treat numerous ailments among which are the following: abscesses, alopecia, amenorrhea, asthma, blenorrhagia, bronchitis, bruises, burns, cachexia, calculus, colds, constipation, cough, debility, dropsy, dysentery, dysmenorrhea, earache, erysipelas, fever, flu, gingivitis, gonorrhea, hematemesis, hemoptysis, jaundice, menorrhagia, nausea, phthisis, rash, scabies, scurvy, sore throat, stomach, swelling, syphilis, toothache, tuberculosis, tumors, typhoid, and wounds.

Source: Duke, J.A. and Wain, K.K. 1981. *Medicinal Plants of the World*. Computer index.

Coconut and coconut oil are used in many traditional forms of medicine. The most well known of these is the Ayurvedic medicine of India. Here coconut products enjoy a place of importance and are essential components of some of the medicinal preparations. Coconut oil is recognized for its healing properties in both Ayurvedic and Indian folkloric medicine to treat a variety of conditions such as burns, wounds, ulcers, skin fungus, lice, kidney stones, and choleraic dysentery.[1, 2]

Modern medical science is just now beginning to unlock the healing secrets of coconut oil. Research is showing that coconut oil has many practical applications as a medicine. As you've seen in Chapter 6 the MCFA in coconut oil have a powerful antimicrobial effect that can kill a large number of infectious organisms, even the supergerms that are resistant to drugs are vulnerable. In Chapter 7 you learned how coconut oil can be used to prevent and treat heart disease. In Chapter 8 coconut oil was revealed to be a super food that is easily digested and utilized to nourish the body. In this chapter you will learn how it can be used as an aid to treat a number of health problems.

AIDS PREVENTION AND TREATMENT

After more than two decades of research, the AIDS epidemic is still going strong. Drugs have been developed to help slow down the progress of the disease, but like other viruses, there is yet no cure.

One of the most exciting and active areas of research with MCFA is in the treatment of those infected with the human immunodeficiency virus (HIV). HIV, like many other microorganisms, has a lipid membrane which is vulnerable to MCFA.

In the 1980s researchers discovered that the medium-chain fatty acids lauric and capric acids were effective in killing HIV in lab cultures. This opened the door to a possible treatment for HIV/AIDS that was far safer than the drugs currently being used.

One of the problems with antiviral drugs used to fight HIV is that they have undesirable side effects including muscle wasting, nausea, vomiting, anorexia, bone marrow suppression, ulcerations, hemorrhaging, skin rash, anemia, fatigue, and altered mental function. Another problem is that the AIDS virus can grow resistant to the drugs, often becoming invulnerable to them. The specific combination of viral resistance varies from patient to patient. To fight these resistant strains of super viruses doctors use a hit-and-miss approach by brewing potent AIDS drug cocktails. The more drugs used, the greater the risk of undesirable side effects.

Unlike the standard drugs used to treat HIV which attack the virus' genetic material, medium-chain fatty acids simply break the virus apart. The MCFA are much like the other fatty acids that make up the virus' lipid membrane and are absorbed by the virus, which weakens the membrane until it breaks apart, killing the virus. It is unlikely that the virus can develop an immunity to this mechanism, so MCFA can attack and kill any of the strains of HIV, even the genetically drug-resistant superviruses.

Over the years many HIV infected individuals have reported a decrease in their viral load (the number of viruses in the blood) and an improvement in overall health after eating coconut or drinking coconut milk. Some have reported lowering their viral loads to non-detectable levels after eating coconut for only a few weeks.

The first clinical study on the effectiveness of coconut oil to treat HIV patients was reported by Cornrado Dayrit, M.D., emeritus professor of pharmacology, University of the Philippines and former president of the National Academy of Science and Technology, Philippines.[3] In this study 14 patients ages 22 to 38 with HIV were separated into three groups. None of the patients had ever received any anti-HIV treatment. The treatment they were testing compared monolaurin (the monoglyceride of lauric acid found in coconut oil (see page 62) and pure coconut oil. One group (four patients) was given 22 grams of monolaurin a day. The second group (five patients) was given 7.2 grams of monolaurin. The third group (five patients) was given 3¹/₂ tablespoons of coconut oil. The amount of coconut oil in the third group contained about the same quantity of lauric acid as supplied by the monolaurin in the first group. After three months of treatment the viral load had decreased in seven of the patients. After six months when the study was completed nine out of the 14 patients had a decreased viral count (two in the first group, four in the second, and three in the third). Eleven of the patients had regained weight and appeared to be improving. This study confirmed the anecdotal reports that coconut oil has anti-HIV effects and has provided solid clinical evidence that both monolaurin and coconut oil are effective in fighting HIV. Additional research is currently underway to further study the use of monolaurin and coconut oil to treat HIV/AIDS.

Unfortunately, the ready availability and low cost of coconut oil and its derivative fatty acids are reasons why research into its use as a treatment for AIDS and other viral illnesses has been slow. There is little monetary incentive for pharmaceutical companies to fund research of a natural, readily available substance that they cannot protect with a patent and charge exorbitant prices for. Currently the cost of standard medications for one person to control the virus can reach over $15,000 a year. If all the hundreds of thousands of people who are infected by HIV spend anywhere near this amount you can easily see the enormous amount of money the pharmaceutical companies pull in. It is no wonder they are reluctant to support a treatment that threatens to end this flood of cash.

HIV-infected individuals often suffer from nutritional deficiencies and recurrent infections. Resistance to infectious illness decreases as the disease progresses. Opportunistic microorganisms such as cytomegalovirus, candida, cryptosporidium, and others quickly take root. In time the body is devastated so greatly by infection that survival is impossible. The fatty acids in coconut oil not only offer the possibility of reducing HIV load, but kill other harmful organisms as well. Combined with the fact that lauric acid and other MCFA improve digestion and energy production, the result is better overall health.

Current research suggests that individuals infected with HIV progress more rapidly to AIDS when they have a higher viral load. Reducing the viral load to undetectable levels greatly increases the patient's chances of avoiding the disease and reduces the chance of infecting others.

A recent study by researchers from Johns Hopkins University showed that the number of individual viruses in the person determines the degree to which the virus can be passed on to others. The study found that someone with 200,000 virus copies (individual viruses per mm of blood) is 2.5 times more likely to spread HIV than someone with only 2,000 copies. The researchers found no transmission of the virus at all by infected people who carried less than 1,500 copies of the virus.

Currently some researchers recommended that HIV-infected individuals consume the equivalent of 24-28 grams of lauric acid a day in order to significantly reduce their viral load. This would amount to about $3^1/_2$ tablespoons (50 grams) of coconut oil.

What does all this mean to you and me? A lot. While it is not yet known if lauric acid may one day be a cure for AIDS, it has been proven to reduce the HIV load in those individuals who are infected by the virus, thus allowing them to live more normal lives and greatly reduce the risk of transmitting the virus to others. It may just as well be able to protect and possibly prevent infection in the first place if a person has sufficient lauric acid in his or her daily diet and exposure to HIV is low.

Currently the AIDS epidemic has spread worldwide. Millions of people are affected by HIV. The numbers who become infected are increasing daily. As yet there has not been an effective means to stop this plague. With coconut oil and lauric acid now there is hope. Many people fear picking up the virus, even those who are not involved in high-risk activities. The simple act of using coconut oil in your ordinary food preparation may provide you with a substantial degree of protection not only against HIV but against measles, herpes, flu, as well as dozens of other of disease-causing viruses.

CHRONIC FATIGUE SYNDROME

Coconut oil may be one of the best solutions to chronic fatigue syndrome currently available. Chronic fatigue syndrome (CFS), once considered to be an imaginary ailment, is now recognized as a bona fide illness. While its cause is still pretty much a mystery, it has become a problem of growing concern. It is estimated that some three million Americans and 90 million people worldwide are affected by it.

CFS is characterized by a relatively sudden onset of extreme fatigue, often following an infectious illness. Symptoms may include any of the following: muscle weakness, headache, memory loss, mental confusion, recurring infections, low-grade fever, swollen lymph glands, severe exhaustion following moderate physical activity, depression, anxiety attacks, dizziness, rashes, allergies, and autoimmune reactions. Symptoms that persist for six months or more are a strong indication of CFS.

The degree and severity of symptoms often fluctuate. An afflicted person may temporarily "recover" and function normally for awhile only to relapse a short time later. Many people are affected without even realizing it. They assume the symptoms are due to age, stress, or seasonal illness and they do nothing to solve the problem.

The exact cause of the illness is still unknown and there is no standard medical test to detect it. Consequently, a cure has yet to be found. The current belief is that CFS does not have a single cause but is the result of many factors. Some believe it is the result of multiple chronic infections which depress the immune system and drain the body of energy. Poor nutrition, excessive stress, food and environmental toxins, and chronic infections all combine to lower immune function and drain energy. Many people believe that a depressed immune system is the primary cause of the problem.

Dr. Murray Susser, M.D. from Santa Monica, California says, "CFS can start with ordinary viral infections like those that cause respiratory infections like the common cold and flu. There are 2,300 viruses which can cause a cold or flu and if one of those hits you and your body isn't able to get rid of it, then you have a chronic infection. That's really what chronic fatigue behaves like, the flu that never got better. I sometimes call it, 'the flu that became always.'"[4]

Any number of viruses, bacteria, fungi, or parasites can contribute to chronic fatigue. The most likely causes are the herpes virus, Epstein-Barr virus, candida, and giardia. Some infections, especially viruses such as herpes, can persist for a lifetime. Herpes can cause fever blisters and genital lesions. The blisters may disappear temporarily only to reappear occasionally, especially as a result of stress.

Herpes zoster is the chickenpox virus. Once the virus enters the body it stays there for the rest of the person's life.* After chickenpox has run its course, the virus manages to survive within the confines of the nervous system and stays there throughout life. For most people it remains dormant. During times of stress, however, when the immune system's efficiency drops, the virus can become reactivated. This new infection is known as shingles.

The Epstein-Barr virus is a member of the herpes family. It causes mononucleosis, often called the kissing disease because it can be transmitted this way. Once in the body it attacks the white blood cells. Recovery takes four to six weeks with rest. The body needs this length of time to allow the immune system to overcome the virus. For two to three months

---

* Herpes virus may also play a role in the development of cervical cancer.

afterwards patients often feel depressed, lack energy, and feel sleepy throughout the day. These conditions may persist at a chronic level giving rise to CFS.

Cold and flu viruses can cause chronic infections that may contribute to chronic fatigue. Often people with viral infections are given antibiotics. There is no antibiotic that can kill a virus. Antibiotics are only effective against bacteria. When we come down with a cold, flu, or other viral infection the only thing we can do is take it easy and let our immune system handle the job. Doctors often give people suffering from viral infections antibiotics because there is nothing else they can do. The antibiotics have no more effect than a placebo, thus making the patient feel he is doing something to hasten recovery. This has been the standard practice among doctors for years. The problem with this, besides wasting the patient's money and subjecting him to worthless medications, is that the antibiotics may do some harm. One of the side effects of antibiotic use is the development of candidiasis. Antibiotics kill friendly bacteria in the intestinal tract. These good bacteria compete for space with disease-causing bacteria and yeast, keeping yeast numbers low and relatively harmless. If these bacteria are killed by antibiotic use, yeasts are able to multiply unrestrained causing a systemic candida infection. Candida can become chronic, burdening the immune system, draining the body's energy, leading to prolonged feelings of fatigue and ill health.

As mentioned in Chapter 6, giardia infections produce symptoms often diagnosed as chronic fatigue syndrome. Low-grade bacterial infections may also drain the body's energy, causing chronic fatigue. Low-grade infections can be near impossible to diagnose accurately. If a virus is part of the cause, little can be done as there are no drugs that can cure viral illnesses. Giving the wrong type of medication can make matters worse, so experimenting with antibiotics and other drugs is not a good solution.

What's the answer? Coconut oil may provide a vital solution to chronic fatigue syndrome. The fatty acids in coconut oil can kill herpes and Epstein-Barr viruses which are believed to be major causes. They kill candida and giardia. They kill a variety of other infectious organisms, any of which could cause chronic fatigue.

Some doctors believe it is not the particular germ or organism that matters; any combination of factors or conditions that depress the immune system can lead to CFS. According to them the key to overcoming CFS is strengthening the immune system. Again coconut oil may be the solution. Coconut oil supports the immune system by ridding the body of harmful microorganisms, thus relieving stress on the body. With fewer harmful organisms taxing the body's energy, the immune system can function better.

Coconut oil provides a quick source of energy and stimulates metabolism. This boost in energy not only lifts the spirit but promotes faster healing. The higher the body's metabolism the more efficient the immune system and the quicker the body can heal and repair itself.

It's like a carpenter doing some repairs on your house. If he is tired and slow, it will take a long time to do the job, but if he is energetic and anxious to complete the task it will take a fraction of the time. When metabolism is functioning at a higher level our cells are like an energized carpenter anxious to complete the repairs while depressed metabolism causes the cells to work slower, and consequently healing and repair progress slower.

I believe coconut oil used regularly can be one of the best natural treatments for chronic fatigue. Here is what one 46-year-old man experienced:

"I never thought I was troubled with chronic fatigue syndrome. I was healthy. I ate what I considered a good diet—low in fat, lots of fruits, vegetables, and whole grains. But I noticed as I was approaching my mid-forties my level of energy was decreasing rapidly. Even modest amounts of yard work became a drudgery. After a couple of hours I came in exhausted and it took me two days to recover. By 8:00 p.m. every day I was exhausted, even though I have a desk job. I found myself going to bed earlier and earlier. Life was slowing down and I missed the energy I once had. I assumed that what I was experiencing was just the consequence of growing older and left it at that. But then I began to wonder. I saw other people, much older than I, who were more physically active and had much more energy. I then suspected something was wrong. I began to seek ways to improve my health. I learned about coconut and began to eat it in place of other oils. I did this not to cure any illness but simply to improve my overall health. It was several months later when I noticed that the energy I used to have had returned. I no longer wanted to go to sleep at 8:00 p.m. but stayed up till 11:00 without problem. I got less sleep but had more energy. Improvement came so gradually that I didn't notice the change until after several months. And it wasn't until later that I even thought it might be related to coconut oil. Since I've been using coconut oil I have not been lethargic during the day, as I was in the past; I have more energy and accomplish more. I feel really good."

OSTEOPOROSIS

One of the advantages of using MCFA in baby formula is that they help with the absorption of other nutrients. The absorption of calcium and magnesium and also amino acids has been found to increase when infants are fed a diet containing coconut oil.[5, 6] Coconut oil has been used for the purpose of enhancing absorption and retention of calcium and magnesium in people when a deficiency of these minerals exists. This is one of the reasons why hospitals give premature and sick infants formulas containing MCFA. It is also used to treat children suffering with rickets which involves a demineralization and softening of the bones similar to osteoporosis in adults.

Regardless of your age your bones can benefit from coconut oil. Dietary fats play a role in the formation of our bones. Researchers at Purdue University found that free radicals from oxidized vegetable oils interfere with bone formation thus contribute to osteoporosis. They also discovered that antioxidants such as vitamin E protected the bones from free radicals. In addition, they found that saturated fats, like those in coconut oil, also acted as antioxidants and protected the bones from destructive free radicals.[7]

Fresh coconut and perhaps virgin coconut oil contains fat-like substances called sterols which are very similar in structure to pregnenolone. Pregnenolone is a substance our bodies manufacture from sterols and is used to make hormones such as DHEA and progesterone. When women's bodies are in need of these hormones pregnenolone is used as the starting material to make them. According to John Lee, M.D., the reason women are often plagued with osteoporosis as they get older is because they have an imbalance of progesterone to estrogen. Environmental estrogens from meat, milk, and pesticides dilute natural progesterone. In clinical practice Dr. Lee has had women use progesterone to increase their body's reserves of this hormone. Bone density tests before and after treatment showed a clear reversal of osteoporosis. Dr. Lee has outlined his findings in the book *What Your Doctor May Not Tell You About Menopause*. It is believed that pregnenolone, which is converted into progesterone in women, has the same bone building effect. If this is true, the pregnenolone-like substances in coconut may also aid in maintaining hormone balance which promotes healthy bones.

This may be why populations who consume coconuts as a major part of their diets are rarely troubled by osteoporosis. For those who are concerned about developing osteoporosis as they get older, coconut oil may be useful in helping to slow down this degenerative process by improving mineral absorption, protecting the bones from free radicals, and maintaining hormone balance.

GALLBLADDER DISEASE

Most anyone who suffers from a digestive disorder can benefit from using coconut oil. More people fit into this category than may realize. Anyone who has had their gallbladder removed would greatly benefit from using coconut oil in place of other oils.

The purpose of the gallbladder is to store and regulate the use of bile. The function of bile in the digestive process is often given little notice, but is essential. The liver produces bile at a relatively constant rate. As the bile is secreted, it drains into and is collected by the gallbladder. The gallbladder, being hollow, functions as a container to hold bile. Fats and oils in our foods stimulate the gallbladder to pump bile into the intestine. An adequate amount of bile is essential for the digestion of fats because it emulsifies or breaks the fat into small particles. Digestive enzymes from the pancreas can break the small particles of fat down into individual fatty acids which can then be absorbed. Without bile, fat digesting enzymes could not complete the job of digestion; this would lead to serious nutritional deficiencies and disease.

When the gallbladder is surgically removed, fat digestion is greatly hindered. Without the gallbladder, the bile, which is continually being secreted by the liver, slowly drains into the small intestine. The tiny amount of bile that drains directly from the liver into the intestine is not enough to function adequately in fat digestion when even moderate amounts of fat are consumed. This leads to malabsorption of fat-soluble vitamins and to digestive problems. Bile must be present in the intestine to properly absorb

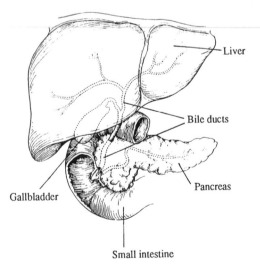

Liver

Bile ducts

Pancreas

Gallbladder

Small intestine

The liver produces bile continuously and stores it in the gallbladder. When we eat a meal containing fat, the gallbladder empties the bile into the intestine where it is used in digesting the fat. If there is not enough bile present in the intestine, fat-soluble vitamins are not properly absorbed from the food, which can lead to vitamin deficiencies. This is a serious problem with those who have had their gallbladders removed.

108

fat-soluble vitamins (vitamins A, D, E, K, and beta-carotene). The consequence of not getting enough of these vitamins may not be immediately noticeable but over time will manifest itself in a variety of ways. Metabolism of MCFA does not require bile or pancreatic enzymes, so someone who has had his or her gallbladder removed or who has trouble digesting fats would greatly benefit from the use of coconut oil.

DIABETES

One of the many plagues of modern society is diabetes. The incidence of diabetes has risen from almost nothing a century ago to a level of major concern today. It is now the sixth biggest killer in America. Diabetes not only can cause death but can lead to kidney disease, heart disease, high blood pressure, stroke, cataracts, nerve damage, hearing loss, and blindness. It is estimated that 45 percent of the population is at risk of developing diabetes.

Diabetes is all about sugar—the sugar in our bodies known as blood sugar or blood glucose. Every cell in our bodies must have a constant source of glucose in order to fuel metabolism. Our cells use glucose to power processes such as growth and repair. When we eat a meal the digestive system converts much of our food into glucose which is released into the bloodstream. The hormone insulin, which is secreted by the pancreas gland, moves glucose from the blood and funnels it into the cells so it can be used as fuel. If the cells are unable to get adequate amounts of glucose, they can literally starve to death. As they do, tissues and organs begin to degenerate. This is what happens in diabetes.

There are two major forms of diabetes: Type I and Type II. Type I, also referred to a insulin-dependent or juvenile diabetes, usually begins in childhood and results from the inability of the pancreas to make adequate amounts of insulin. Type II diabetes is known as non-insulin-dependent or adult-onset diabetes because it usually appears in older adults. In Type II diabetes the pancreas may secrete a normal amount of insulin but the cells are unable to absorb it. Insulin acts like a key to a lock. It goes to the cells and unlocks the door to allow glucose to enter. If the lock is made of cheap materials and breaks, the key no longer works and the door remains locked. This is essentially what happens with Type II diabetes. Insulin is generally available but it can no longer unlock the door because the lock is broken. In both types of diabetes the level of glucose in the blood is elevated while cells are deprived.

In Type I the pancreas is incapable of producing enough insulin to adequately shuttle glucose to all the cells in the body. Treatment involves

109

insulin injections one of more times a day along with adherence to a strict low-sugar diet. About 90 percent of diabetics are of Type II and 85 percent of them are overweight. Excess body weight is a very strong risk factor for Type II. Diet plays a key role in both onset of the disease and in its control. The types of foods we eat can either promote or protect us from diabetes.

In the Pacific islands diabetes is unheard of among those people who eat traditional diets. But when they abandon their native foods and adopt Western ways, diseases of all types surface. One of these new diseases is diabetes. An interesting example of this has occurred on the island of Nauru in the South Pacific. For centuries the people, subsisting on a diet composed primarily of bananas, yams, and coconuts, lived totally free from diabetes. Phosphate deposits discovered on the island brought an influx of wealth and a change in lifestyle. The islanders replaced the coconut and yams they had eaten for centuries with foods made from refined flour, sugar, and processed vegetable oils. The result was the emergence of a never before seen disease—diabetes. According to the World Health Organization up to one-half of the urbanized Nauru population age 30-64 are now diabetic.

Doctors have been able to help patients control diabetes by putting them on a low-fat, high-carbohydrate diet. The diet restricts total fat intake to 30 percent or less of calories. Complex carbohydrates such as whole grains and vegetables comprise 50 to 60 percent of calories. Simple carbohydrates such as refined flour and sugar are to be avoided. The reason for this is because simple carbohydrates can put undue strain on the pancreas and quickly raise blood sugar to dangerous levels. The reason for reducing fat as well as sweets is to promote weight loss. Since overweight is of primary concern with diabetes, losing excess weight is a priority. Another reason for the low-fat diet is to reduce risk of heart disease which is a common consequence of diabetes. Probably the best reason for keeping fat to a minimum is that some fats, particularly oxidized fats, not only promote diabetes but may actually cause it.

Researchers have discovered that the overconsumption of refined vegetable oils leads to diabetes. As far back as the 1920s Dr. S. Sweeney produced reversible diabetes in all of his medical school students by feeding them a high vegetable oil diet for 48 hours. None of the students had previously been diabetic. More recently researchers have been able to cause test animals to develop diabetes by feeding them diets high in polyunsaturated fat.[8, 9] Simply restricting fat intake in diabetic animals has shown to reverse Type II diabetes.[10, 11] Likewise, clinical studies with humans on low-fat diets also show reversal of the disease. Many studies have shown low-fat diets to be effective in controlling diabetes.[12]

The current recommendation is to limit all fats. Monounsaturated fats, such as olive oil, don't seem to adversely affect diabetes and so are allowed in moderation, but because all fats, including olive oil, are high in calories, they are discouraged. Saturated fat is restricted because it is believed to increase risk of heart disease. The biggest culprit, however, seems to be polyunsaturated oil.[13] Studies have shown that when polyunsaturated fats from the diet are incorporated into cellular structure, the cell's ability to bind with insulin decreases, thus lowering their ability to get glucose.[14] In other words, the "locks" on the cells which open the door for glucose to enter degrade when too much polyunsaturated oil is consumed in the diet. Insulin is then unable to open the door. Polyunsaturated oils are easily oxidized and damaged by free radicals. Fats of all types, including polyunsaturated oils, are used as building blocks for cell membranes. Oxidized polyunsaturated fats in the cell membrane can adversely affect the cell's function, including its ability to allow hormones, glucose, and other substances to flow in and out of the cell. Therefore, a diet high in refined polyunsaturated vegetable oils promotes diabetes. A diet low in such oils helps to alleviate symptoms. Because all fats also promote weight gain, it's best to avoid them as much as possible.

There is one fat that diabetics can eat without fear. That fat is coconut oil. Not only does it not contribute to diabetes, but it helps regulate blood sugar, thus lessening the effects of the disease. The Nauru people consumed large amounts of coconut oil for generations without ever encountering diabetes, but when they abandoned it for other foods and oils the results were disastrous.

As mentioned earlier in this chapter, coconut oil puts less of a demand on the enzyme production of the pancreas. This lessens the stress on the pancreas during mealtime when insulin is produced most heavily, thus allowing the organ to function more efficiently. Coconut oil also helps supply energy to cells because it is easily absorbed without the need of enzymes or insulin. It has been shown to improve insulin secretion and utilization of blood glucose.[15, 16] Coconut oil in the diet enhances insulin action and improves binding affinity compared to other oils.[17, 18] The *Journal of the Indian Medical Association* has reported that Type II diabetes in India has increased as the people have abandoned traditional oils, like coconut oil, in favor of polyunsaturated vegetable oils which have been promoted as "heart-friendly." The authors comment on the link between polyunsaturated oils and diabetes and recommend increasing coconut oil consumption as a means to prevent diabetes.[19]

One of the consequences of diabetes is a lack of energy. This is due to the inability of cells to get needed glucose. Without the glucose to power cellular activity, metabolism slows down and the entire body becomes tired.

Exercise has been recommended as a means to help diabetics control blood sugar. One of the reasons exercise is beneficial is that it increases metabolism. A faster metabolic rate stimulates increased production of needed insulin and increases absorption of glucose into cells, thus helping both Type I and Type II diabetics.

Another advantage of increasing metabolism is that more calories are burned. Coconut oil raises metabolic rate causing the body to burn up more calories and thus promoting weight loss. Yes, you can actually lose excess weight by adding coconut oil to your diet. The MCFA in coconut oil are sent directly to the liver for conversion into energy and not into body tissues as fat. (See Chapter 10 for more details on the weight-loss effects of coconut oil.)

If you are diabetic or borderline diabetic, consumption of most fats should be avoided. Coconut oil, on the other hand, is different. Because it helps stabilize blood glucose levels and aids in shedding excess body weight, it is probably the only oil a diabetic should eat.

LIVER DISEASE

The liver is one of the most important organs in the body. It detoxifies, builds proteins and fats, secretes hormones, stores vitamins and minerals, produces bile necessary for digestion, and a hundred or so other functions vital to maintaining proper health. When the liver becomes diseased, any number of health-threatening conditions can arise.

Two of the most common liver problems we hear about are hepatitis and cirrhosis. Both can be fatal. Hepatitis is a general term which indicates inflammation. A number of different conditions can produce hepatitis, among them are alcohol, drugs, viruses, and bacteria. Three types of hepatitis, designated as hepatitis A, B, or C, are caused by viral infections.

Hepatitis A virus is found in feces and is transmitted by poor sanitation and hygiene. It is estimated that in the U.S. about 40 percent of young adults have been exposed to the hepatitis A virus. In some parts of the world where hygiene is poor, almost everyone has been exposed. Hepatitis B and C viruses are most often passed by sexual contact or needle-sharing among drug abusers. They are both less common than hepatitis A. In parts of Africa and Asia up to 20 percent of the population is infected by Hepatitis B. In the U.S. the rate is about 1 percent. hepatitis C is the most severe of the three and often leads to liver cirrhosis.

Chronic hepatitis, alcohol or drug abuse, or infection may lead to cirrhosis. Liver cirrhosis is a degenerative condition characterized by massive tissue destruction and scarring. The liver damage that alcoholics and hepatitis patients experience is caused largely by the destructive action of free radicals. The destruction caused by free radicals seriously affects the liver's ability to function and if left untreated can lead to organ failure and death. Researchers have been finding coconut oil to be of great benefit to liver health. MCFA are immediately funneled to the liver from the digestive tract where they can aid the organ in many ways. Viruses that cause hepatitis are inactivated by MCFA, thus aiding the immune system in fighting off dangerous infections.

MCFA are resistant to free-radical formation and actually help prevent their formation in the liver. A study by H. Kono and others showed that MCFA can prevent alcohol-induced liver injury by inhibiting free-radical formation.[20] Several other studies have also shown that fatty acids, such as those found in coconut and palm oils, protect the liver from alcohol-induced free-radical injury and tissue death; indicating that the use of these oils can not only prevent injury but even rejuvenate diseased tissue. Dr. A. Nanji and other researchers suggest using fatty acids (from tropical oils) as a dietary treatment for alcoholic liver disease.[21, 22]

We can conclude that regular consumption of coconut oil can help protect the liver from two of its most destructive enemies—viruses and free radicals.

CROHN'S DISEASE

If you saw a newspaper headline which stated "Crohn's Disease Patients Find Relief by Eating Cookies" you may think the editor was a little kooky. Dr. L.A. Cohen of the Naylor Dana Institute for Disease Prevention in Valhalla, New York wouldn't think so, not if the cookies were made with coconut. Dr. Cohen notes the ease with which MCFA in coconut are digested and absorbed and says they "have found use in the clinic as a means to provide high energy lipid to patients with disorders of lipid digestion (pancreatitis), lipid absorption (Crohn's disease), and lipid transport (chylomicron deficiency)."[23]

Eating coconut cookies has made an impact on Gerald Brinkley, a Crohn's disease sufferer for 30 years. "When I read that eating coconut macaroons could ease symptoms," Brinkley says, "I decided to try them myself. Coincidence or not, my symptoms have improved since I began eating two cookies a day."

Crohn's disease is an inflammatory intestinal disease characterized by diarrhea, abdominal pain, bleeding ulcers, bloody stools, anemia, and

113

weight loss. Ulcerations can occur anywhere along the digestive tract from the mouth to the rectum. Ulcerative colitis is a similar disease that affects the colon—the lower part of the intestinal tract. At times these chronic conditions can become debilitating. The ability of the intestines to absorb food is hampered which may lead to nutritional deficiencies. Sufferers find that certain foods aggravate symptoms and are, therefore, constantly challenged to find foods that they can tolerate. Like many other chronic illnesses there is no known cure. Drugs can ease the symptoms but if conditions become too severe surgical removal of the infected organ is usually recommended.

Anecdotal reports suggest that coconut may offer relief from symptoms and prevent digestive distress. Teresa Graedon, Ph.D. co-author of *The People's Pharmacy Guide to Herbal and Home Remedies* says during the research for her book she heard enough testimonials about the benefit of using coconut for Crohn's disease that she was convinced that this is one home remedy that may have important medical significance and believes strongly that more research should be pursued in this area. I have also heard similar stories. For example, one occurred in Hawaii and involved a small child that suffered from an intestinal problem so severe that most any food, including milk, aggravated symptoms. The child was wasting away because he couldn't tolerate most of the foods he was given. A native Hawaiian told the mother to feed the child the "jelly" inside an immature coconut. She took the woman's advice and the child thrived eating a diet consisting primarily of coconut jelly.* Knowing what we do scientifically about the digestibility of coconut oil, it makes sense that it would be of benefit to those with digestive problems.

Interestingly enough researchers have demonstrated the benefits of coconut oil on patients with digestive problems, including, Crohn's disease, at least since the 1980s. The anti-inflammatory and healing effects of coconut oil apparently play a role in soothing inflammation and healing injury in the digestive tract which are characteristic of Crohn's disease. Its antimicrobial properties also affect intestinal health by killing troublesome microorganisms that may cause chronic inflammation.

While the cause of Crohn's disease is still unknown, many doctors feel it is the result of a bacterial or viral infection. Stomach ulcers, for example,

---

* Coconut jelly is a term used to describe the gelatinous-like substance inside an immature coconut. As the coconut matures this jelly separates into the meat and water normally found inside the coconut. The jelly is easy for a small child to eat because it is not as chewy as the meat or as liquid as the water. Islanders often consider it a delicacy. It is usually the first solid food Islanders give their children when they start weaning.

are caused primarily by the bacterium H. pyloris. The bacteria bore into the stomach wall causing ulcerations and discomfort characteristic of the condition. It's possible that this bacterium or a similar one could also infect other areas of the digestive tract.

Several studies have shown that the measles and mumps viruses might be involved.[24, 25, 26, 27] A persistent low-grade measles infection in the intestine is common in many Crohn's and ulcerative colitis patients. The infection is localized in the digestive tract so it does not cause a full-scale case of the measles. Those who have had measles or mumps in the past and now suffer from some type of inflammatory bowel disease (IBD) such as Crohn's disease or ulcerative colitis are likely to harbor a low-grade intestinal infection that the body has not been able to overcome. The evidence for measles infection as a cause or at least a contributing factor in IBD is very convincing. In one study, for example, 36 Crohn's disease patients, 22 ulcerative colitis patients, and 89 people free of IBD symptoms (controls) were tested. Twenty-eight of the 36 Crohn's disease patients (78%) and 13 of 22 ulcerative colitis patients (59%) tested positive to the measles virus as compared to only 3 of 89 (3.3%) controls.[28]

H. pyloris bacteria and the measles virus are both killed by the MCFA in coconut oil. If the symptoms characteristic in Crohn's disease and ulcerative colitis are also caused by these or some other microorganism then coconut oil may be beneficial in treating these conditions.

Eating macaroons to ease symptoms of Crohn's disease, as strange as it may sound, does have some scientific backing. For those who have Crohn's disease, ulcerative colitis, stomach ulcers, or other digestive problems you don't have to eat coconut cookies to get relief, any food prepared with coconut oil or coconut milk would work just as well.

PROSTATE ENLARGEMENT

If you are male, chances are you will suffer some type of prostate problem during your lifetime. The most common prostate problem is benign prostatic hyperplasia (BPH) or prostate enlargement. Nearly half of all men between the ages of 40 and 59 and as many as 90 percent of those in their 70s and 80s have some symptoms of BPH. It has become so bad that it's almost an invariable consequence of aging. Prostate enlargement, however, is not simply a result of aging, lifestyle and diet play an important role. BPH is only a major problem in westernized countries. Those men who live in less prosperous localities of the world where local foods are produced and consumed don't appear to be troubled by it as much.

The exact cause of BPH is unknown. The most popular theory focuses on the male hormone dihydrotestosterone (DHT) as the culprit. It is believed that as we age more testosterone is converted into DHT which accumulates in the prostate gland. DHT encourages the growth of prostate cells. This causes the prostate to enlarge, as it does so it pinches off the urethra, the tube through which urine flows from the bladder. This causes frequent and impaired urination, especially at night, and is often associated with inflammation of the gland. While not normally cancerous, it sets the stage for such a condition to exist.

A logical treatment for BPH is to block the conversion of testosterone into DHT. The drug finasteride works on this principle and has been effective. A popular herbal remedy which also appears to block the toxic effect of excess DHT formation is saw palmetto. This subtropical plant is found in the southeastern part of the United States. Native Indians of Florida and early settlers used the berries from this plant as a folk medicine to treat reproductive disorders, urinary diseases, and colds. In women it has been used to increase the supply of mother's milk and to relieve painful periods.

Studies show saw palmetto berries are very effective at reducing the effects of BPH and are remarkably safe. Compared with Proscar (a much-prescribed BPH drug), saw palmetto is more effective in reducing prostate symptoms. Numerous studies have shown saw palmetto extract to be effective in nearly 90 percent of patients usually in a period of four to six weeks. In contrast, Proscar is effective in reducing the symptoms in less than 37 percent after taking the drug for a full year.[29] Saw palmetto has no adverse side effects. Proscar, on the other hand, may cause impotence, decreased libido, and birth defects. Saw palmetto has gained a reputation among both alternative and conventional health care professionals as an effective treatment for BPH. It is one herb that even conventional medicine recognizes as safe and effective.

The medicinal effects of saw palmetto are derived primarily from fatty acids in the berries.[30] It is interesting to note that saw palmetto is a member of the palm family and the berries are relatives to the coconut. Many of the fatty acids in saw palmetto berries are MCFA similar to those in coconut. Dr. Jon Kabara, an expert in lipid (fat) biochemistry, suggests that since the fatty acids in saw palmetto berries inhibit the formation of DHT hormone so should the fatty acids in coconut oil. The conclusion we can derive from this is that coconut oil should be just as effective or even more so in preventing and treating BPH as saw palmetto extract.

CANCER

If you are a woman, your chance of developing breast cancer is one in eight. If you are a man, your chance of getting prostate cancer is one out of nine. One out of every three people alive today in the U.S. will eventually get some form of cancer during his or her lifetime. Cancer is second only to heart disease as the leading cause of death. Like heart disease, there is no sure cure. Often the treatment is as bad as the disease. The best defense is prevention and most forms of cancer are preventable.

Every single one of us has cancerous cells in our bodies. The reason we don't all develop cancer and die is because the immune system destroys these renegade cells before they can get out of hand. As long as the immune system is functioning in the manner for which it was designed, we need not worry about cancer. Arthur I. Holleb, M.D., senior vice president of Medical Affairs for the American Cancer Society states: "Only when the immune system is incapable of destroying these malignant cells will cancer develop."[31] In other words, cancer can only develop in those individuals whose immune systems are so stressed or weakened that they are incapable of mounting an effective defense. Dr. Holleb didn't specify that the efficiency of the immune system affected only lung cancer or breast cancer or leukemia. He referred to all cancers, which means that even if we are exposed to carcinogenic substances, if our immune systems are working as they should, cancer will not develop. A healthy immune system, therefore, is a key element in the prevention of all forms of cancer.

There are several things you can do to improve the efficiency of your immune system and help prevent cancer, such as eating a healthy diet, getting regular exercise, reducing stress, getting proper rest, and such. You should also avoid those things that promote cancer such as smoking and consuming heat-damaged vegetable oils. As noted in Chapter 5, processed vegetable oils depress the immune system and create free radicals that can promote cancer. Another thing you can do to strengthen your immune system is to eat coconut oil on a regular basis. Consuming coconut oil, especially in place of most other oils, can greatly reduce your chances of developing cancer.

We are continually surrounded by troublesome germs, many of which find entrance into our bodies. The white blood cells of our immune system constantly battle invading microbes as well as clean out diseased and cancerous cells. When exposure to germs is excessive or when the immune system is under stress, the white blood cells become overworked. When the immune system is under stress, it is unable to effectively clean out cancerous cells. When this happens cancerous cells can grow and spread without restraint.

The antimicrobial properties of MCFA in coconut oil aid the body in eliminating disease-causing germs, thus relieving stress on the immune system. MCFA take over the job of killing many of the invading microbes. With fewer germs around to cause troubles, white blood cells are free to seek out and destroy cancerous cells. In this manner, coconut oil aids the body in defending itself against germs by allowing the white blood cells to focus their attention on cleaning out toxins and cancerous cells. So a major benefit of coconut oil in the fight against cancer is to reduce stress on the immune system which, in turn, allows the white blood cells to function more efficiently. Therefore, cancerous cells don't have a chance to run amok.

Coconut oil not only assists the white blood cells, but may also take an active part in fighting some forms of cancer. Dr. Robert L. Wickremasinghe, head of the serology division at the Medical Research Institute in Sri Lanka, reports that coconut oil appears to possess anticarcinogenic properties. Researchers have shown that coconut oil inhibits the induction of carcinogenic agents that cause colon as well as mammary (breast) tumors in test animals.[32] Many vegetable oils promote cancer because they are easily oxidized to form carcinogenic free radicals. MCFA have an antioxidant-like effect which prevent free-radical reactions and appear to provide protection at least in the case of breast and colon cancer.[33, 34, 35] So, if cancer is a concern with you, it would be wise to replace the oils you now use in food preparation with coconut oil.

PROTECTION AGAINST DISEASE

Since at least the 1960s coconut oil has been used to treat malabsorption problems in adults and infants. Because of its unique metabolic properties, it can help people shed unwanted weight, thus reducing the risk of many health problems associated with obesity. People who eat coconut oil on a daily basis have little or no cardiovascular disease, indicating that it may be useful in the fight against heart disease and atherosclerosis.

Coconut oil's antimicrobial effects reduce stress on the immune system, allowing the immune system to function more efficiently. The stronger the immune system the better your body is able to defend itself against all types of illnesses, whether infectious or degenerative. Adding coconut oil to your diet can help your body defend itself against most health problems that involve the immune system.

Because of its resistance to free-radical formation and its ability to support the immune system, coconut oil may be useful in preventing or

HEALTH BENEFITS OF COCONUT OIL	*Coconut oil is classified as a "functional food"—a food that provides health benefits beyond its nutritional content. Scientific research is uncovering an impressive list of dietary and medical benefits of coconut oil. For this reason, it is becoming known as "the healthiest oil on Earth."*

treating a wide assortment of conditions, many of which aren't even discussed in this book. I am constantly running across new health benefits. Recently one of my clients told me about a treatment for cataract she found in a book by noted herbalist John Heinerman. The author advised putting several drops of coconut milk* from a fresh coconut into the eyes, then apply hot wet cloths that have been wrung out over the eyes, and lay down for 10 minutes. My client tried it on herself and reported that it worked! According to the book even one application is enough to get significant improvement.

Medical researchers and health care workers are discovering new health benefits associated with coconut oil all the time. Currently several clinics in the United States are testing the efficiency of a dietary supplement composed of monolaurin—a derivative of coconut oil. Doctors have reported remarkable results with patients. One female patient, for example, who suffered with ovarian cysts for 20 years began taking the supplement and within one month the cysts began to shrink and disappear.[36]

Researchers have discovered that coconut oil may be useful in the treatment of kidney and bladder problems. For example, in one study where kidney failure was induced in test animals, those that were given coconut oil had fewer and less severe lesions and survived longer. The researchers concluded that coconut oil has a protective effect on the kidneys.[37] Because of the antimicrobial effects of coconut oil it may also be of benefit to any number of kidney and bladder infections. Recently, one woman came to see me and complained about a bladder infection that first became noticeable that morning. I told her about coconut oil and she began taking it orally

---

* The liquid from a fresh coconut is actually called "coconut water" and is different from the coconut milk which is sold in stores. It was the coconut water which she used for her cataract.

immediately. Without any other treatment, the infection disappeared completely within two days.

Another incredible use researchers have discovered for coconut oil is in the treatment of epilepsy. When added to the diet, MCFA have proven to be effective in reducing epileptic seizures in children. D. L. Ross of the University of Minnesota Medical School showed that seizure frequency decreased by more than 50% in two-thirds of the children in his study during a 10-week treatment period.[38]

What an amazing health food! As coconut oil becomes more widely used we are certain to find many more health benefits with this wonder of nature. It's incredible that some people still ignorantly criticize coconut oil as being unhealthy. If they only knew the facts and stopped letting themselves be deceived by marketing propaganda. Hopefully, the information in this book will help educate doctors, dietitians, and the general public about the healing miracles of coconut oil.

EAT FAT, LOSE WEIGHT

A GROWING PROBLEM

The world's population is growing—at the waist. More people are overweight now than ever before. The number of overweight people has greatly increased over the past few decades and particularly over the last ten years. According to the Centers for Disease Control and Prevention (CDC) the number of obese people in the U.S. has exploded over the past decade from 12 percent of the total population to 17.9 percent. In the United States, 55 percent of the population is overweight, one in four adults is considered obese. As much as 25 percent of all teenagers are overweight. Even our kids are becoming fatter. The number of overweight children has more than doubled in the past 30 years. Figures (and waistlines) are similar in the United Kingdom, Germany, and many other affluent countries.

A person is considered obese if his or her weight is 20 percent or more than the maximum desirable amount. Over the past decade obesity has increased by 70 percent among people aged 18-29. For those 30-39 years of age it has increased 50 percent. All other age groups have likewise experienced a dramatic increase in weight.

Medical problems can escalate the battle of the bulge into a full-scale war. Being overweight increases risk for gallbladder disease, osteoarthritis, diabetes, heart disease, and early death. If you are overweight, losing some pounds could be one of the healthiest things you can do for yourself.

If you are like most people you've noticed a gradual increase in your waistline over the years. Most of us do. I'm no exception. I'd put on an extra 20 pounds over the years. I never considered myself exactly fat, just a little pudgy here and there.

For several years I tried to lose some of this excess weight, and I believed I could. For years I kept several pair of my favorite pants that were too small for me. I knew I would lose enough weight to fit back into them. Well I tried. I reduced my fat intake, ate less food, and was hungry all the time. The only thing dieting accomplished was to make me miserable. My stomach rumbled and complained constantly. I felt denied. It was depressing. Finally, I just gave up; it wasn't worth the trouble. I came to the resolution that I would never lose any weight permanently, so I gathered up all the clothes that wouldn't fit me and I tossed them out. I gave up on weight-reducing diets.

I thought I ate healthfully. My meals were well balanced with the different food groups. I avoided saturated fat and used "healthy" oils like margarine and liquid vegetable oil for all food preparation needs. But as I learned more about diet, health, and coconut oil, I realized I was eating the wrong kind of oils. I replaced the processed vegetable oils I was eating with coconut oil. I used butter instead of margarine. I ate fewer sweets and more fiber. I did this simply because I believed it to be healthier. I didn't reduce the amount of food I was eating. I probably ate more calories than I did before because I began eating *more* fat in the form of coconut oil.

A strange thing happened. I didn't expect it to happen and I didn't even notice it until months later. My pants were becoming looser. I was able to cinch my belt up tighter. I hadn't weighed myself for some time but found that I had lost about 20 pounds. I was shocked because I wasn't dieting. I wasn't trying to lose weight. It just came off on its own. I regretted that I'd tossed out all my favorite pants.

I have been eating this way now for several years. I don't feel deprived. I eat foods cooked in fat. I eat desserts containing fat. The fat I eat is almost exclusively coconut oil. The 20 pounds are still gone. I am at my ideal weight for my height and bone structure. I found a way of eating that wasn't like a weight-loss diet because it worked without trying. It was great. I look better and feel better about myself.

HEALTH PROBLEMS ASSOCIATED WITH OBESITY

• Abdominal hernias	• Arthritis
• Gout	• Coronary heart disease
• Hypertension	• Respiratory problems
• Varicose veins	• Atherosclerosis
• Diabetes	• Gastrointestinal disorders
• Cancer	• Gynecological irregularities

This chapter is for all those who want to lose unwanted weight permanently without struggling with weight-reducing diets. You don't need to diet to lose weight, instead you need to make wise food choices. Your food can be just as tasty and satisfying, yet still be healthy and weight-reducing.

HOW WE GET FAT
Why We Count Calories

What makes people fat? Basically it's consuming more food than our bodies need. The food we eat is converted into energy to power metabolic functions and physical activity. Any excess energy is converted into fat and packed away into fat cells to produce the cellulite on our legs, the spare tire around our middle, and the oversized seat cushions on our backsides. So, the more we eat, the bigger we get.

The energy we obtain from food is measured in calories. Everybody needs a certain number of calories to keep basic metabolic processes functioning. These are the processes that maintain life: keeping the heart beating, lungs breathing, stomach digesting food, and powering every cellular process that goes on in the body.

The rate at which the body uses calories for these maintenance activities is called the basal metabolic rate (BMR). It is equivalent to the number of calories a person would expend while lying down, inactive but awake. Any physical activity, no matter how simple, would require additional calories. At least two thirds of the calories we use every day go to fuel basic metabolic functions.

Each of us has a different BMR. Many factors determine our BMR and the amount of calories our bodies need and use. Young people require more calories than older people. Physically active people use more than less active ones. People who are fasting, starving, or even dieting use less calories than ordinary. Overweight people use fewer calories than lean or muscular people. These last two situations are unwelcome news to people who are overweight and dieting. It means they have to eat even less to see a change. The two most influential factors over which we have control in determining body weight are calorie consumption and physical activity.

Let's look at an example of how food consumption affects weight. A 150 pound man with a sedentary job, such as a computer keyboard operator, needs about 1600 calories for basic metabolic functions and another 800 calories for daily physical activities. He would need to consume a total of 2400 (1600 + 800) calories a day to maintain his body weight. If he ate less, say 2300, he would lose weight, because his body requires 2400 calories.

Since his body uses 2400 calories, if he doesn't get them all from his diet, the extra 100 calories must come from the breakdown of fatty tissues. He loses fat and weight. However, if he eats more than 2400 calories, all the additional calories will be converted into fat and he gains weight.

Now let's look at an example where physical activity changes, but calorie consumption remains the same. If the man in our example (consuming 2400 calories/day) becomes even less active than he already is, his body would use fewer calories. If, for example, he uses only 2300 calories, the excess 100 calories he consumes would be turned into fat and he would gain weight. If, on the other hand, he started an exercise program, the physical activity would increase his daily calorie requirement, for example say up to 2500 a day. He would lose weight because body fat (100 calories worth) would have to be used to supply his energy needs. This is why active people are usually much slimmer than inactive people and why inactive people tend to gain weight.

If the man in our example had a job that required moderate activity, such as janitorial work, he would need about 2600-2800 calories a day to maintain his weight. If he had a heavy job, such as a brick layer, he would need about 2800-3200 calories a day. An average-sized person needs between 2200 and 3200 calories a day depending on physical activity. Women are generally smaller and have less muscle mass than men so they need a little less (about 200-400 calories less).

Lose Weight Quick?

You've seen the advertisements "I lost 50 pound in 4 weeks" or "I went from a size 18 to a size 8 in 30 days!" All sorts of diets claim you can "quickly" lose weight. Is it really possible to lose weight this fast? Let's take a look at the facts.

A pound of body fat stores about 3,500 calories. To lose it, you must reduce your calorie intake by 3,500. On average, a reduction of 500 calories a day (3,500/week) brings about a weight loss of one pound a week. A reduction of 1,000 calories a day equates to a loss of 2 pounds a week.[1] To eliminate 1,000 calories a day, an average-sized person would need to reduce his food intake by nearly half. That's a big reduction! What this means is that true *fat* loss takes time. *You cannot lose 50 pounds of fat in six weeks!* It's just not possible unless you are very obese and don't consume anything except water. Six to 12 pounds is more realistic in this timeframe.

Many people will argue with the above statement saying "I lost 10 pounds in two weeks." Weight loss is deceiving. A pound lost does not necessarily indicate a reduction in body fat. Quick changes in weight are *not* changes in fat, but are due primarily to a loss of water. Look at the numbers. On average, we need about 2,500 calories a day to maintain current weight whether we are over- or underweight. This is the amount needed just to stay even. Out of this number two-thirds or 1,667 calories are needed just to power basic metabolic processes. The remaining 833 calories are used for daily activities. A reduction of 1,000 calories a day is dramatic and borders on starvation because you would not even get enough calories to fuel basic metabolic functions let alone your daily activities. This large of a reduction in calories would also require you to drastically reduce the amount you eat each day even if you chose low-calories foods. At this drastic rate you will only lose 2 pounds of fat a week. In addition, you would be constantly hungry and fatigued due to a lack of energy. Claims in advertisements that state that somebody on a particular diet lost 10 pounds in one week or 40 pounds in four weeks or some other incredible figure may be true, but it wasn't fat they lost, it was muscle mass and water. In time, the water will be added back and weight will increase. If water isn't eventually replaced it can lead to some very serious health problems caused by chronic dehydration.

In order to lose fat and excess weight permanently and healthfully you need to do it slowly. The best way to lose weight is to make little adjustments in the types of food you eat and increase your activity level and stop worrying about counting calories or denying yourself. It can be done.

Metabolic Roller Coaster

Don't you hate them—those people who are as skinny as rails and eat like horses? They're full of pep and vitality, gorge themselves on all types of fattening foods and never gain an ounce. You, on the other hand, eat a celery stick and immediately gain five pounds. Why is that? The answer—metabolism. Your basal metabolic rate (BMR) is slower than theirs. They burn up more calories with the same amount of physical activity as you. They can eat more than you, but weigh less. Wouldn't it be nice to increase your metabolic rate?

The best way you can rev up your metabolism is to exercise. When you exercise regularly metabolism picks up. During exercise metabolism increases and remains elevated even when you're not exercising. A physically fit body also burns more calories than one that is not, because lean body tissue burns more calories than fatty tissue. So a person in good physical shape uses more calories. This is why one person can eat like a gorilla and look as skinny as a bird, while someone else can eat like a bird and still pack on weight.

Metabolism is also affected by the amount of food we eat. If we suddenly start to eat less, it signals our body that there must be less food available and as a means of self preservation our BMR decreases to conserve energy. The problem with this is that when we diet we cut down on calorie consumption and the body thinks it's starving so it slows our metabolic rate down. Slower metabolism also means our bodies produce less energy and we become fatigued easily due to a lack of energy.

Dieting tends to make us feel hungry and tired all the time, because our BMR drops in order to match the lowered intake of calories. So in order to see a significant reduction in weight you must eat even less, essentially starving yourself, consuming fewer calories than your body actually needs for daily activities. If you are overweight and reduce your eating to just enough to match the amount of calories you use each day, you won't lose a thing. You will maintain your current weight level. In order to reduce you must nearly starve yourself. Or you must significantly increase your physical activity. Exercise is beneficial because it keeps your BMR normal or increases it so that your body burns more calories. If you combine exercise with dieting, you get the most weight-reducing effect because you lower your calorie intake and increase both your daily use of calories and your BMR.

Dieting Makes You Fat

Someone once said, "Over the past several years I've lost 200 pounds. If I'd kept it all off I would weigh a minus 20 pounds." Many people can identify with this statement. Dieting hasn't helped. In fact, dieting can actually make you fat! How does it do that? After depriving yourself for a period of time in order to lose weight, you begin to ease up on the diet. Most people experience sensations of intense hunger and respond by eating at least as much as they ate before the diet started, if not more. The diet may have resulted in a loss of 10 or 15 pounds in the first few weeks, most of which was water. After you end the diet your food cravings prompt you to eat and overeat. But now the calories you eat pack a heftier punch. Why? Because your BMR has decreased. The 800 calorie meal will have the same effect as say a 1,000 calorie meal. The result? You regain all the weight you lost and then some. By the time your BMR catches up, you're already overweight again. This time you weigh more than you ever did. With a lower metabolic rate you burn less and less, and it becomes harder and harder to lose. When you do start eating again, you're more likely to store fat rather than burn it because you're burning it at a lower level.

Now bigger than ever, you may build up courage to try dieting again. What happens? You again limit your calorie/food consumption and experi-

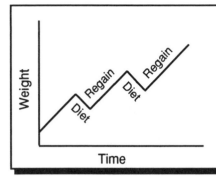

THE YO-YO EFFECT

Quick weight-loss diets are often counterproductive. Repeated cycles of dieting and regaining weight encourages the body to add on more weight after each dieting episode. This can lead to "dieting induced obesity."

ence good results at first as your body sheds water. You hit a plateau, when you've lost all the water your body is willing to give up. You become discouraged and start eating again. You regain all the weight you lost and then some. With each new diet you end up gaining more and more weight.

Only those people who can carefully watch what they eat, stick to it, and exercise regularly keep the weight off permanently. Crash diets don't work. Lifestyle changes do.

A BIG FAT PROBLEM

While some foods provide more calories than others, overeating any food will add additional pounds to our waistlines. There are three nutrients that give us energy or calories—fat, protein, and carbohydrate.* Every gram of protein we eat, whether it comes from meat or wheat, supplies our bodies with 4 calories. Carbohydrate, which is the primary energy source in vegetables, fruits, and grains, also supplies 4 calories per gram. Fat, however, supplies more than twice that—9 calories per gram. You would need to eat more than twice as much protein or carbohydrate to get the same amount of calories as you do from fat.

Reducing the amount of fat we eat is a logical way to reduce total calorie consumption and lose unwanted weight. But few people can stick to a low-fat or no-fat diet for long. Fats make food taste better and are necessary in the preparation of many dishes and baked goods. Statistics show that nearly all those who go on low-fat diets to lose weight regain the weight after a couple of years, often putting on more weight than they had before. Eliminating fat from the diet takes a tremendous amount of will-

---

* Alcohol also supplies energy, but because it provides no nutritive value other than calories it is not considered a nutrient.

power, and to be truly successful has to be a lifelong commitment. Most of us aren't willing to eliminate fat from our diets for the rest of our lives.

Fats are actually important food components and without them we would suffer from nutrient deficiencies. It is through the fats in our food we get the fat-soluble vitamins (A, D, E, K and beta-carotene). Researchers are showing that these nutrients protect us from a myriad of diseases including cancer and heart disease. Fat is required in our foods in order to obtain and absorb these nutrients. A low-fat diet can lead to nutrient deficiencies and increase the risk of numerous degenerative diseases. Some fats are considered essential because our bodies cannot make them from other nutrients. This is why the American Heart Association, the National Heart, Lung, and Blood Institute, and other organizations, all recommend that we get 30 percent of our daily calories from fat. In comparison, these organizations also recommend that we get only 12 percent of our calories from protein. The rest should come from carbohydrates.

A LOW-CALORIE FAT
Not All Fats Are Alike

We have a dilemma here. Fat is, to put it bluntly, fattening. The more fat we eat, the more calories we consume, and the harder it is to lose weight.

Coconut oil can help you lose excess weight.

But if we cut down on fats, we also cut out the essential fatty acids and the fat-soluble vitamins.

What if...what if there was a fat that had fewer calories than other fats and contributed no more to weight gain than protein or carbohydrate, and actually promoted better health, would you be interested? Sounds like a pipe dream doesn't it? It's not. There actually is a fat that can do this. That fat is found in coconut oil.

Replacing the fats you now eat with coconut oil may be the wisest decision you can make to lose excess body fat. We often think that the less fat we eat, the better. However, you don't necessarily need to reduce your fat intake, you simply need to choose a fat that is better for you, one that doesn't contribute to weight gain. You can lose unwanted body fat by eating *more* saturated fat (in the form of coconut oil) and *less* polyunsaturated fat (processed vegetable oils).

One of the remarkable things about coconut oil is that it can help you *lose* weight. Yes, there is a dietary fat that can actually help you take off unwanted pounds. Coconut oil can quite literally be called a low-calorie fat.

All fats, whether they be saturated or unsaturated, from a cow or from corn, contain the same number of calories. The MCFA in coconut oil, however, are different. They contain a little less. Because of the small size of the fatty acids that make up coconut oil, they actually yield fewer calories than other fats. MCT oil, which is derived from coconut oil and consists of 75 percent caprylic acid (C:8) and 25 percent capric acid (C:10), has an effective energy value of only 6.8 calories per gram.[2] This is much less than the 9 calories per gram supplied by other fats. Coconut oil has at least 2.56 percent fewer calories per gram of fat than long-chain fatty acids (LCFA).[3] This means that by using coconut oil in place of other oils your calorie intake is less.

This small reduction in calories is only part of the picture. The amount of calories coconut oil contributes is in effect closer to that of carbohydrate because it is digested and processed differently than other fats. The digestive and metabolic effects are discussed below.

Produces Energy, Not Fat

When people go on diets to lose weight, the foods that are restricted most are those which contain the most fat. Why is fat singled out? We know it is high in calories, but there is also another reason. Because of the way it is digested and utilized in our bodies, it contributes the most to body fat. The fat we eat is the fat we wear—literally.

When we eat fat, the fat is broken down into individual fatty acids and repackaged into small bundles of fat and protein called lipoproteins. These lipoproteins are sent into the bloodstream where the fatty acids are deposited directly into our fat cells. Other nutrients such as carbohydrate and protein are broken down and used immediately for energy or tissue building. Only when we eat too much is the excess carbohydrate and protein converted into fat. As long as we eat enough to satisfy energy needs, fat in our food always ends up as fat in our cells. Only between meals when physical activity outpaces energy reserves is fat removed from storage and burned for fuel.

MCFA, however, are digested and utilized differently. They are not packaged into lipoproteins and do not circulate in the bloodstream like other fats, but are sent directly to the liver where they are immediately converted into energy—just like a carbohydrate. So when you eat coconut oil, the body uses it immediately to make energy rather than store it as body fat. As a consequence, you can eat much more coconut oil than you can other oils before the excess is converted into fat. It has been well documented in numerous dietary studies using both animals and humans that replacing LCFA with MCFA results in a decrease in body weight gain and a reduction in fat deposition.[4-10]

These studies have provided the scientific verification that replacing traditional sources of dietary fat, which are composed primarily of LCFA, with MCFA, yield meals having a lower effective calorie content. MCFA can be a useful tool in controlling weight gain and fat deposition. The simplest and best way to replace LCFA with MCFA is to use coconut oil in the preparation of your food.

A Metabolic Marvel

Wouldn't it be nice to be able to take a pill that would shift our metabolic rate into a higher gear? In a sense that is what happens every time we eat. Food affects our BMR. When we eat, many of our body's cells increase their activities to facilitate digestion and assimilation. This stimulation of cellular activity known as diet-induced thermogenesis, uses about 10 percent of the total food energy taken in. Perhaps you have noticed, particularly on cool days, that you feel warmer after eating a meal. Your body's engines are running at a slightly higher rate, so more heat is produced. Different types of foods produce different thermogenic effects. Protein-rich foods such as meat increase thermogenesis and have a stimulatory or energizing effect on the body.* Protein has a much greater thermogenic effect than either carbohydrate or fat. This is why when people suddenly cut down on meat consumption or become vegetarians they often complain of a lack of energy. This is also one of the reasons high protein diets promote weight loss—the increase in metabolism burns off more calories.

One food that can rev up your metabolism even more than protein is coconut oil. MCFA shift the body's metabolism into a higher gear, so to speak, so that you burn more calories. This happens every time you eat MCFA. Because MCFA increase the metabolic rate, they are dietary fats that can actually promote weight loss! A dietary fat that takes off weight rather than putting it on is a strange concept indeed, but that is exactly what

---

* This is true as long as you don't overeat. Overeating puts tremendous strain on the digestive system which can drain your energy and make you feel tired. This is why we often feel sleepy after a big meal.

happens, so long as calories in excess of the body's needs are not consumed. MCFA are easily absorbed and rapidly burned and used as energy for metabolism, thus increasing metabolic activity and even burning LCFA.[11] So not only are medium-chain fatty acids burned for energy production, but they encourage the burning of long-chain fatty acids as well.

Dr. Julian Whitaker, a well-known authority on nutrition and health, makes this analogy between the long-chain triglycerides (LCT) and medium-chain triglycerides (MCT): "LCTs are like heavy wet logs that you put on a small campfire. Keep adding the logs, and soon you have more logs than fire. MCTs are like rolled up newspaper soaked in gasoline. They not only burn brightly, but will burn up the wet logs as well."[12]

Research supports Dr. Whitaker's view. In one study, the thermogenic (fat-burning) effect of a high-calorie diet containing 40 percent fat as MCFA was compared to one containing 40 percent fat as LCFA. The thermogenic effect of the MCFA was almost twice as high as the LCFA: 120 calories versus 66 calories. The researchers concluded that the excess energy provided by fats in the form of MCFA would not be efficiently stored as fat, but rather would be burned. A follow-up study demonstrated that MCFA given over a six-day period can increase diet-induced thermogenesis by 50 percent.[13]

In another study, researchers compared single meals of 400 calories composed entirely of MCFA and of LCFA.[14] The thermogenic effect of MCFA over six hours was three times greater than that of LCFA. Researchers concluded that substituting MCFA for LCFA would produce weight loss as long as the calorie level remained the same.

Coconut oil contains the most concentrated natural source of MCFA available. Substituting coconut oil for other vegetable oils in your diet will help promote weight loss. The use of refined vegetable oil actually promotes weight gain, not just from its calorie content, but because of its harmful effects on the thyroid—the gland that controls metabolism. Polyunsaturated vegetable oils depress thyroid activity, thus lowering metabolic rate—just the opposite of coconut oil. Eating polyunsaturated oils, like soybean oil, will contribute more to weight gain than any other fat known, even more than beef tallow and lard. According to Ray Peat, Ph.D., an endocrinologist who specializes in the study of hormones, unsaturated oils block thyroid hormone secretion, its movement in the circulation, and the response of tissues to the hormone. When thyroid hormones are deficient, metabolism becomes depressed.[15] Polyunsaturated oils are, in essence, high-fat fats which encourage weight gain more than any other fats. If you wanted to lose weight, you would be better off eating lard, because lard doesn't interfere with thyroid function.

Farmers are always looking for ways to fatten their livestock because bigger animals bring bigger profits. Fats and oils are used as an additive in animal feed to quickly pack on weight in preparing them for market. Saturated fat seems like a good choice to fatten up livestock so pig farmers tried to feed coconut products to their animals for this purpose, but when it was added to the animal feed, the pigs lost weight![16] Farmers found that the high polyunsaturated oil content of corn and soybeans quickly did what the coconut oil couldn't. Animals fed corn and soybeans packed on pounds quickly and easily. The reason these oils worked so well is that their oils suppressed thyroid function, decreasing the animal's metabolic rate. Soybeans are particularly bad because of the goitrogens (anti-thyroid chemicals) they contain.[17, 18] They could eat less food and gain more weight! Many people are in a similar situation. Every time we eat polyunsaturated oils, our thyroid gland is assaulted and loses its ability to function normally. Weight gain is one of the consequences.

Up until now most people have been afraid of using coconut oil because of the propaganda war waged by the soybean industry. People were led to believe that coconut oil was both unhealthy and fattening, neither of which are true. The fats in coconut oil, for the most part, do not become fatty tissues on our bodies. They produce energy. This is one of the reasons why food manufacturers put coconut oil or MCFA in sports drinks and energy bars. It is interesting to note that soybean oil does just the opposite. It promotes weight gain and fat deposition. We use more soybean and hydrogenated oils than ever before. Over the past couple of decades, as soybean oil has replaced tropical oils in our foods, the problem of obesity has mushroomed. Both adults and kids are much fatter than they used to be. It appears that the soybean industry's war on coconut oil has contributed to our expanding weight problem.

If you want to lose unwanted weight, the best thing you can do is to avoid those oils that make you fat and start using coconut oil—the world's only natural low-calorie fat.

THE COCONUT DIET

According to the Mayo Clinic, 95 percent of those people who go on weight loss diets regain all their weight back within five years. Many regain more weight than they had before. The diets not only don't work but can make matters worse. In order for a diet to work it needs to be permanent. This cannot be done with a weight-reducing diet. These types of diets are looked on as temporary restrictions in food, and as soon as the weight is lost we go back to eating the way we did before, the way that made us fat in the first place. You can never stay slim by eating the way you used to. In order to lose weight permanently you must make a permanent change. This, however, is undesirable for most people. Who in their right mind would want to remain on a weight-loss diet forever? These diets are just too restrictive and in many cases unhealthy.

But what if I told you there was a diet that you would like, that you could stay on permanently and still enjoy most of your favorite foods without worrying about counting calories or weighing food? For lack of any better name I call it "The Coconut Diet." I call it this because it is based around coconut and the fact that coconut oil is a reduced-calorie fat which promotes weight loss.

The coconut diet is simple. The most important and most unique feature of this diet is that coconut oil and other coconut products are used as much as possible. Most people are not accustomed to using coconut, so at first they may think this might be difficult, but it's not. You can add coconut products to your ordinary way of eating without noticing much change.

The most important change is replacing all the refined vegetable oils you currently use in your food preparation with coconut oil. Eliminate all margarine, shortening, and other hydrogenated oils from your diet. Olive oil and butter are okay, but use coconut oil whenever possible.

The second thing you should do is use other coconut products as much as possible. Find ways to use fresh and dried coconut. You can find recipes in cookbooks. Coconut milk is a wonderful item that can be used in a wide variety of dishes. It can replace cow's milk and cream in most any recipe and tastes great. Some of the dishes I make using coconut milk include butterscotch pudding, coconut milk pancakes, clam chowder, chicken almondine, and creamy coconut gravy, to mention just a few. Coconut milk that you buy in the can is not sweetened so it can be used for a wide variety of main dishes or desserts. With delicious meals like these, dieting can be a pleasure, and because there are no calorie restrictions to worry about, it can easily be maintained for life without feeling hungry or deprived.

When combined with a high-fiber diet, using coconut oil and coconut products can have a remarkable effect on your weight and your health. For more detailed information about using coconut products to lose unwanted weight I recommend the book *Eat Fat, Look Thin: A Safe and Natural Way to Lose Weight Permanently*. This book outlines a dietary program based on coconut and includes numerous delicious recipes. See Appendix II for more information about this book.

BEAUTIFUL SKIN AND HAIR

For thousands of years coconut oil has been use to make the skin soft and smooth and give hair a rich, shiny luster. Polynesian women are famed for their beautiful skin and hair, even though they are exposed to the hot blistering sun and the chafing of the ocean breeze every day. As a skin lotion and hair conditioner, no other oil can compare.

Because coconut oil has a natural creamy texture, comes from a vegetable source, and is almost always free from pesticides and other chemicals and contaminants, it has been used for years in soaps, shampoos, creams, and other body care products. Its small molecular structure allows for easy absorption, giving both the skin and hair a soft smooth texture. It makes an ideal ointment for the relief of dry, rough, and wrinkled skin. Many people use it as a lip balm because it is safe and natural. Unlike most other body care products it can be used in its natural form without adulteration by harsh chemicals and other additives. For this purpose, it has been for many years and still is commonly used as a body cream.

HAND AND BODY LOTION
Aging and Oils

We use hand and body lotions to soften the skin and make it look younger. Many lotions, however, actually promote dry skin. Commercial creams are predominantly water. Their moisture is quickly absorbed into dry, wrinkled skin. As the water enters the skin, it expands the tissues, like filling a balloon with water, so that wrinkles fade away and skin feels smoother. But this is only temporary. As soon as the water evaporates or is carried away by the bloodstream, the dry, wrinkled skin returns. Have you ever permanently cured dry, wrinkled skin with any body lotion? It can't be done, at least not with most ordinary body care products. Another ingredient in most lotions is oil of some type. These are almost always highly processed vegetable oils devoid of all natural, protective antioxidants. What consequence does this have in a skin lotion? Lots!

The type of oil you put on your skin and eat with your foods affects the tissues of your body. Oils have a pronounced effect on all the tissues of the body, especially the connective tissues. Connective tissue is the most abundant and widely distributed tissue in the body. It is found in skin, muscles, bones, nerves, and all internal organs. Connective tissue consists of strong fibers that form the matrix or supporting framework for all body tissues. In other words, it holds everything together. Without connective fibers we would become a shapeless mass of tissue. As we age part of the reason our bodies sag and become distorted is due to the breakdown of connective tissues. We more or less start falling apart.

Our skin is held together by these connective tissues. They give the skin strength and elasticity. When we are young and healthy the skin is smooth, elastic, and supple. This is the effect of strong connective fibers. As we age these fibers are continually subjected to free-radical attack which breaks them down. As a result, connective tissues become hardened and lose both elasticity and strength. The skin loses its ability to hold itself together and begins to sag and become wrinkled. Once young, soft, and smooth, the skin turns dry and leathery.

Once a free-radical reaction is started it can cause a chain reaction which produces more free radicals, which ultimately damage thousands of molecules. The only way our body has to fight them is with antioxidants. When a free radical comes into contact with an antioxidant, the chain reaction is stopped. For this reason, it's good to have plenty of antioxidants available in our cells and tissues to protect us. The number of antioxidants we have in our tissues is determined to a large extent by the nutrients in our diet.

Free-radical reactions occur in the body constantly. They are an unavoidable result of living and breathing. However, some people experience more free-radical damage than others. The reason is that many environmental factors increase the number of free-radical reactions we are subjected to. For example, a diet low in antioxidant nutrients (vitamins A, C, and E, for example) will lower the number our cells have available to protect themselves. Cigarette smoke and pollution readily create free radicals. Radiation, including ultra-violet light, can stimulate free radical generation. Chemicals such as pesticides and food additives also increase free-radical activity. One substance that is commonly used in our food and even in body care products that leads to a great deal of free radicals is oxidized vegetable oil.

Conventional processing strips polyunsaturated oils from the natural antioxidants that protect them. Without these antioxidants they are highly prone to free-radical generation both inside and outside of the body. This is why eating processed vegetable oils can cause a deficiency in vitamin E and other antioxidants. The antioxidants are used up fighting off free radicals. When we put these types of oils on our skin they create free radicals, causing permanent damage to connective tissues. This is why you should be very careful about the types of oils you use on your skin. If you use a lotion or cream containing this type of oil you are, in effect, causing your skin to age faster. The lotion may bring temporary improvement but accelerate aging of the skin and even promote skin cancer.

One of the classic signs of old age is the appearance of brown, freckle-like spots on the skin. This pigment is called lipofuscin. It is also known as

Coconut oil helps to keep your skin looking young and healthy.

aging spots or liver spots. It is a sign of free-radical deterioration of the lipids (fats) in our skin, thus the name *lipo*fuscin. Oxidation of polyunsaturated fats and protein by free radical activity in the skin is recognized as the major cause of liver spots.[1, 2] Liver spots don't ordinarily hurt or show any signs of discomfort. If we couldn't see them we wouldn't even know they were there. But they do affect our health and our appearance.*

Because cells cannot dispose of the lipofuscin pigment, it gradually accumulates within many cells of the body as we age. Once lipofuscin pigment develops, it tends to stick around for life, but you can prevent further oxidation and perhaps even reduce the spots you already have by using the right kind of oils in your diet and on your skin.

Coconut Oil Protects and Heals Your Skin

The ideal lotion is one that not only softens the skin, but protects it against damage, promotes healing, and gives it a more youthful, healthy appearance. Coconut oil fits that description. Pure coconut oil is the best natural skin lotion available. It prevents destructive free-radical formation and provides protection against them. It can help prevent the skin from developing liver spots and other blemishes caused by aging and overexposure to sunlight. It helps to keep connective tissues strong and supple so that the skin doesn't sag and wrinkle. In some cases it can even restore damaged or diseased skin. I've seen precancerous lesions completely disappear with the daily use of coconut oil.

The Polynesians, who traditionally wear very little clothing, have for generations been exposed to the hot blistering sun, yet have beautiful healthy skin without blemish and without cancer. The reason is they eat coconuts and use the oil on their bodies as a lotion. The oil is absorbed into the skin and into the cell structure of the connective tissues, limiting the

---

* On the surface of the skin, lipofuscin forms the so-called liver spots. While these spots are clearly seen on the skin, they also form in other tissues throughout the body—intestines, lungs, kidney, brain, etc. They represent areas that are damaged by free-radical reactions. The more you have on your skin, the more you have inside your body, and the more damage or "aging" your tissues have undergone. To some degree you can judge the damage free radicals have done to the inside of your body by the size and number of liver spots on your skin. The more you have and the bigger they are, the more free-radical damage has occurred. All the tissues affected are damaged to some degree. If this occurs in your intestine, it can affect the organ's ability to digest and absorb nutrients. In the brain it will affect mental ability. Likewise, free radicals break down connective tissues, causing sagging and loss of function of the skin. And the same thing happens to the internal organs, they sag and become deformed. The skin acts as a window by which we can see inside the body. What we look like on the outside reflects, to a large part, what is happening on the inside.

137

Cross Section of Skin

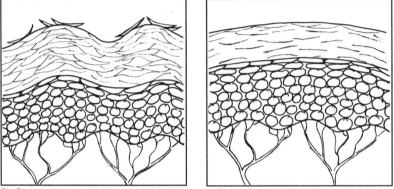

Before   After

Coconut oil can help give flaky, wrinkled skin (left) a more smooth, youthful appearance (right).

damage excessive sun exposure can cause. Their skin remains undamaged even when exposed to long hours in the hot sun.

The difference between coconut oil and other creams and lotions is that the latter products are made to bring immediate, temporary relief. Coconut oil, on the other hand, not only brings quick relief but aids in the healing and repairing process. Most lotions do the skin no lasting benefit and many actually accelerate the aging process. Why take the risk of permanently damaging the skin when you can easily use coconut oil to help bring back its youthful appearance?

Coconut oil can make your skin look more youthful. The surface of the skin consists of a layer of dead cells. As these dead cells fall off, new cells take their place. As we age, this process slows down and dead cells tend to accumulate, giving the skin a rough, flaky texture. Coconut oil aids in removing dead cells on the outer surface of the skin, making the skin smoother, which reflects light more evenly, creating a healthier, more youthful appearance. The skin "shines" because light reflects better off evenly textured skin.

The removal of excessive dead skin and the strengthening of underlying tissues are two of the key advantages to using coconut oil as a skin lotion. Sometimes even young people can be troubled with chapped or excessively dry skin, producing an abnormally thick and often irritating layer of dead cells. Coconut oil can not only provide immediate relief, but often brings lasting improvement as well. People have experienced remarkable results with a variety of skin problems. Many people who have tried it won't use anything else. Read the following testimonial:

"For a number of years I had been troubled occasionally with severely dry, cracked skin on my hands. It would come without warning and persist for a couple of months then gradually get better. Nothing I did seemed to help. The last time it appeared was most severe. At times the skin would be so dry it would crack and bleed. My wife avoided holding my hand because she said it felt like sandpaper. And it did! I tried a variety of creams and lotions without success. The condition persisted for over a year, much longer than it ever had before. I then learned about coconut oil and how good it is for the skin. I bought some coconut oil and began applying it to my hands. Immediately I noticed a difference. I hated to use lotions because they often left a greasy or sticky film on my hands, but coconut oil soaked into the skin without that feeling. Best of all, within a couple of weeks my rough, dry skin went away—permanently. My hands are now very smooth and soft. When I'm out with my wife, she gladly takes hold of my hand, just as she used to do. Coconut oil is without reservation the best skin care product I have ever used."

The pictures on the following page show the condition of the skin on this man's hands before and after he began using coconut oil. Notice the dramatic difference in skin texture and health between the two photographs.

If dryness and cracking is severe, I recommend before going to sleep at night putting a liberal amount of coconut oil on the affected area then wrapping it loosely in plastic so it doesn't drip all over the place. In the morning take off the plastic and wash off the excess oil. Do this every night until the condition improves.

SKIN ELASTICITY TEST

How youthful is your skin? As we age, our skin loses its elasticity, becoming leathery and wrinkled. This is the result of free-radical destruction and is a sign of degeneration and loss of function. Significant changes in the skin become evident at about the age of 45. The following skin test indicates approximately how old functionally the skin has become as a result of free-radical deterioration. Take this test and see how your skin rates as compared with the age groups listed. Test to see if your skin is functionally younger or older than your biological age.

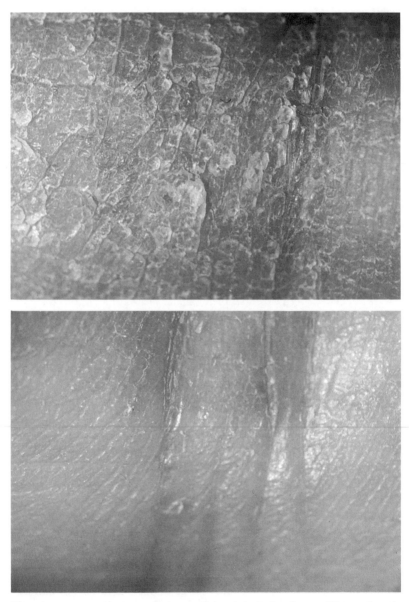

The photo at top shows a close-up of the right index finger, illustrating the condition of the subject's skin prior to using coconut oil. The skin is severely dry and rough. The picture at the bottom is the same finger a couple of months after he began using coconut oil.

140

For this test, pinch the skin on the back of your hand with the thumb and forefinger and hold it for five seconds. Let go and time how long it takes for the skin to completely flatten back out. The shorter the time, the younger the functional age of the skin. Compare your results to the table below.

SKIN ELASTICITY TEST	
Time (sec)	Functional Age (years)
1-2	20-30
3-4	30-44
5-9	45-50
10-15	60
35-55	70
56 or more	over 70

How did you fare? Did your skin test older than your true age or were you right on target? If you want to prevent further degeneration and perhaps even regain some youthfulness in your skin, the best thing you can do is use coconut oil in place of other creams and lotions. I'm in my 50's and when I perform this test, my skin bounces back within 1-2 seconds—just as you would expect from a 20-year-old.

HAIR CARE

What coconut oil does for the skin it can also do for the hair. It makes a great hair conditioner. Noted New York hair stylist Amanda George gives credit to coconut oil for her luxurious hair. "I massage two teaspoons of warm coconut oil into my hair before bed, then wash it out in the morning," says Amanda.[2] The result is hair that is soft and shimmering. To warm the oil you can place the bottle in warm water or hold it briefly under hot running tap water.

Beauticians who are familiar with coconut oil swear by it. They claim that it can be just as effective for conditioning hair as a $40 or $50 salon treatment—at only a fraction of the cost. And you can do it yourself at home.

A little oil (a couple of teaspoons) can be applied at night and washed out in the morning or you can use a little more and thoroughly soak the hair for an hour or two before washing. Some people prefer to put the oil on, cover the head with a shower cap, and then take a long relaxing bath. After

Coconut oil is an excellent hair conditioner that can help give your hair a healthy, luxurious look.

about an hour the oil is washed off. This process can be repeated every few days.

If you take a long warm bath make sure to apply coconut oil on your skin to replace the natural oils that have been washed off. In fact, any time you use soap you are removing your body's protective layer of oil and changing the pH of your skin. Applying coconut oil will help reestablish a healthy skin environment.

Another advantage of using coconut oil as a hair conditioner is that it will help control dandruff. I found this out for myself. I've been plagued with dandruff since I was a teenager. The only thing that could control it was to use medicated shampoos which I did for many years. Whenever I tried switching to a non-medicated shampoo, the dandruff came right back within a few days. As I learned more about the harsh chemicals used in many body care products I decided I didn't want to use medicated shampoos anymore. I started to use more natural herbal soaps and shampoos. As before, the dandruff came roaring back in full force. I tried everything natural I could find in an attempt to control it. Nothing seemed to work. I eventually put some coconut oil in my hair as described above and washed it out several hours later. The result was phenomenal. After a single application all the dandruff was gone. I couldn't believe it was that easy. Nothing except medicated shampoos had worked this well before. I now had a natural product that not only cleared up my dandruff but was good for my hair and scalp as well. Coconut oil is now a regular part of my personal care regimen.

SKIN HEALTH

Whether it is applied topically or taken internally, coconut oil helps to keep skin young, healthy, and free of disease. Antiseptic fatty acids in coconut oil help to prevent fungal and bacterial infections in the skin when it is consumed in the diet, and to some extent, when it is applied directly to the skin. The Polynesians who use it regularly are rarely troubled by skin infections or acne.

Our skin acts as a protective covering shielding us from harm much like a suit of flexible armor. It provides a protective barrier between us and literally millions of disease-causing germs which we come into contact with each day. If it were not for our skin, we could not survive; even organisms that are ordinarily harmless would become deadly.

The only way to gain entry into the body other than through the natural openings, such as the nose and mouth, is by penetrating the skin. When the skin's defenses break down, infections can result. Acne, ring-worm, herpes, boils, athlete's foot, and warts are just some of the infectious conditions that can affect the skin and body.

Our skin is more than simply a covering. If that was all it was, we would literally be covered with disease-causing germs just waiting for an opportunity to gain entry into the body. The slightest cut, even a tiny scratch, would allow a multitude of these troublemakers into the body, causing disease and perhaps death. Fortunately, the skin provides not only a physical barrier but a chemical one as well. The chemical environment on the surface of healthy skin is inhospitable to most harmful germs. As a consequence, organisms that cause disease are few in number. Most cuts do not end up becoming infected because the skin is relatively free from harmful germs. However, if a wound is made by an object such as a dirty nail that is covered in dangerous microorganisms, they bypass the skin's physical and chemical barriers and infection often results.

The biggest chemical barrier to infectious organisms is the acid layer on the skin. Healthy skin has a pH of about 5, making it slightly acidic. Our sweat (containing uric and lactic acids) and body oils promote this acidic environment. For this reason, sweat and oil do us good. Harmless bacteria that can tolerate the acid live on the skin, but troublesome bacteria can't thrive and their numbers are few.

The oil our bodies produce is called sebum. Sebum is secreted by oil glands (sebaceous glands) located at the root of every hair as well as other places. This oil is very important to skin health. It softens and lubricates the skin and hair and prevents the skin from drying and cracking. Sebum also contains medium-chain fatty acids, in the form of medium-chain triglycerides, that can be released to fight harmful germs.[3]

Our skin is home to many tiny organisms, most of which are harmless; some are even beneficial. At least one variety of bacterium is essential to the healthy environment on our skin. It feeds on the sebum, breaking down the triglycerides into free fatty acids.

Let me refresh your memory about triglycerides. A triglyceride is simply three individual fatty acids joined together by a glycerol molecule. Sebum as well as all dietary fats (e.g. corn oil, soybean oil, etc.) are composed primarily of triglycerides. These bacteria feed on the glycerol molecule which holds the fatty acids together. When the glycerol is removed, the fatty acids are freed and become independent of one another. This is what is called a *free* fatty acid. Medium-chain fatty acids bound together as triglycerides have no antimicrobial properties, but when broken down into free fatty acids, they become powerful antimicrobials. Okay, now let's get back to the discussion.

These bacteria convert the medium-chain triglycerides in the sebum on our skin into free fatty acids that can kill disease-causing bacteria, viruses, and fungi. The combination of the pH and MCFA provides a protective chemical layer on the skin that prevents infection from disease-causing microorganisms.

Most, if not all, mammals utilize the antimicrobial property of medium-chain fatty acids to protect themselves from infection. As in humans, these fatty acids make up a part of the oil excreted by the skin. In the wild, animals are left to nature and instinct to heal from injury. Bites and scratches are common occurrences, especially from encounters with predators. Wounds from these animals can often cause infection in a victim who is lucky enough to escape with its life. Instinctively, injured animals will lick the wound to clean it out *and* to spread body oils into the injured tissue. These oils disinfect the wound, thus protecting the animal from infection. Likewise, when we cut a finger we instinctively put the injured part of the finger in our mouths.

The saliva also helps to increase the amount of MCFA on the skin. Saliva contains an enzyme called lingual lipase which begins the process of breaking fats down into individual fatty acids. This enzyme readily breaks down the medium-chain triglycerides in dietary fats and body oils (sebum) into free medium-chain fatty acids.*

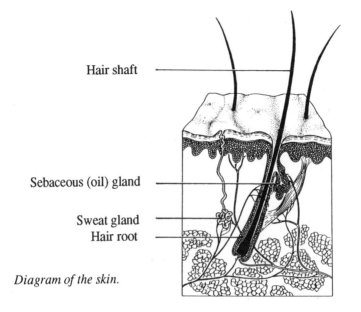

Hair shaft

Sebaceous (oil) gland

Sweat gland
Hair root

Diagram of the skin.

Animals often cleanse themselves by licking their fur, coating it with salivary enzymes that can convert body oils into protective free MCFA. Licking a wound also mixes saliva with the oils on the skin and hair, producing more medium-chain fatty acids that can help fight infection.

Some animals seem to produce more of these protective fatty acids than others. The porcupine is one of these. The porcupine's quills make an intimidating weapon, unfortunately they can accidentally impale themselves or other porcupines. Dr. Uldis Roze, a biology professor at Queens College in New York, speculates that the high amount of protective fatty acids is a defense against self-inflicted wounds.

Dr. Roze found out about the antimicrobial properties of fatty acids on porcupine quills the hard way. His research involves tracking porcupines, capturing them, and attaching radio collars. One day he followed a porcupine up a tree and in his attempt to capture it took a quill in his upper arm. He said his arm was "paralyzed from pain." Unable to remove the quill, he waited for it to work itself out. A few days later when the quill came through, Dr. Roze was surprised that the deep puncture wound remained free from infection. He reasoned that a wood splinter traveling the same path would almost certainly have caused a serious infection. Roze theorized that the oil on the quill contained antibiotic properties that protected him.

---

* Fats and oils made of long-chain fatty acids, as most all dietary fats are, need the addition of gastric and pancreatic enzymes to break them all the way down to individual fatty acids.

This theory was verified when the oil was analyzed and tested. The medium-chain fatty acids in the oil proved to be the secret. His studies showed that these fatty acids could kill several types of bacteria that are often treated by penicillin, including streptococcus and staphylococcus.[4]

He approached the pharmaceutical industry in an attempt to interest them in producing an antibiotic ointment or medication using these fatty acids. He was turned down because medium-chain fatty acids are readily available, natural substances and, therefore, products based on them could not be protected by a patent.

We all have this non-patentable protection on our skin to various degrees. Due primarily to the action of friendly bacteria, the oil on the surface of your skin and hair is composed of between 40 to 60 percent free fatty acids. Among these fatty acids are medium-chain fatty acids that have anitmicrobial properties. These medium-chain fatty acids in the sebum provide the protective layer on the skin that kills harmful germs.

Adults produce more sebum than children and, therefore, have a greater degree of protection from skin infections. The antimicrobial effects of MCFA in sebum have been observed at least as far back as the 1940s. At the time it was noted that children suffering with scalp ringworm (a skin fungus) were cured spontaneously when sebum secretion increased as they reached puberty.[5]

Medium-chain fatty acids similar to those in sebum are found abundantly in coconut oil. The fatty acids in coconut oil, like all other dietary oils, are joined together as triglycerides. Triglycerides, as such, have no antimicrobial properties even when they are made of MCFA. However, when we eat medium-chain triglycerides, our bodies convert them into monoglycerides and free fatty acids which do have antimicrobial properties.

When coconut oil, which is made of triglycerides, is put on the skin it doesn't have any immediate antimicrobial action. However, bacteria which are always present on the skin turn these triglycerides into free fatty acids, just as they do with sebum. The result is an increase in the number of antimicrobial fatty acids on the skin and protection from infection. The free fatty acids also help to contribute to the acidic environment on the skin which repels disease-causing germs. After all, fatty acids are acidic and, therefore, support the acid layer on the skin.

When bathing or showering, soap washes the protective layer of oil and acid off our skin. Often afterwards the skin becomes tight and dry. Adding moisturizers helps the skin feel better, but it does not replace the acid or the protective MCFA that were removed. Your skin is vulnerable to infection at this time. You would think that your body would be clean and germ-free after a bath. But germs are everywhere, floating in the air, on our clothes and everything we touch. Many germs survive washing by hiding in cracks and folds of the skin. Before long your skin is again teaming with microscopic life, both good and bad. Until sweat and oils return to reestablish the body's chemical barrier, your skin is vulnerable to infection. If you have a cut or cracked skin, this can allow streptococcus, staphylococcus, and other harmful germs entry into the body. By using a coconut or palm kernel oil based lotion you can quickly help reestablish the skin's natural antimicrobial and acid barrier.* If you are troubled with skin infections or want to avoid infections, it would be to your benefit to use coconut oil after every bath.

NATURE'S MIRACLE HEALING SALVE

While the antimicrobial power of MCFA in coconut oil has been experimentally tested in the laboratory, used in biology, and seen in everyday life, there is another side to the healing power of coconut oil when applied topically. This was shown to me by accident.

I experienced the healing power of coconut oil in an unusual way. I was unloading a carload of cement blocks. If you've ever worked with cement blocks you know they are heavy. When I went to set one down I accidentally pinched a piece of the flesh of my hand between two of the blocks. The pain was intense, but hardly life threatening, so I continued on with the task. Immediately a dark red blood blister started to form. When I finished unloading the blocks, I washed my hands and applied some coconut oil, simply as a moisturizer, and thought nothing more of it.

A few hours later I looked at the blister and it had shrunk from the size of a split pea to that of a pin head. I was amazed. I'd never seen a blood blister fade away that quickly. Usually they take a week or two to heal. Since I hadn't done anything except put coconut oil on it, my first thought was perhaps the oil was somehow involved in the rapid healing. I immediately dismissed the idea as silly and ignored it. I knew coconut oil was good when eaten but to speed the healing of an injury on the skin seemed too remarkable.

Later I began to see similar miracles in others who had used the oil topically. For example, one of my clients told me he had a flare up with hemorrhoids that were causing him a great deal of pain and discomfort. He tried various creams, but they didn't help. He had just purchased a jar of coconut oil and thought he might try that. So he began applying the oil to the affected area, and to his joy and amazement it relieved the irritation. By the next day the swelling was also gone.

---

* While coconut oil can provide a significant degree of protection from infection on the skin, it must be broken down into individual fatty acids by skin bacteria first. Fresh oil will *not* disinfect an open wound.

In another case a man had been troubled with psoriasis on his face and chest, essentially all his adult life. He tried every cream, ointment, and salve that came along and nothing worked. Every few days the condition would flare up, skin would become dry and scaly and sometimes it would get so bad it would crack and bleed. It affected his forehead, eyebrows, nose, cheeks, chin, and chest. As he got older the condition worsened to the point that inflammation and peeling became a constant nuisance. He'd gone to several doctors and they told him there was nothing they could do to cure the problem and that he might get some temporary relief using a prescription cream. The cream provided only minor temporary relief. Because he didn't get the help he sought from medical doctors, he turned to alternative therapies and began to focus on solving his problem through diet. He cut out convenience foods, reducing sugar and vegetable oil consumption. Eventually he replaced most of the oils in his diet with coconut oil. The condition gradually improved, but still didn't go away. While the severity of the psoriasis was much reduced, inflammation and scaling still persisted. One day when the inflammation was flaring up he applied a little coconut oil to see what that would do. It worked! He did it again the next day and the next. Within just a few days the skin on his face that was once almost constantly dry and leathery now became soft and smooth. No inflammation and no scaling. He says it's the best his skin has looked in over 20 years!

One lady told me, "I like using coconut oil on my face. It keeps my skin moist without making it greasy." She compared it to the medicated cream Retin-A which has been touted by some as a wonder drug. "I used to use Retin-A to prevent pimples, but since I've been using coconut oil I haven't needed it. It works just as good as Retin-A."*

Coconut oil makes the perfect medium for most any herbal salve. One such salve is called GOOT (garlic oil ointment) which consists of crushed raw garlic in coconut oil. It's an ointment you can make yourself and is effective against skin infections. Mark Konlee editor of *Positive Health News* says, "I have never ceased to be amazed at what this ointment can accomplish. Last fall, I met 'Dan' a local resident who told me he had a bad case of plantar warts and athlete's foot. When he showed me the soles of his feet, it was the worst looking set of feet I have ever observed."

Mark made some GOOT, put it in a small jar, and gave it to Dan. He told him to keep the bottle in the refrigerator (shelf life of about 30 days) and put a little on his feet every day. Two weeks later he met Dan again. "He took off his socks to show me what looked like a magical transformation—both the fungal infection and the plantar warts were completely gone. He had what looked like a brand new set of feet, totally normal in color and appearance." Dan reported, "After about 10 days, the plantar warts just peeled off."

148

One of the best uses for coconut oil is to soften and heal dry, flaky skin. When first applied it may seem like you're spreading a very oily substance on your skin, but because it is quickly absorbed, it doesn't leave a layer of greasy film like many commercial lotions and oils do. If you apply too much oil all at once the skin becomes saturated and will not absorb it all. This will leave a greasy film. So it is best to apply a small amount and reapply it as often as necessary. People with extremely dry skin need to reapply the oil often when they first start using it. Some people with this problem desire the greasiness common with many lotions to soften extremely dry or hardened skin. At first they don't think the coconut oil does enough because it is absorbed so quickly. With coconut oil you will need to reapply the oil more often when the skin is very dry. The real benefit with coconut oil will come with repeated use over time. While other lotions temporarily soften dry skin, they won't heal it. Coconut oil will gradually soften the skin, removing dead layers, and encourage the growth of new, healthier tissues.

Many people claim that when applied to the skin coconut oil helps protect them from sun burn and, consequently, from problems related to overexposure to ultraviolet light such as the development of skin cancer and aging spots. Premature wrinkling and dry skin can also be a consequence of too much sun. Coconut oil helps protect the skin from the damaging rays of the sun while allowing the body to gradually adapt so it can withstand greater and greater amounts of exposure. Unlike sunscreen, coconut oil doesn't necessarily block UV light, but allows the body to adjust naturally to sun exposure, naturally increasing the body's tolerance level over time. Because of different skin types, everybody's level of tolerance is different, so each person needs to experiment, getting a little more sun each day until he or she reaches a level of exposure that feels comfortable. Traditionally the Polynesians wore very little clothing and exposed themselves to the hot tropical sun nearly all day long. This was especially true when they traveled long distances over open oceans for days or weeks at a time. Coconut oil supplied them with the protection they needed to withstand the hot glaring sun. For this reason, coconut oil is a common ingredient in commercial sunscreen and suntan lotions.

Why is coconut oil able to stimulate healing and repair? I think it is, in part, because of the metabolic effect MCFA have on the cells. Cellular activity, including healing of injuries, is regulated by the metabolism. When

---

* Retin-A is a medicated cream prescribed by doctors to prevent acne and improve skin texture. While it provides some benefits, it also causes undesirable side effects, the worst of which is making the skin hypersensitive to sunlight which increases the potential for sunburn and skin cancer. This is why it is only available by prescription from a medical doctor.

metabolic rate is high, cellular activity is accelerated and processes such as healing damaged tissues, removing toxins, fighting germs, replacing damaged or diseased cells with healthy new ones, and such are all performed at a heightened rate of activity. Therefore, the healing process is accelerated. MCFA provide a quick source of energy to the cells, boosting their metabolic level and healing capacity.

One of the things that impressed me most about the topical use of coconut oil is its ability to reduce inflammation. I've witnessed it relieve chronic skin inflammation within days. At first this effect was a surprise to me, for at the time I had not found any reference in the scientific literature to coconut oil's effect on inflammation. With further searching I did locate a study that demonstrated that coconut oil does indeed have an anti-inflammatory effect. In a study reported by Dr. S. Sadeghi and others, coconut oil decreased pro-inflammatory chemicals in the body. The researchers suggested that coconut oil might be useful in therapies involving a number of acute and chronic inflammatory diseases.[6] This would help explain my observation that psoriasis and other inflammatory skin conditions seem to improve with the application of coconut oil. I have found, however, that it doesn't work in all cases. If inflammation is severe, coconut oil alone isn't enough to eliminate it. But for mild cases it has worked well.

It is interesting to note that when it is taken internally, the healing characteristics coconut oil exhibits on the skin are also in effect inside the body. Conditions associated with inflammation (especially within the gastrointestinal tract) such as colitis, ulcers, hepatitis, and hemorrhoids may find relief with this natural, harmless oil. It may also help relieve inflammation in other parts of the body as seen in multiple sclerosis (MS), arthritis, lupus, and as noted in Chapter 7, inflammation in the arteries (phlebitis) which can lead to hardening of the arteries and heart disease.

Some of these inflammatory conditions are caused by infections from microorganisms. Most ulcers are caused by bacteria. Inflamed arteries and heart disease can be caused by viruses and bacteria. Hepatitis is usually caused by viral infections in the liver. Coconut oil's antimicrobial effects can eliminate the offending organism and relieve the inflammation and pain they cause.

It appears that coconut oil, whether used inside or outside the body, provides numerous health benefits. Coconut is truly one of nature's miracle foods. It is no wonder that the early European explorers who visited the Pacific Islands were greatly impressed by the natives' excellent health and physical condition.

COOKING WITH COCONUT OIL

THE TROPICAL OILS

Palm, palm kernel, and coconut oils are referred to as the tropical oils. They come from different species of palm trees. The tropical oils have similar characteristics when used in food preparation. Their nutritional and fatty acid content, however, is somewhat different. All the tropical oils are rich in valuable nutrients and health-promoting fatty acids.

Unlike most other vegetable oils, the tropical oils are composed primarily of saturated fatty acids. The unique thing about the tropical oils, especially palm kernel and coconut oils, is that their saturated fatty acids are predominantly of the health-promoting medium-chain variety.

Palm and palm kernel oil are two different oils that come from the same species of tree, one from the seed and the other from the husk surrounding the seed. Palm oil is obtained from the husk by steaming, heating, or pressing. Unlike other tropical oils, palm oil has only a small amount of MCFA. Palm kernel oil is extracted from the seed. The seed kernel is only an inch or so in diameter and resembles a miniature coconut. The appearance of the two oils is quite different. Palm oil has a deep orange-red color which is due to the high concentration of beta-carotene and other carotenoids. Palm kernel oil, like coconut oil, is derived from the white meat inside the shell of the seed and is pure white in appearance.

Coconut oil is produced from the seed of a species of palm tree which is different from that which produces palm and palm kernel oils. Because of the high oil content (33%), extracting oil from coconuts is a relatively simple process and has been the major source of vegetable oil for people in the tropics for thousands of years. Traditionally the oil is extracted from either fresh or dried coconut by boiling and/or fermentation. When boiled in water the oil separates from the meat and floats to the surface where it can easily be scooped out. Fermentation allows the oil and water to separate out naturally. The juice or "milk" of the coconut is squeezed out of the meat. The milk is then allowed to ferment for 24-36 hours. During this time, the oil separates from the water. The oil is removed and then heated slightly for a short time to evaporate all moisture. Heat such as this isn't harmful because the oil is very stable even under moderately high temperatures.

Palm and palm kernel oils are not readily available to the average consumer in most Western countries; they're most commonly used by the food processing industry. You may run across some palm oil, however. A few ethnic or specialty stores carry it for household use. Coconut oil, however, is commonly sold for kitchen use and is rapidly increasing in popularity because it is the richest natural source of health-promoting MCFA. Coconut oil is available in many health food stores or by mail order.

COOKING WITH COCONUT OIL

To enjoy the health benefits of coconut oil and reduce the harmful effects caused by other dietary fats, you should use coconut oil for most all of your cooking and food preparation needs. Most brands of coconut oil have a very mild flavor and can be used to cook any type of food. Because it is primarily a saturated fat, the heat of cooking does not create a free-radical soup like it does with other vegetable oils. You can feel safe knowing that you aren't damaging your health when you eat it. Coconut oil, however, has a moderately low smoking point so you need to keep the temperature below 350° F (177° C) when cooking foods on the stove. If you don't have a temperature gauge on your stove top, you can tell when it goes over this point because the oil will begin to smoke. This is a moderately high cooking temperature and you can cook anything at this heat, even stir-fry vegetables. When baking breads, muffins, and casseroles using coconut oil you can set the oven at temperatures above 350° F (177° C) because the moisture in the food keeps the inside temperature below 212° F (100° C).

Coconut oil melts at about 76° F (25° C), becoming a clear liquid that looks like most any other vegetable oil. Below this temperature, it solidifies and takes on a creamy white appearance. At moderate room temperatures it has a soft buttery texture and is sometimes called coconut butter. Because it has a buttery consistency at normal room temperature, it isn't generally used as a salad dressing. Olive oil or some other high-quality, cold pressed oil is better for cold salads.

Coconut oil can be spread on bread as a replacement for butter or margarine. Some brands have a mild, pleasant coconut flavor that make an excellent spread. If you like the taste of real butter, you can make a more flavorful spread using half butter and half coconut oil whipped together.

You don't need any special instructions or recipes to use coconut oil. Simply use it in place of other oils in recipes that call for butter, shortening, margarine, or vegetable oil. Try it in cookies, cakes, muffins, pie crusts, and pancake batter. It is great for stir frying or any skillet or stove top use. Use a melted coconut-butter mixture with seasonings poured over rice, pasta, or vegetables instead of butter or cream sauce.

For frying, nothing beats coconut oil. It isn't absorbed into foods as much as other vegetable oils, it doesn't splatter as much, and can be used over again. I don't ordinarily recommend eating fried foods because most vegetable oils become toxic when fried, but if you use coconut oil, fried foods could be *good* for you, so long as you don't overheat it. Any oil, including coconut oil, will produce toxic by-products if overheated.

Coconut oil is very stable and does *not* need to be refrigerated. It will stay fresh for at least two or three years unrefrigerated. If kept in a cool place it will last even longer, so it makes a good storage oil. I buy several jars of oil at a time and keep one in the refrigerator. I do this only because I prefer to use hardened oil as opposed to the liquid. To me it's easier to scoop a little out of the jar with a knife or spoon then it is to pour it out. When pouring, it's too easy to spill and drip. Oil can be messy. If I need liquid oil, all I do is heat up a little in a hot pan or I will pull the entire jar out of the refrigerator an hour or so before it's needed. It melts quickly.

RBD AND VIRGIN COCONUT OILS

There are many different methods of processing coconut oil that affect the quality, appearance, flavor, and aroma of the finished product. Coconut oil is commonly divided into two broad categories—RBD and virgin. The difference between the two depends on the amount of processing the oil undergoes. RBD stands for "refined, bleached, and deodorized." The term "virgin" is not an official classification, it simply signifies an oil that has been subjected to less intense refining; that usually means lower temperatures and without chemicals.

RBD oil is typically made from dried coconut known as copra. Copra is made by drying coconut in the sun, smoking it, heating it in a kiln, or

153

some combination of these. Oil made from copra is the most common coconut oil used in the cosmetic and food industries. While high temperatures and chemical solvents are used to produced this oil it is still considered a healthy dietary oil because the fatty acids in coconut oil are not harmed in the refining process. RBD oil is generally clear, tasteless, and odorless. Many people prefer this type of oil for all-purpose cooking and body care needs because it doesn't affect of flavor of foods or leave an odor when used on the skin.

Most virgin coconut oils are made from *fresh* coconuts. The oil is extracted by any number of methods—boiling, fermentation, refrigeration, mechanical press, or centrifuge. Since high temperatures and chemical solvents are not used, the oil retains its naturally occurring phytochemicals (plant chemicals) which produce a distinctive coconut taste and smell.

Virgin coconut oil made from fresh coconuts is a pure white when the oil is solidified, or crystal clear like water when liquefied. RBD oil made from copra can be just as clear and white. You often can't tell the difference between them just by looking. The way to distinguish between them is by the smell and taste. RBD oils are bland. Virgin oils have a delightfully mild coconut flavor and aroma.

There are some oils that may be labeled "virgin" which are made from sun dried copra rather than fresh coconut. These are called cochin oils. They have undergone less processing than most RBD oils. This doesn't mean they are more natural than refined copra oil (RBD), they are actually a lesser or inferior quality. The term "cochin" is derived from a place in India, Cochin, where cheap copra oil is popular. These oils have a strong smell and taste and are slightly discolored. When coconut is dried in the open air it is common for the copra to become moldy. The oil made from this type of copra has a yellowish or gray color because of the mold. The mold residue is considered harmless because the heat used in the processing has rendered it sterile. You can tell the difference between these oils and true virgin coconut oil by the color. Because cochin oil contains a higher level of impurities than other coconut oils it has a relatively short shelf life, about six months. Cochin oil is used mostly in the making of soaps and cosmetics. It is often sold as a cooking oil in Asian markets.

Another product you are likely to encounter is hydrogenated coconut oil. All hydrogenated coconut oils are refined, bleached, and deodorized. Unfortunately, some oils packaged primarily for body care use may not state if they are hydrogenated or not. Unadulterated coconut oil melts at 76° F (25° C), hydrogenated coconut oil melts at about 96° F (35° C) and partially hydrogenated oils somewhere in between these two. If the oil is not completely liquid when its temperature is above 76° F (25° C), it's been hydrogenated—don't use it. I've had oil like this in our bathroom on hot summer days with the temperature in the 90s and only about a third of the oil turned into liquid. So I knew it was hydrogenated even though it did not say so on the label. Unadulterated coconut oil would be totally liquid after a couple hours at this temperature.

When used as a skin lotion, food grade coconut oil is preferred. Oil is readily absorbed through the skin and into the body. It's almost the same as eating it. So if you wouldn't eat it, don't put it on your skin.

COCONUTS AND COCONUT PRODUCTS

Besides pure coconut oil, another source of the oil comes directly from eating the fruit or nut of the seed. Fresh coconut meat is about 33 percent oil. Adding coconut to your recipes can provide a significant amount of this life-giving oil.

Coconut is a good source of fiber, which is known to be valuable in proper digestive function. One cup of dried, shredded coconut supplies 9 grams of fiber. This is 3 to 4 times as much as most fruits and vegetables. For example, broccoli contains only 3 grams of fiber per cup and raw cabbage has only 2 grams per cup. A cup of white bread has a mere 1 gram.

Besides fiber, coconut supplies a wide variety of nutrients necessary for good health. It contains as much protein as an equal amount of green beans, carrots, and most other vegetables. It contains vitamins B-1, B-2, B-3, B-6, C, E, folic acid and the minerals calcium, iron, magnesium, phosphorus, potassium, sodium, and zinc, among others.

Fresh coconut is a delight to eat as a snack. Most good grocery stores everywhere sell it. Buy whole coconuts that are as fresh as you can find. All three eyes should be intact, it should not be cracked, leaking, or moldy. Shake the shell to detect if it still contains the water inside. If not, put it back.

Before opening, you must first drain the liquid. To do this use an ice pick and puncture a hole in at least two of the three eyes. The thin membrane over the eyes is relatively soft and easy to pierce. Once the holes are made, drain the liquid into a glass. Just put the coconut on the glass and let it drain. It should take only a few minutes. Once the liquid is removed, you are ready to crack the shell.

Coconut shells are tough. If you've ever tried to open one, you know how difficult it can be. Fresh coconuts straight from the tree have a softer shell and can be opened by a sharp blow with a large knife. The coconuts sold in most grocery stores are older and have much harder shells. The easiest way to open one of these coconuts is to place it in a corner to hold it and strike it with a hammer. The force to break the shell may be substantial so choose a corner that will not be harmed. Your kitchen countertop may not be the best place to do this. Cement or hardwood stairs make a good location. Another method you may want to try is to use a saw, but this can take a long time. I find it easier to just break it open.

When you buy a coconut at the store you have no way of telling how old it is. A fresh young coconut will stay fresh for many weeks. An older coconut may be rotten the day you buy it. Once a coconut has been opened, it should be refrigerated and used within a few days. Because of its high moisture content it spoils quickly after opening.* The liquid extracted should be used within a couple of days.

After the shell is opened, pull the white meat off. A brown fibrous membrane will be on the side that was in contact with the shell. Peal this off with a vegetable peeler. Your coconut is now ready to eat and enjoy.

Most of the coconut available to us in stores has been dried and shredded. When dried, the moisture content is reduced from 52 percent to about 2.5 percent. The fat content remains pretty much unchanged. Since the saturated fat is highly resistant to oxidation and spoilage, shredded coconut will last for many months.

Another common coconut product is coconut milk. Technically speaking coconut milk is *not* the liquid that develops naturally inside the coconut. This liquid is called *coconut water* although the two terms are commonly interchanged. True coconut milk is a manufactured product made from the flesh of the coconut. It is prepared by mixing water with grated coconut, squeezing and extracting the pulp, leaving only the liquid. Coconut milk contains between 17 and 24 percent fat. Canned coconut milk is available in many grocery and health food stores.

There was a time when many foods contained or were cooked in coconut or palm kernel oils, but that isn't true any more. Because of the negative campaign launched by the soybean industry, coconut oil has been replaced by hydrogenated vegetable oils in most of our foods. In order to get it in your diet you must put it there yourself. You can do this by simply buying coconut oil and using it at home in your food preparation. You may also add coconut meat and milk to your diet.

At the present, food-grade coconut oil is still difficult to find in some areas. The best places to look for it are in health food stores. If your local

---

* The remarkable antimicrobial properties of coconut oil become effective only after it has entered our bodies. Therefore, the oil in the fresh nut will not prevent mold or bacteria growth.

store doesn't carry it, ask them to order it for you. If you can't find a source of coconut oil in your area, check the resources at the back of this book.

COCONUT MILK

Coconut milk is a good source of MCFA. It contains about 24 percent oil. It makes a wonderful substitute for cow's milk and cream in most recipes. You can use it to make creamy fruit smoothies, rich sauces, gravies, and soups, or you can pour it over a bowl of fruit or breakfast cereal. Canned coconut milk is available in most grocery or health food stores.

Sweetened Coconut Milk

Coconut milk straight from the can is very thick, creamy, and not very sweet, which makes it great for use in soups and sauces. But it is too thick and rich to drink by the glass. Straight from the can its more like a thick, non-sweetened cream. With just a little preparation, however, you can make an excellent substitute for cow's milk.

The recipe below will show you how to turn a can of coconut milk into a creamy coconut beverage that is good enough to drink by the glass, pour over cereal, or combine with freshly cut fruit in a bowl. Diluting the milk slightly and adding a little honey gives it a mild, pleasant sweetness that will have you wanting to drink it by the glass.

1 can (14 oz) coconut milk

7 oz water (one half can)

2 tablespoons honey (or other sweetener)

salt

Empty 1 can of milk in quart container. Add one half can of water (7 oz), 2 tablespoons of honey, and a pinch of salt. Mix thoroughly, chill, and serve. Note: the honey will dissolve in mixture easily if liquid is at room temperature. For sweeter milk add more honey. For less creamy milk add more water.

Flavored Coconut Milk

The coconut milk can be flavored by adding 1 teaspoon of vanilla or almond extract to the mixture. These flavors give the milk a wonderful added taste. Other extracts may also be added for variety.

Peaches and Milk

For a wonderful treat, pour coconut milk over freshly sliced peaches. Makes a delicious simple and natural dessert. You may try it on a variety of different fresh fruits such as strawberries, blackberries, raspberries, etc. A little honey may be added if the fruit isn't sweet enough for your taste.

ALLERGIES AND FOOD SENSITIVITIES

Coconut products make excellent choices for people with food allergies. While some people can be allergic to most any type of food, relatively few people have allergic reactions to coconut.

One of the most common allergy-causing foods is cow's milk. This includes all dairy products—cheese, yogurt, cream, buttermilk, ice cream, butter, etc. When you look at the many foods that are made with some type of dairy product, being allergic can seem like a major handicap. Refraining from dairy in one form or another is difficult for most people. We grow up eating dairy products and if we suddenly are told not to have them we feel greatly deprived. We love the creamy taste so much it's like asking us to cut off an arm to quit eating it completely. Even if eating dairy causes headaches, stomach cramps, sinus congestion, or skin rashes, the temptation is often too great. Those with allergies often eat dairy even though they know they will pay for it later. With coconut milk you can have milk without the symptoms. You can enjoy cereal for breakfast as well as rich creamy soups, milkshakes, sauces, and desserts without fear of suffering an allergic reaction afterwards. Coconut milk provides a safe, healthy alternative to cow's milk.

Another group of foods that is also one of the most common causes of allergies is nuts—peanuts, almonds, walnuts, pecans, etc. Peanuts are especially troublesome. They can cause severe allergic reactions and even death in some people. Like cow's milk, nuts make many foods taste better. Also, many of the oils used in foods come from nuts. Peanut oil is very common. If you are allergic to nuts and nut oils, you don't necessarily have to eliminate them all from your diet. You may be able to replace them with coconut and coconut oil.

According to one study, over 60 percent of all food allergies are cause by milk and nuts.[1] For the person who has food allergies, and is not allergic to coconut, coconut products may provide a safe and tasty alternative. Coconut milk and other coconut products can be used in a surprising variety of food products from delicate desserts to hearty main courses.

158

A NATURAL WAY TO BETTER HEALTH

LIVE HEALTHY FOR A LIFETIME

My goal is to live healthy for a lifetime. I expect to live a long healthy life without suffering with crippling pain and degenerative disease and without taking dangerous drugs or submitting myself to abusive medical treatments. You won't find me wasting away in some retirement home. When I'm 80 years old I'll still be running around full of life and energy. The way I plan on accomplishing this goal is to live a healthy lifestyle. One of the primary aspects of a healthy lifestyle is diet, so the principle fat in my diet is coconut oil. I already know my plan is working. I've seen the results.

One of the keys to good health is having an efficient immune system. Chronic illness and degenerative disease are most prevalent among those whose immune systems are weak or overworked. If your immune system remains young and vital, the odds of living longer and healthier are greatly enhanced. One clue to the level of health of our immune systems and, consequently, our future health, is how often we become sick. The more often we come down with seasonal illnesses and are troubled with allergies and other autoimmune conditions, the less efficient is our immune system.

Several years ago I tried a little experiment. In my 20s I considered myself relatively healthy. I rarely missed a day of work due to illness, although I would go to the office when I wasn't feeling in the best of health. If the illness wasn't too severe, I usually headed off to work. Don't you do the same?

If someone asked me how often I was sick each year, I would think back to how many days I missed work. It seemed like only two or three.

By adding coconut oil to your diet you can enjoy a healthier, happier life.

Somehow, I lost track of all the many days I went to work knowing I was battling some infection. So I decided to run an experiment.

I kept a detailed record of every illness I had, whether or not I went to work. If I knew I was fighting an infection or felt one coming on, or experienced allergy-like symptoms, I wrote it down. I kept a record of the symptoms, when they started, and when they subsided. At the end of the year I was shocked. It had been a normal year for me healthwise, but I recorded 74 days of illness of one sort or another. This was not the simple aches and pains from everyday life or stress, but definite sickness. I continued this record for six years!

In that time I found that I was sick, on average, for 54.5 days each year!* This was surprising because I was still young and considered myself far healthier than most people. I ate a so-called "balanced" diet that included plenty of fruits and vegetables, exercised faithfully an average of four days a week, and did not eat many sweets or junk foods. I had always

---

* Studies by The Centers for Disease Control and Prevention have shown that the average number of sick days each person experiences per year is about 65. This includes major illness as well as minor sniffles, upset stomachs, etc. which we all ignore and quickly forget about. If you kept a detailed diary you would be surprised how often you feel "under the weather."

believed in natural health and tried to live healthfully. So why was I sick so often?

I did eat a lot of processed vegetable oil, shortening, and margarine. I grew up on these oils because we thought they were healthy. I know better now. Even when I began reducing the total amount of fat and oil in my diet, my health didn't seem to improve much.

The big change occurred when I switched from eating processed vegetable oils and margarine to coconut oil and other more saturated fats (butter and olive oil). As a result, since I've been on this new program, I've had no sick days...zero...no colds, no flus, no stomach aches, no sore throats, no fevers, no allergies, nothing! I haven't been sick for even a single day in years and I've been around some very sick and contagious people.

Because I use coconut oil for most of my food preparation needs, I believe I am protected from many infectious diseases and enjoy improved digestive health—two major benefits of coconut oil. I'm totally free from all chronic degenerative disease. I'm in my 50's and enjoy better health now than at any other time in my life. Do the healing properties of coconut oil work? I think so. Why else have I come from 54 days of illness a year, when I was young and supposedly healthy to none now when I'm middle aged? I've seen many people younger than I who have died of heart disease, cancer, and other illnesses. With the aid of the antimicrobial medium-chain fatty acids in coconut oil, my immune system has been able to fight off every disease-causing germ I have come into contact with over the past several years and kept me free from degenerative disease.

No matter what I say, some people express concern about eating saturated fat. I'm not worried about it. I know the fats in coconut oil are heart healthy. High blood pressure is one of the strongest risk factors associated with heart disease. It's more closely associated with heart disease than high cholesterol. I'm in my 50's yet I have the blood pressure reading of a 20-year-old (110/60). The average reading for a healthy adult is 120/80. By the time we reach 60 years of age, doctors tell us it's typical for blood pressure to be 130/90 or more which is considered on the high side. As blood pressure increases, cardiovascular health deteriorates and risk of heart disease and stroke increase. Because I eat coconut oil, ten years from now I'll probably still have the cardiovascular health of someone in his 20s. Coconut oil protects me from heart disease just as it does Pacific Islanders who use it as a part of their everyday diet.

HOW MUCH COCONUT OIL DO YOU NEED?

In order to gain the marvelous benefits available from MCFA, we must eat those foods which contain them. The only significant dietary sources of MCFA are coconuts, palm kernels, and whole milk/butter. The butterfat in cow's milk contains a small amount of MCFA. Most milk and dairy products nowadays are low- or non-fat and, therefore, provide essentially none of these health-giving fatty acids. Butter consists of about 6 percent MCFA. A better source are the tropical oils. Palm kernel oil is 58 percent MCFA, but the only place you will find this oil is as an ingredient in a few commercially prepared foods. Coconut oil contains 63 percent MCFA and fresh or dried coconut is 33 percent fat. Coconut milk is 24 percent fat. So coconut products—the meat, oil, and milk—are by far the most readily available and richest dietary sources of MCFA.

How much coconut oil do you need for optimal health benefit? How much do you need to prevent infection? How much should you take on a daily basis? Researchers have yet to satisfactorily answer these questions. However, based on the amount of MCFA found in human breast milk, which is known to be effective in its role to protect and nourish infants, we can estimate the amount that may be suitable for adults. Based on this premise, an adult of average size would need 3¹/₂ tablespoons (50 grams) of coconut oil a day to equal the proportion of MCFA a nursing baby receives. The same amount of MCFA can be obtained from 10 ounces of coconut milk or 7 ounces of raw coconut (about half a whole coconut).

Studies have shown the antimicrobial effects of MCFA are additive, so the greater the number of these infection fighting fatty acids available in our bodies, the greater our protection.[1] Eating more should provide greater health benefits, not only in preventing illness but in improving digestion and nutrient absorption, protecting against heart disease, etc.

The question you might ask now is can you get too much, and if so, how much is too much? Again there is no definite answer. Coconut oil is essentially non-toxic to humans.[2] It's considered safer than soy which many people eat by the pound. The FDA has included coconut oil on its list of foods that are generally regarded as safe (GRAS). This is a very exclusive list. Only those foods that have passed stringent testing and have a history of safe usage can qualify for inclusion on the GRAS list. Soy and soybean oil are *not* on the list as well as many other foods we commonly consider healthy and eat every day. You can consume more than 3¹/₂ tablespoons a day of coconut oil without worry.

Animals which have been fed enormous quantities of coconut oil appear to have no adverse effects.[3] Diets containing as much as 9.54g of

MCFA per kilogram of body weight have proven to be safe in these studies.[4] If we extrapolate that and place it in human terms it would equate to a 150 pound person consuming 46 tablespoons of oil a day. Animals, however, don't always respond to foods the same way humans do. So how much coconut oil can a human consume? We know that certain island populations consume large amounts of coconut oil, as much as 10 tablespoons a day and have excellent health. This is far more than you would normally want to eat, so you probably don't need to worry about eating too much. Several clinical studies have shown MCFA levels up to at least 1 gram per each kilogram of body weight to be safe.[5] For a 150 pound person that would equate to 5 tablespoons. For a 200 pound person that would be 6.5 tablespoons.

I think 2-4 tablespoons of coconut oil daily is a reasonable amount for most adults. Taking as much as 4 tablespoons a day may sound like a lot to some people. You don't have to take this much. Even 1 tablespoon a day can be beneficial. It has been shown that the equivalent of 1 tablespoon a day can significantly reduce the viral load in HIV-infected patients (see study on page 101).

You could get a daily dose of MCFA by taking coconut oil like you would any other liquid dietary supplement—by the spoonful or mixing it in a beverage. Another way to get coconut oil into the body is by applying it

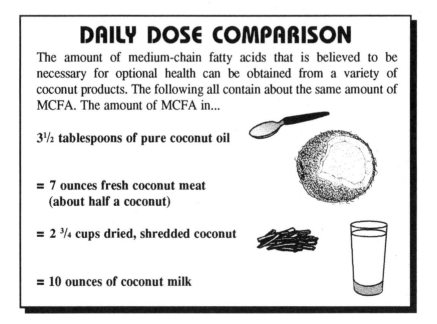

DAILY DOSE COMPARISON

The amount of medium-chain fatty acids that is believed to be necessary for optional health can be obtained from a variety of coconut products. The following all contain about the same amount of MCFA. The amount of MCFA in...

3½ tablespoons of pure coconut oil

= 7 ounces fresh coconut meat (about half a coconut)

= 2 ¾ cups dried, shredded coconut

= 10 ounces of coconut milk

on the skin. Oils are readily absorbed by the skin. Spreading a thin layer of coconut oil over the entire surface of the body after a shower is one convenient method you can use. The only problem with this method is that you can't really tell how much oil is actually absorbed since absorption varies depending on skin texture and thickness. Also, too much oil applied to any one area tends to sit on the surface of the skin where it is easily rubbed off. I feel the most accurate and most palatable way to get coconut oil working in your body is by using it with your food (see Appendix I).

Replacing the cooking oils you currently use with coconut oil would be an easy step to take to add MCFA into your diet without increasing your total fat intake. Also incorporate more coconut meat and milk into your diet. Seven ounces of dried coconut provides about 3^1/$_2$ tablespoons of oil. Ten ounces of coconut milk also provides 3^1/$_2$ tablespoons of oil. The more coconut oil you can add to your diet this way the better. Coconut oil is one fat you can eat without feeling guilty. From all the research that has been done to this point, it appears that coconut oil is the healthiest all-purpose oil you can use.

WHAT TO DO WHEN YOU'RE SICK

In coastal Africa and South and Central America and other tropical areas of the world, people are known to drink coconut or palm kernel oil whenever they become sick. To them the tropical oils are both a food and a medicine. You could also use this oil, as many cultures have done for thousands of years, as a medicine to overcome illness.

Coconut oil can be helpful in fighting many common seasonal illnesses. In the case of a virus which includes the flu, there is no medication that can destroy the organism. Medications given in these circumstances are primarily to relieve symptoms. The body has to mount its own defense and you simply must wait it out. Even if you have a bacterial infection and are given antibiotics, your body must still fight off the infection. Whether you have a viral or bacterial infection, you're going to need to eat. You might as well be eating foods prepared in coconut oil. This will provide your body with valuable antimicrobial fatty acids that will aid it in overcoming the illness.

Some people prefer to avoid drugs whenever possible because they don't want the side effects that accompany medications. Coconut oil provides a natural way to fight infection without harmful or unpleasant side effects. Whether you choose to use medications or not, coconut oil can help you fight the infection and get better quicker.

Although there is no recommended dosage to take when you are sick, I would suggest 4-8 tablespoons a day until you feel better. Spread your dosage over the day by taking a couple of tablespoons at each meal. A large person would need to take more than a smaller individual. You can take it by the spoonful if you like, but it is more palatable if you mix it with food. A couple of tablespoons in a glass of orange juice is a quick and easy way to do it. Orange juice, or other beverages, should be at room temperature or warmer to prevent the oil from solidifying. Juice and oil do not mix well. So add the oil, stir, and drink promptly. If you let the mixture sit, the oil will float to the surface of the juice. If this is too much oil for your taste then you can use one of the recipes given in Appendix I. Once you're back to normal, continue to take the equilivent of 3-4 tablespoons (42-56 grams) daily for maintenance.

If someone is very sick and vomiting it may not be possible to take coconut oil orally. In this case you can massage the oil into the skin. Oils are easily absorbed into the body though the skin. This bypasses the digestive tract providing the body needed nourishment, a source of energy, and antimicrobial fatty acids to fight the infection. Even if the infectious organism is not vulnerable to MCFA, the nourishment the oil provides will strengthen the body helping it to heal quicker. I suggest massaging 2-4 tablespoons of oil, two or three times a day over the entire body. Several thin layers of oil are absorbed much better than one thick layer because too much oil in any one place saturates the tissues and limits absorption, plus excess oil often rubs off on clothing and sheets. When applying the oil make sure to massage it into the skin closest to the most infected part of the body. For a sore throat massage the oil around the neck; for a chest or lung infection be sure to apply plenty of oil on the chest and back.

The most active antimicrobial ingredient in coconut oil is lauric acid or more specifically monolaurin (see page 62). You can purchase lauric acid (monolaurin) as a dietary supplement. This provides a concentrated dose of the most potent germ-fighting fatty acid. It can be taken with a glass of water like any other supplement. This lauric acid supplement known by the trade name Lauricidin® is available at some health food stores or by mail order (see resources in Appendix II). The recommended dose of monolaurin is as follows: at the first sign of infection take 1,800-3,600 mg (6-12 300mg capsules) daily for four to five days, then taper down to 2-4 capsules until free of symptoms.

Self-diagnosis and treatment may be all right for minor illnesses like a cold, however, I recommend that before treating any serious illness you consult with a physician or other health care provider first. After reading about all the wonderful things coconut oil can do, it's tempting to think of it as a panacea for all illnesses. While coconut oil is good, keep in mind that it's *not* a cure-all. The MCFA in coconut oil won't kill all germs and medical care may be needed.

I think the best use of coconut oil is as a potent nutrient that can help to prevent disease and illness. It is much easier to prevent an illness from developing than it is to cure it once it gets started. If you take 3-4 tablespoons of coconut oil every day and eat a healthy diet you probably won't get sick. If you do get sick, it will probably be from an infection that is not vulnerable to MCFA. In this case you may want to use some other natural remedy or standard medication.

ESSENTIAL FATTY ACIDS
I need to include a few words about the essential fatty acids (EFA). To be healthy and avoid deficiency disease, you must get all the nutrients your body needs. Fatty acids are vital nutrients necessary for good health. Some of the fatty acids are classified as being "essential" because our bodies cannot make them from other nutrients. We must get the essential fatty acids from our foods. The two basic essential fats are omega-6 (linoleic) and omega-3 (alpha-linolenic) fatty acids. Medium-chain fatty acids, like those found in coconut oil, are also important and are considered *conditionally essential*, that is, under certain circumstances they are just as important as other essential fatty acids.

EFA fats are contained in most vegetable oils but are often damaged by refining and processing or destroyed by free radicals. Therefore, conventionally processed vegetable oils are inferior sources for EFA. In addition, trans fatty acids from hydrogenated oils, including margarine and shortening, block or interfere with the body's utilization of EFA. For these reasons, if you eat conventionally processed vegetable oils and hydrogenated oils you may be deficient in EFA.

You can get the EFA your body needs directly from your foods, unrefined cold-pressed vegetable oils, or from dietary supplements. Coconut oil, however, has a very small percentage of these fats (only 2%). A benefit of using coconut oil in your daily diet is that MCFA work synergistically with the essential fatty acids improving the body's utilization of these fats. A diet rich in coconut oil can enhance the efficiency of essential fatty acids by as by as much as 100 percent.[6] Not only that, but coconut oil also acts as antioxidant protecting EFA from destructive oxidation inside the body.

The World Health Organization says we need to get about 3 percent of our daily calories from the essential fatty acids.[7] There is no set minimum for the MCFA, although we know infants probably need somewhere around 5-10 percent of calories from this source. We also know from island populations that people can get as much as 50 percent of their calories from coconut oil without harm and probably provides them with much benefit. So it appears that for optimal health we should consume a little EFA along with a significantly larger amount of MCFA.

THE CHALLENGE

Scientific knowledge regarding the health benefits of coconut oil began emerging over 40 years ago. During this time its unique health promoting properties have been recognized by only a small number of researchers. Although products containing coconut oil derivatives have been used to nourish patients in hospitals for many years, the vast majority of doctors, nutritionists, and food scientists have been unaware of its potential health benefits. Consequently, they have often equated coconut oil with the idea of unhealthy saturated fats that raise blood cholesterol. Most have unjustly and ignorantly criticized coconut oil as doing the same. Fortunately, this is beginning to change as knowledge of the many benefits of coconut oil increases. One of the purposes of this book is to educate the public as well as health care professionals about the great potential of coconut oil and to dispel untruths created by the marketing efforts of competitive industries.

Despite the evidence presented in this book, many health care workers and writers will continue to argue and say coconut oil is bad for you. It's hard to accept a new truth when you have been conditioned to believe something else for many years. However, if you have an open mind and are willing to accept new truths, you will welcome the knowledge about coconut oil. There are too many benefits to ignore. I didn't make this stuff up. The information in this book came from published studies and clinical observations as well as historical and epidemiological research. The facts are there, you can read them yourself if you want to wade through the medical literature (see the references at the end of the is book). If you stop to think about it and use a little common sense, it's clear that coconut oil is not harmful. People who consume large quantities of coconuts and coconut oil have been shown to be some of the healthiest on earth. However, you are likely to hear criticism of coconut oil for years to come. But who are you going to believe, the soybean industry and misinformed writers and doctors who are dying right and left from degenerative diseases, or the healthy Pacific Islanders and the researchers making the discoveries? I put my trust in the facts and not the marketing propaganda of the soybean industry.

HEALTH BENEFITS OF COCONUT OIL

Research and clinical observation have shown that medium-chain fatty acids, like those found in coconut oil, may provide a wide range of health benefits. Some of these are summarized below:

- Kills viruses that cause mononucleosis, influenza, hepatitis C, measles, herpes, AIDS and other illnesses
- Kills bacteria that cause pneumonia, earache, throat infections, dental cavities, food poisoning, urinary tract infections, meningitis, gonorrhea, and dozens of other diseases
- Kills fungi and yeast that cause candida, jock itch, ringworm, athlete's foot, thrush, diaper rash and other infections
- Expels or kills tapeworms, lice, giardia, and other parasites
- Provides a nutritional source of quick energy
- Boosts energy and endurance enhancing physical and athletic performance
- Improves digestion and absorption of fat-soluble vitamins and amino acids
- Improves insulin secretion and utilization of blood glucose
- Relieves stress on pancreas and enzyme systems of the body
- Reduces symptoms associated with pancreatitis
- Helps relieve symptoms and reduce health risks associated with diabetes
- Reduces problems associated with malabsorption syndrome and cystic fibrosis
- Improves calcium and magnesium absorption and supports the development of strong bones and teeth.
- Helps protect against osteoporosis
- Helps relieve symptoms of gallbladder disease
- Relieves symptoms associated with Crohn's disease, ulcerative colitis, and stomach ulcers
- Relieves pain and irritation caused by hemorrhoids
- Reduces chronic inflammation
- Supports tissue healing and repair
- Supports and aids immune system function
- Helps protect the body from breast, colon, and other cancers
- Is heart healthy; does not increase blood cholesterol or platelet stickiness

- Helps prevent heart disease, atherosclerosis, and stroke
- Helps prevent high blood pressure
- Helps prevent periodontal disease and tooth decay
- Functions as a protective antioxidant
- Helps to protect the body from harmful free-radicals that promote premature aging and degenerative disease
- Does not deplete the body's antioxidant reserves like other oils do
- Improves utilization of essential fatty acids and protects them from oxidation
- Helps relieve symptoms associated with chronic fatigue syndrome
- Relieves symptoms associated with benign prostatic hyperplasia (prostate enlargement)
- Reduces epileptic seizures
- Helps protect against kidney disease and bladder infections
- Helps prevent liver disease
- Is lower in calories than all other fats
- Supports thyroid function
- Promotes loss of excess weight by increasing metabolic rate
- Is utilized by the body to produce energy in preference to being stored as body fat like other dietary fats.
- Helps prevent obesity and overweight problems
- Applied topically helps to form a chemical barrier on the skin to ward off infection
- Reduces symptoms associated with psoriasis, eczema, and dermatitis
- Supports the natural chemical balance of the skin
- Softens skin and helps relieve dryness and flaking
- Prevents wrinkles, sagging skin, and age spots
- Promotes healthy-looking hair and complexion
- Provides protection from the damaging effects of ultraviolet radiation from the sun
- Controls dandruff
- Helps you look and feel younger
- Is resistant to oxidation, so has a long shelf life
- Does not form harmful by-products when heated to normal cooking temperatures like other vegetable oils do
- Has no harmful or discomforting side effects
- Is completely non-toxic to humans

If naysayers don't want to believe it, don't let that hold you back. You have a great opportunity awaiting you. By eating coconut oil on a regular basis you will have the potential power of these antimicrobial MCFA protecting your body and supporting your immune system. Eating coconut oil may provide you with a harmless and inexpensive way of preventing or even fighting off many illnesses. Research may eventually find coconut oil to be just as effective as many of the antimicrobial drugs and vaccines that are currently used. It is definitely safer. Eating coconut oil has no undesirable side effects.

Despite the benefits, you're not likely to see big expensive ad campaigns promoting the use of coconut oil. The food and drug industries have more profitable products to market. Hydrogenated soybean oil is the product of choice for most of the food industry, and they're not likely to change anytime soon. The drug industry isn't too excited about the potential use of coconut oil to prevent or treat disease. They will merely consider it competition like other natural products in which they have no interest. They will no doubt ignore developments in MCFA research and continue promoting their highly profitable medications and vaccines.

Keep in mind that doctors after graduation from medical school are, for the most part, educated by the pharmaceutical industry. The literature they receive and the seminars they go to are funded almost entirely by these companies. The information they are exposed to is naturally extremely biased, focusing only on drug therapy. For this reason, most doctors know very little about nutrition and even less about current research involving MCFA. Most doctors will probably be completely ignorant of the research and developments regarding MCFA for several years to come. They will continue advising you to avoid all saturated fats, including coconut oil, because they don't know any better. They may never have even heard of medium-chain fatty acids or even know that there are many different types of saturated fat. Don't wait for them to catch up with you.

After reading this book, you are armed with knowledge that could greatly enhance your health and improve your quality of life. The simple act of eliminating refined vegetable oils from your diet and replacing them with coconut oil will work wonders for you. You will be replacing a toxic substance by one that offers many marvelous health benefits.

This change should be a lifelong commitment. Eating coconut oil isn't something you should do for only a few months like so many people do with fad diets. To gain permanent benefit, you need to do it permanently. Ignore the negative comments you may get from others who know nothing about the health benefits of coconut oil. Have them read this book and let them discover the healing miracles of coconut oil for themselves. One of the best presents you can give a friend is the gift of health. Give your friends copies of this book. You will not only help them gain better health but you will gain friends who will encourage and support you.

If you still have doubts, I challenge you to try it for six months—just six months, that's all. After six months see if you don't look and feel better than you did before. My challenge to you is to eliminate all processed vegetable oils from your diet, especially hydrogenated oils (including shortening and margarine). A little butter* and *organic, cold pressed*, vegetable oils are okay, but for maximum benefit remove all other commercial vegetable oils. Use coconut oil for *all* your cooking needs and use extra virgin olive or another high-quality, cold-pressed oil in your salad dressing.

The hardest thing about this challenge is that if you go out to eat in a restaurant, you often don't know what type of oils they use. If you have a choice, request olive or coconut oil whenever possible. Choose butter over margarine. Otherwise, I suggest you avoid eating in places where you don't know what you're getting. Restaurants are notoriously negligent in regards to customers' health, especially when it comes to oils. They often use the cheapest, degraded, processed oils around. Oils are often heated to very high temperatures repeatedly for days and even weeks at a time, causing them to become extremely rancid and highly toxic. Deep fried foods such as french fries, chicken nuggets, and donuts are the most toxic foods you can get at a restaurant. If you have to have fried foods, they should be fried in coconut oil because it does not degrade into free radicals or create toxic trans fatty acids when heated as other vegetable oils do.

I know this dietary change will work for you. I've seen it happen in others. I would like to hear from you. Write and tell me how coconut oil has affected your life. You can write to me at HealthWise Publications, P.O. Box 25203, Colorado Springs, CO 80936. For more information on oils and health write and ask for a free copy of the HealthWise Newsletter.

---

* Many people refrain from using butter with the belief that it is bad for them. Milk contains many of the health-promoting MCFA, including lauric acid. Butter provides a modest source of this important fatty acid. Population studies have shown that when people remove butter from their diets and replace it with margarine their rate of heart disease actually *increases!*[7]

YOUR DAILY DOSE

The simplest way to take coconut oil on a daily basis is by the tablespoonful like a dietary supplement. The recommended daily dosage for adults is 3¹/₂ tablespoons. Keep in mind that people have achieved good results from eating less oil per day. So if you only eat 1 or 2 tablespoons daily you will still benefit.

Oil, any oil, straight from the spoon is difficult for most people to take. Some people can handle it without problem but for most, the oily taste and texture are hard to stomach (figuratively speaking).* Take heart, there are other ways to get the daily dose without having to consume it by the spoonful. This chapter contains recipes which use a high amount of coconut oil in order to easily supply the recommended dose in more palatable ways.

The recipes in this chapter are useful for people who don't ordinarily use any oil in cooking or food preparation and what to get the full recommended dose all at one time. Keep in mind that it isn't necessary to take 3¹/₂ tablespoons of oil in one single meal, in fact, I prefer to spread it out over the entire day. The amount of oil used in these recipes is more than what is generally called for, if you want to use less do so. Use these recipes as they are or as examples to create your own and adjust the oil content to suit your needs.

---

* Virgin coconut oil extracted from fresh coconut milk produces a very delicate flavored product that is so good it can easily be eaten by the spoonful. It is so good it is almost like eating coconut cream.

SWEETENED COCONUT MILK

The Sweetened Coconut Milk recipe on page 157 makes an excellent beverage and substitute for cow's milk. It can be enjoyed by the glass or poured over hot or cold cereal or fresh fruit. The recipe makes a little more than $2^{1}/_{2}$ cups of milk. Each $^{1}/_{2}$ cup serving of this milk contains 1 tablespoon of coconut oil. A 12-ounce glass ($1^{1}/_{2}$ cups) will supply you with 3 tablespoons of oil, and $1^{3}/_{4}$ cups supplies $3^{1}/_{2}$ tablespoons. A 14-ounce glass ($1^{3}/_{4}$ cups) of this milk eaten with an ordinary breakfast it will supply you with a complete daily dose of coconut oil to start off your day.

FRUIT SMOOTHIE

You can combine coconut milk with fruit to make a creamy and delicious fruit smoothie. Coconut milk is usually sold in 14-ounce cans; 10 ounces of coconut milk supplies $3^{1}/_{2}$ tablespoons of oil. Using an electric blender mix 10 ounces ($1^{1}/_{4}$ cups) of coconut milk with 2 cups of frozen fruit. Most any type of fruit will work strawberries, raspberries, pineapple, bananas, peaches, apricots, etc. It's best to buy fresh fruit, cut it up, and freeze it until you're ready to make the smoothie. Using frozen fruit will give your smoothie the consistency of a milkshake. You may add a little honey to sweeten it to your satisfaction. This recipe makes 2 cups (16 ounces) which supplies $3^{1}/_{2}$ tablespoons of oil. This drink makes a pleasant way to get your daily dose.

HOT CEREAL

When you make hot cereal like oatmeal, creamed wheat, cracked wheat, and such you can mix into it coconut oil. I recommend 3 tablespoons of oil for every bowl ($1^{1}/_{2}$ cups) of cereal, this amounts to 1 tablespoon per half cup of cooked oatmeal. Top the cereal anyway you like with milk, yogurt, honey, fruit, etc.

You can reduce the amount of pure oil you mix into the cereal if you use coconut milk. A half cup of Sweetened Coconut Milk described above will supply a half tablespoon of oil. A half cup of canned coconut milk will supply you with $^{3}/_{4}$ tablespoon of oil.

HASH BROWNS

Fried potatoes absorb a lot of fat when they are cooked. Coconut oil is an excellent frying fat because of its stability under heat. You can easily use

4 or more tablespoons of oil to cook 1 medium-sized potato which would be one full serving. Here's how you do it.

Grate the potato and set aside. Heat 4 tablespoons of coconut oil in a fry pan at 300° F (149° C). Add the grated potato to the hot pan, spread it out evenly over the bottom of the pan, then push it down with a pancake turner so the potato pieces form a mat. You want the potato to be in contact with the bottom of the pan and the oil. Cover the pan and cook for about 10-12 minutes. Remove the cover. The potatoes are completely cooked. You do not need to turn the hash browns over and cook the other side. Serve by placing the toasted side up. Season to taste. One serving (one potato) cooked this way will supply about $3^1/_2$ tablespoons of oil.

BRAN MUFFINS

Muffins can contain a large amount of oil without adversely affecting the taste. These muffins made with bran and whole wheat make a healthy breakfast or mid-day snack. The ingredients are as follows:

1 cup water
1 $^1/_4$ cup whole wheat flour
$^1/_4$ cup wheat bran
$^1/_3$ cup honey
9 tablespoons coconut oil (this is equilivent to $^1/_2$ cup plus 1 tablespoon)
1 egg
$^1/_2$ cup nuts
1 tablespoon vanilla
1 teaspoon cinnamon
$^1/_2$ teaspoon nutmeg
2 teaspoon baking powder
$^1/_4$ teaspoon salt

Combine water, vanilla, honey, egg, and bran in a bowl and let sit for 10-15 minutes. The bran will absorb some of the moisture as it sits which will improve the texture of the final product. In another bowl mix flour, baking powder, salt, cinnamon, and nutmeg together. Preheat oven to 400° F (204° C). Add melted (not hot) coconut oil to the liquid ingredients, add the nut and mix together. Combine the wet and dry ingredients into one bowl and mix just until moist. Do not over mix or the muffins will not rise as well. Fill muffin cups half full. Bake for 15 minutes. Makes one dozen muffins.

Each muffin contains ³/₄ tablespoon of coconut oil, two muffin supplies 1¹/₂ tablespoons, four muffins supplies 3 tablespoons, five muffins 3³/₄ tablespoons. These muffins are medium to small in size so you can easily eat three, four, or five at a meal without problem.

WHOLE WHEAT MUFFINS
This recipe is similar to the one above but without the bran and with applesauce added.

1³/₄ cups whole wheat flour
³/₄ cup water
¹/₂ cup applesauce
9 tablespoons coconut oil (¹/₂ cup plus 1 tablespoon)
2 teaspoons baking powder
¹/₄ teaspoon salt
¹/₃ cup honey
1 egg
1 teaspoon vanilla

Preheat oven to 400° F (204° C). Combine lukewarm water, eggs, honey, applesauce, vanilla, and melted coconut oil (not hot) in a bowl and mix thoroughly. In a separate bowl mix together flour, baking powder, and salt. Add the dry ingredients to the liquid mixing just until moistened. Fill muffin cups. Bake for 15-18 minutes. Makes one dozen muffins. Each muffin contains about ³/₄ tablespoon of oil. Five muffins supplies 3³/₄ tablespoons.

BLUEBERRY MUFFINS
This recipe makes delicious whole wheat blueberry muffins.

1¹/₂ cups whole wheat flour
¹/₂ cup water
1 cup fresh blueberries
9 tablespoons coconut oil
2 tablespoons baking powder
¹/₄ teaspoon salt
¹/₂ cup honey
1 egg
1 teaspoon vanilla

175

Preheat oven to 400° F (204° C). Combine lukewarm water, eggs, honey, vanilla, and melted coconut oil (not hot) in a bowl and mix thoroughly. In a separate bowl mix together flour, baking powder, and salt. Add the dry ingredients to the liquid mixing just until moistened. Fold in the blueberries. Fill muffin cups. Bake for 15-18 minutes. Makes one dozen muffins. Each muffin contains about ³/₄ tablespoons of oil. Five muffins supplies 3³/₄ tablespoons.

As a variation to this recipe you can substitute another fruit such as raspberries or cherries for the blueberries. You can create a variety of delicious muffins using different types of fruits.

WHOLE WHEAT PANCAKES

The simple pancake can easily be made with additional oil. Try this recipe using whole wheat flour.

1¹/₂ cups whole wheat flour
¹/₄ teaspoon salt
¹/₂ cup applesauce
2 teaspoons baking powder
1 egg
³/₄ cup water
¹/₂ cup coconut oil (8 tablespoons)

Heat ¹/₂ cup of coconut oil in skillet over *low* heat until melted. Mix flour, salt and baking powder into a bowl. In a separate bowl beat egg and *lukewarm* water, applesauce, and melted (not hot) oil together. Leave the coconut oil residue in the skillet and increase temperature to moderate heat about 325° F (163° C). As the pan is heating combine liquid and dry ingredients and mix only until well dampened. Do not over mix as this will make pancakes heavier. Use about 3 tablespoons batter for each pancake. Cook until bubbles form over surface, turn gently, and brown flip side. Serve hot with honey, maple syrup, fruit or other topping. Makes one dozen pancakes.

Each pancake contains ²/₃ tablespoon of oil. Three pancakes supplies 2 tablespoons and six pancakes 4 tablespoons. If six pancakes are too much for you to eat and you want more oil you can increase the amount of oil in the mix by 2 tablespoons for a total of 10. This will give you ⁴/₅ tablespoon per pancake; three pancakes supplies 2¹/₂ tablespoons and six supplies 5 tablespoons.

CREAMY CHICKEN GRAVY

This is a tasty dish that can make a hearty breakfast, a satisfying lunch, or an easy dinner. This is one of my favorite recipes because it can be used in a variety of delicious ways.

1 14-oz can of coconut milk
1 cup chicken
2 tablespoons coconut oil
2 tablespoons flour
1 cup water
1 tablespoon dried onion or 2 tablespoons fresh, copped
$1/4$ teaspoon celery seed
Salt and pepper

Melt coconut oil in medium-sized sauce pan at about 300° F (149° C). Add flour and brown, stirring frequently. When oil/flour mixture turns a light golden brown (if you're using whole wheat flour its color will not change much because it is already brown) add 1 cup of water stirring constantly. Be careful because mixture is hot and will splatter a bit. Add celery salt, onions, coconut milk, and chicken. Reduce heat and simmer for about five minutes until gravy thickens. Add salt and pepper to taste. You may also try adding another herb or spice such as dried sage, curry powder, lemon pepper, garlic, or diced chili peppers for a variety of different flavored gravies.

Serve gravy over toast, bisques, mashed potatoes, pasta, rice, or most any cooked vegetable (broccoli, asparagus, cauliflower, green beans, peas, etc.). This recipe makes about $3^{1}/2$ cups of gravy containing a total of 7 tablespoons of coconut oil, enough to supply two people with $3^{1}/2$ tablespoons of oil each.

For variation you can replace the chicken with any other type of meat—turkey, tuna, salmon, hamburger, sausage, etc.—or you can leave the meat out entirely. Sliced mushrooms makes a good replacement for meat in this recipe.

A vegetarian gravy mixed with sautéed vegetables (carrots, onions, cauliflower, mushrooms, peas, etc.) in place of the meat and served over mashed potatoes, rice, or pasta is delicious.

CREAM OF ASPARAGUS SOUP

This is a very creamy, rich flavored soup made with coconut milk. Makes a great lunch or dinner.

2 14-ounce cans coconut milk
^{1}/$_4$ cup water
2 cups asparagus, chopped
4 tablespoons coconut oil
6 tablespoons flour
^{1}/$_2$ cup onion, chopped
^{1}/$_2$ cup celery, chopped
^{1}/$_2$ tablespoon marjoram
Salt and pepper

Heat coconut oil in sauce pan over medium heat. Add flour and cook stirring frequently until mixture turns a golden brown. Do not burn. Add onions, celery, and asparagus to pan and sauté for about 5 minutes stirring frequently. Add coconut milk and water. Stir frequently and simmer until vegetables are tender (about 10-15 minutes). Add marjoram, salt, and pepper to taste. Makes about 6 ^{3}/$_4$ cups of soup, enough for three 2^1/$_4$ cup servings. Each serving contains 3^1/$_2$ tablespoons of oil.

SEASONED DIP

A dip popular at some Italian restaurants combines olive oil and seasonings. Bread is dipped into the mixture and eaten as an appetizer. You can make a similar dip using coconut oil in place of olive oil.

3^1/$_2$ tablespoons coconut oil
2 tablespoons of onion, finely diced
1 tablespoon of garlic, finely diced
^{1}/$_2$ teaspoon of basil
^{1}/$_2$ teaspoon of oregano
^{1}/$_4$ teaspoon paprika
^{1}/$_4$ teaspoon salt
^{1}/$_8$ teaspoon black pepper (or cayenne pepper)

Combine all ingredients in a small saucepan. Heat until mixture just begins to simmer. Turn off the heat and let sit until cool. Don't over heat, you're goal is not to cook it, but just help the flavors blend. You can use this as a dip or as a spread for bread. It also makes a great seasoning for pasta.

II

RESOURCES

For additional information about the health and dietary aspects of fats oils, particularly coconut oil and medium-chain fatty acids, refer to the resources listed below. If you can't find these books at your local bookstore they are available from the publishers or from Amazon.com.

BOOKS

Eat Fat, Look Thin:
A Safe and Natural Way to Lose Weight Permanently
Bruce Fife, N.D., HealthWise Publications, 2002. (719)550-9887
Fat can be good for you and can help you lose unwanted weight—if it's the right kind of fat. This book explains the "Coconut Diet" which will help you shed excess weight without counting calories or giving up favorite foods. Includes recipes.

Know Your Fats: The Complete Primer for Understanding the Nutrition of Fats, Oils, and Cholesterol
Mary G. Enig, Ph.D., Bethesda Press, 2000. (301) 680-8600
An accurate overview of the health aspects of fats and oils including the benefits of coconut oil.

Heart Frauds: Uncovering the Biggest Health Scam In History
Charles T. McGee, M.D., HealthWise Publications, 2001. (719) 550-9887
The cholesterol theory of heart disease was disproved years ago, yet everyone is paranoid about their cholesterol levels. The medical, pharmaceutical, and food industries continue to promote the so-called cholesterol

myth all for the sake of profit. This book reveals the history of the cholesterol theory and explains why the medical profession is so reluctant to abandon it. For the sake of your health you should read this revealing book.

Nourishing Traditions: The Cookbook that Challenges Politically Correct Nutrition and the Diet Dictorats
Sally Fallon, Mary G. Enig, Ph.D., Patricia Connolly, New Trends Publishing, 1999. (877) 707-1776
More than just a cookbook, this volume is about eating the kinds of real food that has nourished people all over the world for centuries. It combines the wisdom of the ancients with the latest accurate scientific research. Contains insights from a variety of doctors and nutritionists. Great recipes that include healthy oils like coconut oil.

WEBSITES
www.lauric.org
The Center for Research on Lauric Oils, Inc. maintains this website summarizing recent research in lauric and capric acids. Contains some very interesting information and links to other web sites.

www.price-pottenger.org
The Price-Pottenger Nutrition Foundation promotes principles of sound nutrition based on the discovers and work of Weston A. Price, D.D.S. and Francis M. Pottenger, Jr., M.D.

www.westonaprice.org
This is a fantastic resource for dietary and nutritional information. Sponsored by the Weston A. Price Foundation which is dedicated to educating the public about the facts regarding diet and nutrition and dispelling myths perpetuated by commercial enterprises. This site contains lots of excellent articles on a variety of nutritional topics including coconut and other oils.

www.coconut-info.com
This website is devoted to providing accurate information about the health and dietary aspects of coconuts. Contains many interesting articles and resources. Also includes access to a coconut discussion group where people can ask questions, voice opinions, and express concerns.

PRODUCTS

Most grocery stores carry coconut milk, shredded coconut, and fresh coconuts. Coconut oil, however, is a little more difficult to find. Most health food stores are beginning to stock coconut oil. If your local store doesn't stock it, ask them to order it. If you can't get a good quality coconut oil in your area you can order directly from the distributors below or search the Internet under coconut or coconut oil. The companies listed below sell a variety of coconut products including dietary supplements, soaps, and lotions.

Befit Enterprises, Ltd.
P.O. Box 5034, Southampton, NY 11969, USA. Tel (800) 497-9516, www.cutcat.com
This company sells a variety of health related products including virgin coconut oil,

Cardiovascular Research Ltd.
Ecological Formulas, 1061-B Shary Circle, Concord, CA 94518, USA. Tel (925) 827-2636
A respected health food company that distributes dietary supplements containing the most potent MCFA. Has probably the widest variety of MCFA supplements available.

Carotec, Inc.
P.O. Box 9919, Naples, FL 34101-1919, USA. Tel (800) 522-4279, www.carotecinc.com
This company sells a variety of dietary supplements including lauric acid, caprylic acid, and other coconut/palm products.

Coconut Connections Ltd.
5 Sycamore Dene, Chesham, Bucks HP5 3JT, UK. Tel 01494 771419 (UK), (+44)1494 771419 (Europe), www.coconut-connections.com
This company distributes virgin coconut oil and other related products in the UK and Europe.

Essential Foods NW
219 212th Street SW, Bothell, WA 98021, USA. Tel (206) 200-4846, e-mail essentialfoodsnw@aol.com.
This company distributes a variety of health products including virgin coconut oil.

The Grain & Salt Society
273 Fairway Drive, Asheville, NC 28805, USA. Tel (800) 867-7258, www.celtic-seasalt.com
This company sells a wide variety of helath products including coconut and other oils.

Mid-American Marketing Corporation
P.O. Box 295, Eaton, OH 45320, USA. Tel (800) 922-1744, www.coconutoil-online.com
They sell quality virgin coconut oil and related products.

NatureSecrets AG
Industriestr. 12, CH-8212 Neuhausen, Switzerland. Tel 0041-52-670-0161 (Switzerland) 0049-7121-677-283 (Germany), www.naturesecrets.com
A resource for virgin coconut oil in Europe.

Nature's First Law
P.O. Box 900202, San Diego, CA, 92190, USA. Tel (619) 596-7961, www.rawfood.com
A variety of products are offered by this company including unrefined coconut oil with full flavor and aroma.

Omega Nutrition
6515 Aldrich Road, Bellingham, WA 98226, USA. Tel (800) 661-3529, www.omegahealthstore.com
Specializes in the sale of organic oils including coconut oil. They call their coconut oil "Coconut Butter." This is a very good quality, flavorless, all-purpose cooking oil. The oil can be purchased through them or from most any health food store.

Pure Fiji
www.purefiji.com.fj
This company produces a variety of soaps and hand lotions from pure virgin coconut oil. Very good quality. They have distributors in the USA, UK, and Australia listed on their website.

Quality First International Inc.
6852 Wellington Road #34, R.R. #22, Cambridge, ON, N3C 2V4, Canada. Tel (877) 441-9479, www.qualityfirst.on.ca
They call their oil "Virgin Oil De Coco-Creme." It is extracted from coconut milk and has a delightfully delicate flavor and aroma.

Tropical Traditions
PMB #219, 823 S. Main Street, West Bend, WI, 53095, www.tropical traditions.com
This company distributes virgin coconut oil produced in the Philippines using traditional methods by local farmers. They can ship anywhere in the world.

Wilderness Family Naturals
Box 538, Finland, MN 55603, USA. Tel (866) 936-6457, www.wildernessfamily-naturals.com
This company sells virgin coconut oil as well as a variety of other related products such as palm oil, soaps, and herbs.

REFERENCES

Chapter 1—A Miracle Food

1. Konlee, M. 1997. Return from the jungle: an interview with Chris Dafoe. *Positive Health News* No. 14 Summer Issue
2. Price, W.A. 1939. *Nutrition and Physical Degeneration*. Keats Publishing 1998 edition
3. Prior, I.A.M. 1971. The price of civilization. *Nutrition Today*, July/Aug, p. 2-11
4. Okoji, G.O. et al. 1993. Childhood convulsions: a hospital survey on traditional remedies. *Aft. J. Med. Med. Sci.* 22(2):25

Chapter 2—Why Pacific Islanders Don't Get Heart Disease

1. Price, W.A. 1939. *Nutrition and Physical Degeneration*. Keats Publishing, 1998 edition. Chapters 5 and 6
2. Anonymous, 1998. Bad teeth and gums a risk factor for heart disease? *Harvard Heart Letter* 9(3):6
3. Millman, C. 1999. The route of all evil. *Men's Health*. 14(10):102
4. Prior, I.A. 1981. Cholesterol, coconuts, and diet on Polynesian atolls: a natural experiment: the Pukapuka and Tokelau island studies. *Am. J. of Clin. Nutr.* 34 (8):1552
5. Stanhope, J.M., et al. 1981.The Tokelau Island migrant study. Serum lipid concentrations in two environments. *J. Chron. Dis.* 34:45
6. Ibid
7. Prior, I.A.1981. Cholesterol, coconuts, and diet on Polynesian atolls: a natural experiment: the Pukapuka and Tokelau island studies. *Am. J. of Clin. Nutr.* 34 (8):1552
8. Hegsted, D.M., et al. 1965. Qualitative effects of dietary fat on serum cholesterol in man. *Am. J. of Clin. Nutr.* 17:281
9. Hashim, S.A., et al. 1959. Effect of mixed fat formula feeding on serum cholesterol level in man. *Am. J. of Clin. Nutr.* 1:30
10. Bray, G.A., et al. 1980. Weight gain of rats fed medium-chain triglycerides is less than rats fed long-chain triglycerides. *Int. J. Obes.* 4:27
11. Geliebter, A. 1983. Overfeeding with medium-chain triglycerides diet results in diminished deposition of fat. *Am. J. of Clin. Nutr.* 37:104
12. Baba, N. 1982. Enhanced thermogenesis and diminished deposition of fat in response to overfeeding with a diet containing medium chain triglycerides. *Am. J. of Clin. Nutr.* 35:678

13. Greenberger, N.J. and Skillman, T.G. 1969. Medium-chain triglycerides: physiologic considerations and clinical implications. *N. Engl. J. Med.* 280:1045

14. Fino, J.H. 1973. Effect of dietary triglyceride chain length on energy utilized and obesity in rats fed high fat diets. *Fed. Proc.* 32:993

15. Sindhu Rani, J.A., et al. 1993. Effect of coconut oil and coconut kernel on serum and tissue lipid profile. *Ind. Coco. J.* XXIV(7):2

16. Ibid

17. Kurup, P.A., and Rajmohan, T. 1994. Consumption of coconut oil and coconut kernel and the incidence of atherosclerosis. Coconut and Coconut Oil in Human Nutrition, Proceedings. Symposium on Coconut and Coconut Oil in Human Nutrition. 27 March. Coconut Development Board, Kochi, India, 1995, p.35

18. Thampan, P.K. 1994. *Facts and Fallacies About Coconut Oil.* Asian and Pacific Coconut Community. p.31

19. Kaunitz, H. and Dayrit, C.S. 1992. Coconut oil consumption and coronary heart diseas. *Philippine Journal of Internal Medicine* 30:165

20. Mendis, S. and Kumarasunderam, R. 1990. The effect of daily consumption of coconut fat and soya-bean fat on plasma lipids and lipoproteins of young normolipidaemic men. *British Journal of Nutrition* 63:547

21. Kurup, P.A., and Rajmohan, T. 1994. Consumption of coconut oil and coconut kernel and the incidence of atherosclerosis. Coconut and Coconut Oil in Human Nutrition, Proceedings. *Symposium on Coconut and Coconut Oil in Human Nutrition.* 27 March. Coconut Development Board, Kochi, India, 1995, p.35

22. Prior, I.A., et al. 1981. Cholesterol, coconuts, and diet on Polynesian atolls: a natural experiment: the Pukapuka and Tokelau Island studies. *Am. J. of Clin. Nutr.* 34:1552

23. Enig, M.G. 1993. Diet, serum cholesterol and coronary heart disease, in Man G.V. (ed): *Coronary Heart Disease: The Dietary Sense and Nonsense.* Janus Publishing p.36

24. Enig, M.G. 1999. Coconut: In support of good health in the 21st century, 36 session Asian Pacific Coconut Community

25. Thampan, P.K. 1994. *Facts and Fallacies About Coconut Oil.* Asian and Pacific Coconut Community. p.31

26. Hornung, B., et al. 1994. Lauric acid inhibits the maturation of vesicular stomatitis virus. *Journal of General Virology* 75:353

Chapter 3—The Tropical Oils War

1. Blonz, Edward R. Scientists revising villain status of coconut oil. *Oakland Tribune* Jan 23, 1991

2. Enig, M.G. 1999. Coconut: in support of good health in the 21st century. 36th meeting of APCC

3. Heimlich, J. 1990. *What Your Doctor Won't Tell You.* Harper Perennial

4. Spencer, P. L. 1995. Fat faddists. *Consumers' Research* 78(5):43

5. Enig, M.G. 2000. *Know Your Fats* Bethesda Press p.196

Chapter 4—Why Coconut Oil is Different

1. Belitz, H.D. and Grosch, W. 1987. *Food Chemistry,* 2nd Ed. Translated by D. Hadziyev. Springer-Verlag p.480

Chapter 5—Oils and Your Health

1. Thomas J. Moore, 1989 Sept. The Cholesterol Myth, *The Atlantic Monthly*

2. McCully, Kilmer S. 1997. *The Homocysteine Revolution.* Keats Publishing

3. *Atherosclerosis, Thrombosis and Vascular Biology.* November, 1997. Cited in High fat indulgence invites strokes and clots. *Energy Times* March, 1998

4. Passwater, R. A. 1985. *The Antioxidants*. Keats Publishing
5. Passwater, R. A. 1992. *The New Superantioxidant—Plus*. Keats Publishing. p.15
6. Addis, P.B. and Warner, G. J. 1991. *Free Radicals and Food Additives*. Aruoma, O.I. and Halliwell, B. eds. Taylor and Francis p.77
7. Loliger, J. 1991. *Free Radicals and Food Additives*. Aruoma, O.I. and Halliwell, B. eds. Taylor and Francis. p.121
8. Carroll, KK. and Khor, H.T. 1971. Effects of level and type of dietary fat on incidence of mammary tumors induced in female sprague-dawley rates by 7, 12-dimethylbenzanthracene. *Lipids* 6:415
9. C.J. Meade and J. Martin, 1978. *Adv. Lipid Res.* 127. Cited by Ray Peat, *Ray Peat's Newsletter* 1997 Issue, p.3
10. Raloff, J. 1996. Unusual fats lose heart-friendly image. *Science News* 150(6):87
11. Willett, W.C., et al. 1993. Intake of trans fatty acids and risk of coronary heart disease among women. *Lancet* 341(8845):581
12. Kummerow, F.A. 1975. *Federation Proceedings* 33:235
13. Thampan, P.K. 1994. *Facts and Fallacies About Coconut Oil*. Asian and Pacific Coconut Community, p. 20
14. Booyens, J. and Lousrens, C.C. 1986. The Eskimo diet. Prophylactic effects ascribed to the balanced presence of natural cis unsaturated fatty acids. *Med. Hypoth.* 21:387
15. Kritchevsky, D., et al, 1967. *Journal of Atherosclerosis Research* 7:643
16. Calabrese, C. et al. 1999. A cross-over study of the effect of a single oral feeding of medium chain triglyceride oil vs. canola oil on post-ingestion plasma triglyceride levels in healthy men. *Altern. Med. Rev.* 4(1):23
17. Jiang, Z.M. et al. 1993. A comparison of medium-chain and long-chain triglycerides in surgical patients. *Ann. Surg.* 217(2):175
18. Tantibhedhyangkul, P. and Hashim, S.A., 1978. Medium-chain triglyceride feeding in premature infants: effects on calcium and magnesium absorption. *Pediatrics* 61(4):537
19. Ball, M.J. 1993. Parenteral nutrition in the critically ill: use of a medium chain triglyceride emulsion. *Intensive Care Med.* 19(2):89

Chapter 6—Nature's Marvelous Germ Fighter

1. Food-borne illnesses a growing threat to public health. June 10, 1996. *American Medical News*
2. Wan, J.M. and Grimble, R.F. 1987. Effect of dietary linoleate content on the metabolic response of rats to Escherichia coli endotoxin. *Clinical Science* 72(3):383-5
3. Isaacs, E.E., et al. 1994. Inactivation of enveloped viruses in human bodily fluids by purified lipid. *Annals of the New York Academy of Sciences* 1994; 724:457
4. Kabara, J.J. 1978. Fatty acids and derivatives as antimicrobial agents—A review, in *The Pharmacological Effect of Lipids* (JJ Kabara, ed) American Oil Chemists' Society, p.1-14
5. Kabara, J.J. 1984. Antimicrobial agents derived from fatty acids. *Journal of the American Chemists Society* 61:397
6. Hierholzer, J.C. and Kabara, J.J. 1982. In vitro effects of monolaurin compounds on enveloped RNA and DNA viruses. *Journal of Food Safety* 4:1
7. Thormar, H., et al. 1987. Inactivation enveloped viruses and killing of cells by fatty acids and monoglycerides. *Antimicrobial Agents and Chemotherapy* 31:27
8. Petschow, B.W., et al. 1996. Susceptibility of Helicobacter pylori to bactericidal properties of medium-chain monoglycerides and free fatty acids. *Antimicrobial Agents and Chemotherapy* 145:876
9. Bergsson, G., et al. 1998. In vitro inactivation of Chlamydia trachomatis by fatty acids and monoglycerides. *Antimicrobial Agents and Chemotherapy* 42:2290

10. Holland, K.T., et al. 1994. The effect of glycerol monolaurate on growth of, and production of toxic shock syndrome toxin-1 and lipase by, Staphylococcus aureus. *Journal of Anti-microbial Chemotherapy* 33:41

12. Enig, M.G. 1999. Coconut: in support of good health in the 21st century. 36th meeting of APCC

13. Isaacs, C.E. and Thormar, H. 1991. The role of milk-derived antimicrobial lipids as antiviral and antibacterial agents in *Immunology of Milk and the Neonate* (Mestecky, J., et al., eds) Plenum Press

14. Isaacs, C.E., et al. 1992. Addition of lipases to infant formulas produces antiviral and antibacterial activity. *Journal of Nutritional Biochemistry* 3:304

15. Kabara, J.J. 1978 *The Pharmacological Effect of Lipids, Vol I*. The American Oil Chemists' Society p. 10

16. Monolaurin, 1987. *AIDS Treatment News*, 33:1

17. Isaacs, C.E. and Thormar, H. 1991. The role of milk-derived antimicrobial lipids as antiviral and antibacterial agents in *Immunology of Milk and the Neonate* (Mestecky, J. et al., eds) Plenum Press

18. Merewood, A. 1994. Taming the yeast beast. *Women's Sports and Fitness*. 16:67

19. Crook, W., 1985. *The Yeast Connection*. Professional Books

20. Anonymous, 1998. Summertime blues: It's giardia season *Journal of Environmental Health*, Jul/Aug, Vol 61, p 51

21. Galland, L. 1999. Colonies within: allergies from intestinal parasites. *Total Health* Vol 21, Issue 2, p. 24

22. Novotny, T.E., et al. 1990. Prevalence of Giardia lamblia and risk factors for infection among children attending day-care...*Public Health Reports* 105:4

23. Galland, L. and Leem, M. 1990. Giardia lamblia infection as a cause of chronic fatigue. *Journal of Nutritional Medicine* 1:27

24. Hernell, O., et al. 1986. Killing of Giardia lamblia by human milk lipases: an effect mediated by lipolysis of milk lipids. *Journal of Infectious Diseases* 153:715

25. Reiner, D.S., et al. 1986. Human milk kills Giardia lamblia by generating toxic lipolytic products. *Journal of Infectious Diseases* 154:825

26. Crouch, A.A., et al. 1991. Effect of human milk and infant milk formulae on adherence of Giardia intestinalis. *Transactions of the Royal Society of Tropical Medicine and Hygiene* 85:617

27. G.S. Chowan, et al. 1985. Treatment of Tapeworm infestation by coconut (Concus nucifera) preparations. *Association of Physicians of India Journal*. 33:207

28. Bockus, William Jr., personal communication

Chapter 7—A New Weapon Against Heart Disease

1. Kaunitz, H. 1986. Medium chain triglycerides (MCT) in aging and arteriosclerosis. *J. Environ. Pathol. Toxicol. Oncol.* 6(3-4):115

2. Ross, R. 1993. The pathogenesis of atherosclerosis: A perspective for the 1990s. *Nature* 362:801

3. Fong, I.W., 2000. Emerging relations between infectious diseases and coronary artery disease and atherosclerosis. *CMAJ* 163(1):49

4. Danesh, J and Collins, R, 1997. Chronic infections and coronary heart disease: Is there a link? *Lancet* 350:430

5. Gura, T. 1998. Infections: A cause of artery-clogging plaques? *Science* 281:35

6. Muhlestein, JB, 2000. Chronic infection and coronary artery disease. *Med. Clin. North Am.* 84(1):123

7. Leinonen, M. 1993. Pathogenic mechanisms and epidemiology of Chlamydia pneumoniae. *Eur. Heart J.* 14(suppl K):57

8. Gaydos, C.A. 1996. Replication of Chlamydia pneumoniae in vitro in human macrophages, endothelial cells, and aortic artery smooth muscle cells. *Infect Immunity* 64:1614

9. Kaunitz, H. 1986. Medium chain triglycerides (MCT) in aging and arteriosclerosis. *J. Environ. Pathol. Toxicol. Oncol.* 6(3-4):115

10. Sircar, S. and Kansra, U. 1998. Choice of cooking oils—myths and realities. *J Indian Med Assoc* 96(10):304

11. Ascherio, A. and Willett, W.C, 1997. Health effects of trans fatty acids. *Am J Clin Nutr* 66(4 Suppl):1006S

12. Enig, M.G., 2000. *Know Your Fats: The Complete Primer for Understanding the Nutrition of Fats, Oils, and Cholesterol.* Bethesda Press. p.100

13. Heimlich, J. 1990. *What Your Doctor Won't Tell You.* Harper Perennial

14. Ascherio, A. and Willett, W.C., 1997. Health effects of trans fatty acids. *Am. J. Clin. Nutr.* 66(4 Suppl):1006S

15. Ibid

Chapter 8—Eat Your Way to Better Health

1. Thampan, P.K. 1994. *Facts and Fallacies About Coconut Oil.* Asian and Pacific Coconut Community. p.8

2. Kiyasu G.Y., et al. 1952. The portal transport of absorbed fatty acids. *Journal of Biological Chemistry* 199:415

3. Fushiki, T. and Matsumoto, K. 1995, Swimming endurance capacity of mice is increased by chronic consumption of medium-chain triglycerides. *Journal of Nutrition* 125:531

4. Applegate, L. 1996. Nutrition. *Runner's World* 31:26

5. Azain, M.J., 1993. Effects of adding medium-chain triglycerides to sow diets during late gestation and early lactation on litter performance. *J. Anim. Sci.* 71(11):3011

6. Vaidya, U.V., et al. 1992 Vegetable oil fortified feeds in the nutrition of very low birthweight babies. *Indian Pediatr.* 29(12):1519

7. Tantibhedhyangkul, P. and Hashim, S.A., 1978. Medium-chain triglyceride feeding in premature infants: effects on calcium and magnesium absorption. *Pediatrics* 61(4):537

8. Jiang, Z.M., et al. 1993. A comparison of medium-chain and long-chain triglycerides in surgical patients. *Ann. Surg.* 217(2):175

9. Francois, C.A., et al. 1998. Acute effects of dietary fatty acids on the fatty acids of human milk. *Am. J. Clin. Nutr.* 67:301

10. Ibid

Chapter 9—Coconut Oil As A Medicine

1. Macalalag, E.V. et al. 1997. Buko water of immature coconut is a universal urinary stone solvent. Read at the padivid Coconut Community Conference, Metro Manila, August 14-18.

2. Anzaldo, F.E. et al 1975. Coconut water as intravenous fluid. *Phil J. Pediatrics* 24:143

3. Dayrit, C.S. 2000. Coconut oil in health and disease: Its and monolaurin's potential as cure for HIV/AIDS. Read at the XXXVII Cocotech Meeting. Chennai, India

4. Goldberg, B. ed, 1994 *Alternative Medicine*, Future Medicine Publishing. p. 618

5. Thampan, P.K. 1994. *Facts and Fallacies About Coconut Oil.* Asian and Pacific Coconut Community. p.9

6. Tantibhedhyangkul, P. and Hashim, S.A, 1978. Medium-chain triglyceride feeding in premature infants: effects on calcium and magnesium absorption. *Pediatrics*, 61(4):537

7. Watkins, B.A. et al. Importance of vitamin E in bone formation and in chondroncyte function, Purdue University. Cited by Fallon, S. and Enig, M.G. 2000. Dem bones—do high protein diets cause osteoporosis? *Wise Traditions* 1(4):38

8. Parekh, P.I., et al. 1998. Reversal of diet-induced obesity and diabetes in C57BL/6J mice. *Metabolism* 47 (9):1089

9. Oakes, N.D. et al. 1997. Diet-induced muscle insulin resistance in rats is ameliorated by acute dietary lipid withdrawal or a single bout of exercise: parallel relationship between insulin stimulation of glucose uptake and suppression of long-chain fatty acyl-CoA. *Diabetes* 46(12):2022

10. Parekh, P.I., et al. 1998. Reversal of diet-induced obesity and diabetes in C57BL/6J mice. *Metabolism* 47 (9):1089

11. Anonymous, 1999. Low-fat diet alone reversed type 2 diabetes in mice. *Compr. Ther.* 25(1):60

12. Barnard, R.J., et al. 1983. Long-term use of a high-complex-carbohydrate, high-fiber, low-fat diet and exercise in the treatment of NIDDM patients. *Diabetes Care* 6 (3):268

13. Berry, E.M.. 1997. Dietary fatty acids in the management of diabetes mellitus. *Am. J. Clin. Nutr.* 66 (suppl):991S

14. Ginsberg, B.H., et al 1982. Effect of alterations in membrane lipid unsaturation on the properties of the insulin receptor of Ehrlich ascites cells. *Biochim. Biophys. Acta.* 690(2):157

15. Thampan, P.K. 1994. *Facts and Fallacies About Coconut Oil.* Asian and Pacific Coconut Community. p.15

16. Garfinkel, M., et al. 1992. Insulinotropic potency of lauric acid: a metabolic rational for medium chain fatty acids (MCF) in TPN formulation. *Journal of Surgical Research* 52:328

17. Ginsberg, B.H., et al 1982. Effect of alterations in membrane lipid unsaturation on the properties of the insulin receptor of Ehrlich ascites cells. *Biochim. Biophys. Acta.* 690(2):157

18. Yost, T.J. and Eckel, R.H., 1989. Hypocaloric feeding in obese women: metabolic effects of medium-chain triglyceride substitution. *Am J Clin Nutr* 49(2):326

19. Sircar, S. and Kansra, U. 1998. Choice of cooking oils—myths and realities. *J Indian Med Assoc* 96(10):304

20. Kono, H, et al. 2000. Medium-chain triglycerides inhibit free radical formation and TNF-alpha production in rats given enteral ethanol. *Am. J. Physiol. Gastrointest. Liver Physiol.* 278(3):G467

21. Cha, Y.S. and Sachan, D.S. 1994. Opposite effects of dietary saturated and unsaturated fatty acids on ethanol-pharmacokinetics, triglycerides and carnitines. *J. Am. Coll. Nutr.* 13(4):338

22. Nanji, A.A., et al. 1995. Dietary saturated fatty acids: a novel treatment for alcoholic liver disease. *Gastroenterology* 109(2):547

23. Cohen, L.A. 1988. Medium chain triglycerides lack tumor-promoting effects in the n-methylnitrosourea-induced mammary tumor model. In *The Pharmacological Effects of Lipids* vol III. Jon J. Kabara editor. The American Oil Chemists' Society

24. Montgomery, S.M., et al. 1999. Paramyxovirus infections in childhood and subsequent inflammatory bowel disease. *Gastroenterology* 116(4):796

25. Wakefield, A.J., et al. 1999. Crohn's disease: the case for measles virus. *Ital J Gastroenterol Hepatol* 31(3):247

26. Daszak, P., et al. 1997. Detection and comparative analysis of persistent measles virus infection in Crohn's disease by immunogold electron microscopy. *J Clin Pathol* 50(4):299

27. Lewin, J., et al. 1995. Persistent measles virus infection of the intestine: confirmation by immunogold electron microscopy. *Gut* 36(4):564

28. Balzola, F. A., et al, 1997. IgM antibody against measles virus in patients with inflammatory bowel disease: a marker of virus-related disease? *Eur J Gastroenterol Hepatol* 9(7):661

29. Murray, M. 1994. *Natural Alternatives to Over-the-Counter and Prescription Drugs*: William Morrow

30. Shimada, H. et al. 1997. Biologically active acylglycerides from the berries of saw-palmetto. *J. Nat. Prod.* 60:417

31. Holleb, A.I. 1986. *The American Cancer Society Cancer Book*, Doubleday & Co.

32. Reddy, BS, 1992. Dietary fat and colon cancer: animal model studies. *Lipids* 27(10):807

33. Cohen, L.A. 1988. Medium chain triglycerides lack tumor-promoting effects in the n-methylnitrosourea-induced mammary tumor model. In *The Pharmacological Effects of Lipids* vol III. Jon J. Kabara editor. The American Oil Chemists' Society

34. Cohen, L.A. and Thompson, D.O., 1987. The influence of dietary medium chain triglycerides on rat mammary tumor development. *Lipids*. 22(6):455

35. Hopkins, G.J., et al. 1981. Polyunsaturated fatty acids as promoters of mammary carcinogenesis induced in Sprague-Dawley rats by 7, 12-dimethylbenz[a]anthracene. *J. Natl. Cancer Inst.* 66(3):517

36. Kabara, Jon, personal communication

37. Monserrat, A.J. et al. 1995. Protective effect of coconut oil on renal necrosis occurring in rats fed a methyl-deficient diet. *Ren Fail* 17(5):525

38. Ross, DL, et al 1985. Early biochemical and EEG correlates of the ketogenic diet in children with atypical absence epilepsy. *Pediatr Neurol* 1(2):104

Chapter 10—Eat Fat, Lose Weight

1.Whitney, E.N., et al. 1991. *Understanding Normal and Clinical Nutrition* 3rd ed. West Publishing Company. p.359

2. Ingle, D.L., et al. 1999. Dietary energy value of medium-chain triglycerides. *Jour. of Food Sci.* 64(6):960

3. Thampan, P.K. 1994. *Facts and Fallacies About Coconut Oil*. Asian and Pacific Coconut Community. p.1-2

4. Baba, N. 1982. Enhanced thermogenesis and diminished deposition of fat in response to overfeeding with diet containing medium-chain triglyceride. *Am. J. Clin. Nutr.* 35:678

5. Bach, A.C., et al. 1989. Clinical and experimental effects of medium chain triglyceride based fat emulsions-a review. *Clin. Nutr.* 8:223

6. Hill, J.O., et al. 1989. Thermogenesis in humans during overfeeding with medium-chain triglycerides. *Metabolism* 38:641

7. Hasihim, S.A. and Tantibhedyangkul, P. 1987. Medium chain triglyceride in early life: Effects on growth of adipose tissue. *Lipids* 22:429

8. Geliebter, A. 1980. Overfeeding with a diet containing medium chain triglyceride impedes accumulation of body fat. *Clinical Research* 28:595A

9. Bray, G.A., et al. 1980. Weight gain of rats fed medium-chain triglycerides is less than rats fed long-chain triglycerides. *Int. J. Obes.* 4:27-32

10. Geliebter, A., et al. 1983. Overfeeding with medium-chain triglycerides diet results in diminished deposition of fat. *Am. J. Clin. Nutr.* 37:1-4

11. Baba, N. 1982. Enhanced thermogenesis and diminished deposition of fat in response to overfeeding with diet containing medium chain triglyceride. *Am. J. of Clin. Nutr.* 35:678-82

12. Murray, M. T. 1996. *American Jouranal of Natural Medicine* 3(3):7

13. Hill, J.O., et al. 1989. Thermogenesis in man during overfeeding with medium chain triglycerides. *Metabolism* 38:641-8

14. Seaton, T.B., et al. 1986. Thermic effect of medium-chain and long-chain triglycerides in man. *Am. J. of Clin. Nutr.* 44:630

15. Peat, R. *Ray Peat's Newsletter* 1997 Issue, p.2-3

16. *Encyclopedia Briticanica Book of the Year*, 1946. Cited by Ray Peat, *Ray Peat's Newsletter*, 1997 Issue, p.4

17. Shepard, T.H. 1960. Soybean goiter. *New Eng J. Med.* 262:1099

18. Divi, R.L. et al., 1997. Anti-thyroid isoflavones from soybean: isolation, characterization, and mechanisms of action. *Biochem. Pharmacol.* 54(10):1087

Chapter 11—Beautiful Skin and Hair

1. Harman, D. 1986. Free radical theory of aging: role of free radicals in the origination and evolution of life, aging, and disease processes, In: Free Radicals, Aging and Degenerative Diseases. Alan R. Liss, p.3-50

2. Cross, C.E., et al. 1987. Oxygen radicals and human disease. *Ann. Intern. Med.* 107:526

3. Wooley, Bruce, personal communication

2. Anonymous. Shine to dye for. *Redbook*, Feb 99 192(4):24

3. Kabara, J.J. editor 1978 *The Pharmacological Effects of Lipids, Vol I*. The American Oil Chemists' Society. p.8-9

4. Noonan, P., 1994. Porcupine antibiotics. *Omni*, 16:32

5. Rothman, S, et al. 1945. Fungistatic action of hair fat on microsporon audouini, *Proc. Soc. Exp. Biol. NY* 60:394

6. Sadeghi, S. et al. 1999. Dietary lipids modify the cytokine response to bacterial lipopolysaccharide in mice. *Immunology* 96(3):404

Chapter 12—Cooking with Coconut Oil

1. May, C.D., 1980. Food allergy: Perspective, principles, and practical management. *Nutrition Today* Nov/ Dec P28-31

Chapter 13—A Natural Way to Better Health

1. Isaacs, C.E. and Thormar, H., 1990. Human milk lipids inactivated enveloped viruses. In *Breastfeeding, Nutrition, Infectin and Infant Growth in Develped and Emerging Countries* (Atkinson S.A., Hanson, L.A., Chandra R.K, eds) Arts Biomedical Publishers and Distributors

2. Traul, KA, et al 2000. Review of the toxicologic properties of medium-chain triglycerides. *Food Chem. Toxicol.* 38(1):79

3. Kabara, J.J., 1984. Laurcidin: the nonionic emulsifier with antimicrobial properties. In *Cosmetic and Drug Perservation, Principles and Practice*, Jon J. Kabara ed. Marcel Dekker

4. Traul, K.A. et al. 2000. Review of the toxicologic properties of medium-chain triglycerides. *Food Chem. Toxicol.* 38(1):79

5. Ibid

6. Gerster, H. 1998. Can adults adequately convert alpha-linolenic acid (18:3n-3) to eicosapentaenoic acid (20:5n-3) and docosahexaenoic acid (22:6n-3)? *Int. J. Vitam Nutr. Res.* 68(3):159

7. W.H.O./F.A.O. 1977. Dietary fats and oils in human nutrition. Report of an Expert Consultation U.N. Food and Agriculture Organization Rome

INDEX

191